OTHER TITLES OF INTEREST FROM ST. LUCIE PRESS

Competitive Global Management: Principles and Strategies

Economic Theory for Environmentalists

Ecological Integrity and the Management of Ecosystems

Everglades: The Ecosystem and Its Restoration

Environmental Effects of Mining

From the Forest to the Sea: The Ecology of Wood in Streams, Rivers, Estuaries, and Oceans

Development, Environment, and Global Dysfunction: Toward Sustainable Recovery

Environmental Fate and Effects of Pulp and Paper Mill Effluents

Agricultural Dimensions of Global Climate Change

The Forest Certification Handbook

For more information about these titles call, fax or write:

St. Lucie Press
100 E. Linton Blvd., Suite 403B
Delray Beach, FL 33483
TEL (407) 274-9906 • FAX (407) 274-9927

S^{t}L

RESOLVING ENVIRONMENTAL CONFLICT
Towards Sustainable Community Development

Chris Maser

St. Lucie Press
Delray Beach, Florida

Copyright ©1996 by St. Lucie Press

All rights reserved. No part of this publication may be reproduced, stored in a retrieval system or transmitted in any form or by any means, electronic, mechanical, photocopying, recording or otherwise, without the prior written permission of the publisher.

Printed and bound in the U.S.A. Printed on acid-free paper.
10 9 8 7 6 5 4 3 2 1

ISBN 1-57444-007-1

All rights reserved. Authorization to photocopy items for internal or personal use, or the personal or internal use of specific clients, is granted by St. Lucie Press, provided that $.50 per page photocopied is paid directly to Copyright Clearance Center, 222 Rosewood Drive, Danvers, MA 01923 USA. The fee code for users of the Transactional Reporting Service is ISBN 1-57444-007-1 1/96/$100/$.50. The fee is subject to change without notice. For organizations that have been granted a photocopy license by the CCC, a separate system of payment has been arranged.

The copyright owner's consent does not extend to copying for general distribution, for promotion, for creating new works, or for resale. Specific permission must be obtained from St. Lucie Press for such copying.

Direct all inquiries to St. Lucie Press, Inc., 100 E. Linton Blvd., Suite 403B, Delray Beach, Florida 33483.

Phone: (407) 274-9906
Fax: (407) 274-9927

S^t_L

Published by
St. Lucie Press
100 E. Linton Blvd., Suite 403B
Delray Beach, FL 33483

In memory of
Margaret Thomas,
who always treated me kindly—
especially when I needed it most and felt I deserved it least.

And in memory of Nene Maser,
who taught me that we can overcome
our fears with love if we so choose,
and in that spirit gave all the love she had,
including her very last moment.

*The clearsighted do not rule the world,
but they sustain and console it.*

Agnes Repplier
American essayist

*History does not reveal its alternatives,
and thus one cannot say with certitude
where this road not taken would have led.*

John G. Stoessinger

CONTENTS

Preface xiii

Acknowledgments xxi

Author xxiii

Part I: Resolving Destructive Environmental Conflict

1 Approaches to Facilitation 3
Facilitation at the Crossroad 3
A Brief Look at the Facilitation I Practice 5
   Introduction 7
   Body 8
   Conclusion 10

2 Conflict Is a Choice 13
What Is a Right? 14
The Equality of Differences 16
Environmental Justice Is Predicated on Human Equality 18
Perceived Resource Scarcity Accentuates Destructive
   Environmental Conflict 21
Resource Overexploitation: A Matter of Perceived Loss 23
Destructive Conflict Is a Mistake 25
Destructive Conflict Is Usually Based on the Misjudgment
   of Appearances 26

3 Environmental Principles: The Need to Know and the Fear of Knowing 29

All Resources Are Interconnected, Interactive, Interdependent, and Ultimately Finite   30
    Air: The Breath of Life—And of Death   31
    Soil: The Great Placenta   32
    Water: A Captive of Gravity   33
    Biodiversity: The Variety of Life   33
    Human Population: A Matter of Gender Equality   34
    Sunlight: The Source of Global Energy   35
    Climate: The Global Arbiter   35
    The Key to the Gate   37
Nature Keeps Its Own Scorecard   38
Nature Is Governed by Impartial Laws   38
Destructive Conflict Over a Given Resource Lies in Its Perceived Value   39
Change: The Dynamic Constant   40

4 The Human Equation 45

A Child's Gift   47
We Take Our Families with Us   48
Dysfunctional Family Dynamics Lead to Ongoing Destructive Conflict   48
Homeostasis Is Designed to Hide Dysfunction   49
Boundaries, The Silent Language   50
Coping Mechanisms: Unconscious Thoughts that Manifest as Recognizable Behaviors   52
    Anger and Aggression   54
    Appraisal   55
    Defensiveness   55
    Denial   56
    Displacement   57
    Filters   58
    Projection   58
    Rationalization   59
    Repression   60
    Resistance   60
    Standards and Judgment   61
    Victim   63
The Capacity for Rational Thought   64

Everyone Is Right from His or Her Point of View   65
Acceptance of Circumstances Offers the Choices of
  What Might Be   67

5 Communication: The Interpersonal Element 69
Language as a Tool   69
The Use of Silence in Communication   72
The Need to Be Heard   73
The Basic Elements of Communication   74
  Sender   75
  Symbols   75
  Receiver   75
Communication Barriers   76
  Lack of a Common Experience or Frame of Reference   76
  General Personality Traits   77
Use of Abstractions   82
Inability to Transfer Experiences from One Situation
  to Another   84

6 The Process Is the Decision 87
Faith in the Process Is Belief in the Outcome   87
The Primacy of Process   90
Perception Is Truth; Facts Are Relative   92
Reframing the Issue   95

7 Conflict Is a Learning Partnership 99
I Am at All Times a Guest and a Leader Simultaneously   100
  Leadership: The Art of Being a Servant   100
  Hidden Agendas   102
    Facilitator   102
    Participant   103
  Facilitator as Teacher   105
    The Foundation of Learning   105
    How People Learn   106
    Factors Affecting Perception   106
    Insights   108
    Motivation   108
  The Fallacy of Rescuing   110
  My Role in Participant Relationships   111
  Facilitation Means Total Participation   112

Detachment and Equanimity   113
　　　I Am a Sieve, Not a Sponge   115
　　　I Am the Keeper of Each Participant's Dignity   117
　　　Having a Beginner's Mind   119
　　　Being Myself   121
　　The Continual Learning Curve   123
　　　Not Knowing an Answer Is Okay   123
　　　Success or Failure Is the Interpretation of an Event   124

8 Practicing Transformative Facilitation 131
　　Compromise and the Point of Balance   134
　　A Curriculum of Compassion and Justice   134
　　Facilitation as a Gift Is Free, But as a Trade Has a Cost   136

9 Resolution: Destructive Conflict Brought to a Shared Vision ... 139
　　Who Are We as a Culture?   140
　　What Legacy Do We Want to Leave Our Children?   143
　　Vision, Goals, and Objectives   146

Part II: Beyond Destructive Conflict: Social/Environmental Sustainability

10 Sustainable Development 157
　　Sustainable Development within the Context of our
　　　World View   158
　　　　Mechanistic World View   158
　　　　The Transition   161
　　　　Unified World View   163
　　Sustainable Development: A Conscious Process of
　　　Self-Determination and Social Evolution   163
　　At What Scale Is Sustainable Development Possible?   165

11 Local Community Development 167
　　Is Local Community the Appropriate Scale for
　　　Sustainable Development?   168
　　Understanding Local Community Development   169
　　　Local Community Development   170
　　　Local Community Development and the Local Economy   171
　　　The Sustainability of Local Community Development   172
　　Sustainable Community Development   173

Sustainable Community Development Means Change as a
  Local Creative Process   175
The Role of Local Government   178
  Increasing Local Adaptability   180
  Improving Citizen Participation   180
Sustainable Community Development in Relation to
  Its Landscape   182
Information Feedback Loops   185

12 Modifying Our Belief Systems Regarding Change 187

Endnotes 191

References 195

PREFACE

It is now the twilight of the twentieth century, a century in which once abundant natural resources have rapidly dwindled to scarcity while the world's human population grows at an exponential rate. We citizens of this planet must now address a moral question for the next century: Do those living today owe anything to the future? If your answer is no, read no further!

If your answer is yes, then we must now determine what and how much we owe future generations, lest our present collision course continue unabated into the twenty-first century, eventually to destroy environmental options for all generations to come. Be forewarned, however, that meeting the obligation we say we have—whatever we determine it is—will require a renewed sense of personal and social justice, one that causes us as individuals and society to act now for the simultaneous benefit of both the present and the future. But what direction must our renewed sense of personal and social justice take?

Civilizations have evolved by similar steps: growth of intelligence through discoveries and inventions, through the ideas of government, family, and property, all based on a slow accumulation of experimental knowledge. As such, civilizations have much in common, and their evolutionary stages are connected with one another in a natural sequence of cultural development.

The arts of subsistence and the achievements of technology can be used to distinguish the periods of human progress. People lived by gathering fruits and nuts; learned to hunt, fish, and use fire; and invented the spear and atlatl and then the bow and arrow. They developed the art of making pottery, learned to domesticate animals and cultivate plants, began using adobe and stone in building houses, and learned to smelt iron and use it in tools. Finally, what we call "civilization" began with the invention of the phonetic alphabet, culminating in all the twentieth-century wonders.

Each civilization has also been marked by its birth, maturation, and demise, the latter brought about by uncontrolled population growth that outstripped the source of available energy, be it loss of topsoil or deforestation. In olden times, the survivors could move on to less populated, more fertile areas as their civilizations collapsed. Today, however, there is nowhere left on Earth to go!

Having learned little or nothing from history, our civilization is currently destroying the very environment from which it sprang and on which it relies for continuance. Civilization as we know it cannot, therefore, be the final evolutionary stage for human existence. But what lies beyond our current notion of civilization? What is the next frontier for "civilized" people to conquer? Is it outer space, as so often stated? No, it is not outer space. What then? It is inner space, the conquest of oneself, which many assert is life's most difficult task. As the Buddha said: "Though he should conquer a thousand men in the battlefield a thousand times, yet he, indeed, who would conquer himself is the noblest victor."

In the material world, self-conquest means bringing one's thoughts and behaviors in line with the immutable physical/biological laws governing the world in which one lives, such as the law of cause and effect. In the spiritual realm, this means disciplining one's thoughts and behaviors in accord with the highest spiritual/social truths handed down throughout the ages, such as love your neighbor as yourself and treat others as you want them to treat you.

The outcome of self-conquest is social/environmental sustainability, which must be the next cultural stage towards which we struggle. Social/environmental sustainability is the frontier beyond self-centeredness and its child, destructive conflict. I specify *destructive* conflict because conflict itself is not necessarily destructive. Conflict can be personally and socially constructive, such as a focused debate on an issue that brings about increased growth in personal and social consciousness. In other instances, one can view conflict as somewhat neutral, such as differences of opinion in which two people amicably agree to disagree. A conflict becomes destructive when it destroys human dignity, degrades the productive capacity of an ecosystem, or forecloses options for present and/or future generations.

Fulfilling our acknowledged obligation to future generations requires fundamental changes in our social consciousness and cultural norms, changes that will demand choices different from those we have heretofore made, which means thinking anew. But "a great many people," as American psychologist William James observed, "think they are thinking when they are merely rearranging their prejudices." *Resolving Environmental Conflict* is thus about choices, those with which we free ourselves and those with which we imprison ourselves.

To change anything, we must, through the choices we make, reach beyond where we are, beyond where we feel safe. We must dare to move ahead, even if we do not fully understand where we are going or the price of getting there, because we will never have perfect knowledge. And we must become students of processes and let go our advocacy of positions and embattlements over winning agreement with narrow points of view. This is important because our ever-increasing knowledge rapidly outstrips the ability of our current paradigm, based on old knowledge, to explain the new in terms of the old.

True progress toward an ecologically sound environment and a socially just culture will be initially expensive in both money and effort, but in the end not only will be mandated by shifting public values but also will be progressively less expensive over time. The longer we wait, however, the more disastrous becomes the environmental condition and the more expensive and difficult become the necessary social changes.

No biological short-cuts, technological quick fixes, or political rhetoric can mend what is broken. Dramatic, fundamental change is necessary if we are really concerned with bettering the quality of life, even that of next year. It is not a question of can we or can't we change, but one of will we or won't we change. Change is a choice, a choice of individuals reflected in the collective of society and mirrored in the landscape.

Can destructive environmental conflicts be resolved? Emphatically, yes! But thus far I find only one kind of facilitative approach that can begin to accomplish such resolution. It is the largely ignored "transformative approach" described by Bush and Folger in their 1994 book, *The Promise of Mediation,* which is "a change or refinement in the consciousness or character of individual human beings...individual moral development."

To resolve destructive environmental conflicts, the facilitation process not only must have the greatest and longest-lasting personal and social effect possible but also must be as healing as possible because outcomes of environmental conflicts are, above all, intergenerational. This means that it is the present generation's responsibility to serve the future, not the future generations' responsibility to serve the present. (Facilitation, in the sense that it is used in this book, means to conduct a process of communication whereby people are assisted in freeing themselves from difficulties and obstacles in making decisions that either avoid or eliminate destructive conflict by forging commonly held values into a shared vision towards which to collectively build.)

Destructive conflicts are created by the choices people make and therefore can be resolved by electing different choices with resolution so firmly in mind that it naturally leads to a shared vision of the future towards which to build. Because people are often consciously blind to the motives of their choices, however, some kind of facilitative process is needed to help resolve destructive conflicts by overcoming blind spots, the first step towards a shared vision.

There are many reasons why facilitation is necessary to the resolution of a destructive environmental conflict, but only a few are interwoven into this book by helping people understand that:

1. Nature—not humanity—is ultimately in control and sets impartial rules for the intergenerational experiment of life.

2. Solar energy is the only "free" resource over geological time. Earth-based resources are ultimately finite, a condition now exacerbated by a global overpopulation of humans and an unjust distribution of available resources.

3. Science can do the job it was designed to do only when we have resolved our destructive conflicts and can accept scientific data for what it is meant to be: tentative insight into universal relationships.

4. The environment and our children, their children, and their children's children are the silent parties in almost every environmental conflict.

5. People are one another's learning partners, and conflict is one of life's classrooms.

6. Through conflict resolution we can reframe our understanding of the issues, renegotiate our participation with one another and our environment, and in so doing realize what costs we are committing our children and those of the future to pay for *our* decisions and behavior.

7. Destructive conflict and its squandering of finite resources through the primacy of competition is a luxury society cannot afford.

8. Destructive conflict is a choice, and we always have the option of choosing to choose again.

9. Social/environmental sustainability is also a choice, but it requires a collective vision to see beyond destructive conflict.

This book covers some of the basic transformative concepts that over the years I have found vital in helping resolve destructive environmental conflicts, bringing these conflicts to closure in a shared vision of the future, and then implementing that vision as sustainable community development. Because one must learn the basic philosophy from which the art is born before procedural "do's" and "don'ts" make any sense, *Resolving Environmental Conflict* is meant as a synthesis of essential transformative principles rather than a "how to" book of facilitation procedures.

Although some important procedural aspects of facilitation per se are discussed, there is a standard, well-documented literature on facilitation (mediation) procedures which does not need to be repeated here. The discussion shall therefore be confined specifically to points concerning transformative facilitation.

This book was written to give people the necessary philosophical underpinnings for practicing transformative facilitation. Although I always endeavor to leave behind a working knowledge of the process itself each time I facilitate the resolution of a dispute, I cannot impart in so short a time that which has taken me much of my life to learn. It is therefore my hope that this book will not only help to close that gap but also encourage the many would-be facilitators springing up around the world to consider the transformative approach as the best way to achieve long-term social/environmental sustainability.

Before discussing how this book is set up, I want it clearly understood that how and why I facilitate the resolution of destructive environmental conflicts and the processes of sustainable community development as I do does *not* make it the only way, the right way, or even the best way. It is one way. Therefore, to prevent the discussion from coming across as my notion of what you, the reader, should or should not do, I shall write, as much as possible, in the first person while reflecting on what I think I have learned over the years. Although it is my hope that you find something of value within these pages, you are your own final authority on which parts fit into your work and life.

To become a facilitator, one must learn to be a sifter, taking something from here and something from there, which is incorporated into one's own style. Sifting is essential to one's continual growth as a servant of the parties in destructive environmental conflicts and in sustainable community development.

Resolving Environmental Conflict is presented in two parts. Part I opens with a brief comparison of facilitation approaches and a quick look at how I generally facilitate destructive environmental disputes, which creates a context for what follows. The rest of Part I is an examination of what goes into the facilitation process, beginning with the "givens" of any environmental conflict. The "givens" are those things so basic that they must be understood, accepted, and acted on if a destructive environmental conflict is to be resolved. One of my main purposes is to help people understand the debt they are committing their children and their children's children to pay through decisions they make during the resolution process, however the conflict comes out.

It is imperative that people become aware of the long-term effects of their decisions. I say this because I believe children are one of the two silent parties in all environmental conflicts; the land and its productive capacity is the other. All parties must understand the environmental and economic circumstances to which they are committing the future, because if the conflict is destructive and the outcome is a deficit in terms of either future options for the children or the productive capacity of the ecosystem, it is analogous to taxation without representation, and that goes against everything democracy stands for.

I do not presume to cover all the possible "givens" for resolving destructive environmental conflicts, but only to provide those basic concepts that I find to be essential and recurring. Anything more is beyond the scope of this book.

An environmental conflict is facilitated towards its natural conclusion, a shared vision of a sustainable future towards which to build. Such a vision is the necessary culmination of every facilitation process dealing with resolving destructive environmental conflict if society, as we know it, is to survive the twenty-first century. This is a critical idea, because parts are often mistaken for wholes, and ideas are often viewed as complete when in fact they are not. Such is often the case with the resolution of a destructive environmental conflict, when the goal is seen only as the solution of an immediate problem.

Part II goes beyond shared vision to examine notions of development, sustainability, and community. The process plans for sustainable community development within the context of a sustainable landscape. This means that a community committed to sustainable development is not seeking some mythical "balance" between its economics and its environment. Rather, it seeks the synergism of ecology and culture, including economy, to promote a healthy, sustainable environment that enriches the lives of all its inhabitants—both human and nonhuman. Sustainable community development gives people a chance to employ such cardinal principles of culture as democracy, beauty, utility, durability, and sustainability in the planning process.

The sustainable community development of the future must begin in the elementary schools of today, and it must begin by children learning the art of facilitating differences before they become destructive conflicts. This does not mean that every child must necessarily become a skilled facilitator. But it does mean that every child would have available a basic understanding of transformative facilitation and the ability to use its principles in deciding the best way to deal with stressful personal issues and interpersonal differences, beginning at home while growing up.

I think it possible that learning transformative facilitation skills at a young age can begin to break the escalating dysfunctional cycle of family abuse by helping children understand that there are behavioral models other than those at home from which to choose. In addition, the principles of transformative facilitation can help a child learn how to retain or take back his or her personhood by revealing that empowerment is a viable alternative to the role of being a victim. Thus, every child from a dysfunctional family who chooses a peaceful model of resolving differences will carry forward into his or her own family a greater degree of socially functional behavior.

If learning transformative facilitation skills can help shift a child's focus from socially dysfunctional to socially functional behaviors, then destructive environmental conflicts may decline in both frequency and intensity, which would go a long way towards protecting the options of future generations. In this way, we could give children the peaceful tools of empowerment with which to begin helping themselves in the present for the future. The gift of such tools sums up, for me, the purpose of transformative facilitation, which, I believe, is our best chance of achieving sustainable community development.

Bear in mind, however, that the future is always rooted in the present. It is therefore necessary to commence teaching and using the principles and skills of transformative facilitation now if present generations are to grow toward social/environmental sustainability while there is still time to approach it.

ACKNOWLEDGMENTS

I have often been told that my thinking is too idealistic, too impractical, and too philosophical, but then anything less than the ideal is not worth striving for. Be that as it may, in writing *Resolving Environmental Conflict,* I found myself in good company. There are four special references that found their way to my desk and closely parallel my own thinking. They are so important to me that referring to them in the bibliography is not enough; I thus acknowledge them here.

First, I gave a guest lecture on "The Nature of Sustainability" to a class in the University of Oregon's Department of Planning, Public Policy, and Management, in Eugene in April 1992. Three or four months later Christine Kirk, a student in that class, sent me a copy of her senior thesis ("Community Development: The Inlet for Sustainable Change"), with the following comment: "I very much enjoyed your style of presentation and your perception of sustainable development. Enclosed is my senior thesis. I would like for you to read it because I believe that our perceptions of sustainable development are similar." Christine was indeed correct, and it is with great pleasure that I include her as my co-author on Chapters 10 and 11.

Second is Max DePree's 1989 book, *Leadership Is an Art,* which I used in Chapters 7 and 11. Third is Fred Kofman and Peter M. Senge's 1993 paper, "Communities of Commitment: The Heart of Learning Organizations," parts of which are scattered throughout the text, and fourth is Robert Rodale's 1988 paper, "Big New Ideas—Where Are They Today?," which he sent to me before he died and which I offer with pleasure in Chapter 11.

There is yet another body of work dealing with communication and learning that I found surprisingly good and useful. It is hidden, of all places, in the 1977

Aviation Instructor's Handbook. I have used the ideas in it liberally in portions of Chapters 5 and 7.

The following people, listed in alphabetical order, were kind enough to review the manuscript and help me improve it: John Baldwin (Director, Institute for a Sustainable Environment, University of Oregon, Eugene), Joyce K. Berry (Assistant Professor, Human Dimensions and Policy in Natural Resources, Colorado State University, Fort Collins), Ron Clarke (Professor Emeritus, Religious Studies, Oregon State University, Corvallis), David Hunt (Mediation Trainer, Salem, Oregon), James R. Karr (Director, Institute for Environmental Studies, University of Washington, Seattle), Christine Kirk (Community Policing, Albany Police Department, Albany, Oregon), Deen Selwood (Program Coordinator, Turtle Island Earth Stewards Society, Vancouver, British Columbia, Canada), Bob Tarrant (Retired Director, USDA Forest Service Pacific Northwest Research Station, Portland, Oregon, and Professor Emeritus, Forest Science, Oregon State University, Corvallis), and Julia Wondelleck (Assistant Professor, Resource Policy and Behavior, University of Michigan, Ann Arbor).

I am also deeply grateful to Sandy Pearlman, at St. Lucie Press, for her superb editing.

And once again my wife, Zane, graciously accepted being a writer's widow while I worked on this book. I am sincerely grateful for all the help.

AUTHOR

Chris Maser spent over 20 years as a research scientist in natural history and ecology in forest, shrub steppe, subarctic, desert, and coastal settings. Trained primarily as a vertebrate zoologist, he was a research mammalogist in Nubia, Egypt (1963–1964) with the Yale University Peabody Museum Prehistoric Expedition and was a research mammalogist in Nepal (1966–1967) for the U.S. Naval Medical Research Unit #3 based in Cairo, Egypt, where he participated in a study of tick-borne diseases. He conducted a three-year (1970–1973) ecological survey of the Oregon Coast for the University of Puget Sound, Tacoma, Washington. He was a research ecologist with the U.S. Department of the Interior Bureau of Land Management for twelve years (1975–1987)—the last eight studying old-growth forests in western Oregon—and a landscape ecologist with the Environmental Protection Agency for one year (1990–1991).

Today he is an independent author as well as an international lecturer and facilitator in resolving environmental disputes, vision statements, and sustainable community development. He is co-founder and Chief Facilitator for the Center of Resolution, Vision, and Change, based in Corvallis, Oregon. He is also an international consultant in forest ecology and sustainable forestry practices. He has written over 240 publications, including *The Redesigned Forest* (1988), *Forest Primeval: The Natural History of an Ancient Forest* (1989, listed in School Library Journal as best science and technical book of 1989), *Global Imperative: Harmonizing Culture and Nature* (1992), *Sustainable Forestry: Philosophy, Science, and Economics* (1994), *From the Forest to the Sea: The Ecology of Wood in Streams, Rivers, Estuaries, and Oceans* (1994, with James R. Sedell), and *The Seasons of My Ditch* (1996). Although he has worked in Canada, Egypt, France, Germany, Japan, Malaysia, Nepal, Slovakia, and Switzerland, he calls Corvallis, Oregon, home.

PART I

RESOLVING DESTRUCTIVE ENVIRONMENTAL CONFLICT

If we could read the secret history of our enemies,
we should find in each man's life,
sorrow and suffering enough to disarm all hostilities.
                    Henry Wadsworth Longfellow

1

APPROACHES TO FACILITATION

The following comparative discussion of facilitation approaches is drawn from the introduction and Chapter 1 of Bush and Folger's excellent book, *The Promise of Mediation*.[1] (For those interested in a comparison of facilitative approaches, this is the book to read.) Facilitation, according to Bush and Folger, is generally understood as an informal process in which a neutral third party, one powerless to impose resolution, helps disputing parties seek a mutually acceptable settlement. As such, facilitation has within itself the unique transformative potential to engender moral growth in people by helping them—in the very midst of conflict—to wrestle with difficult inner and outer circumstances and bridge human differences.

Bush and Folger point out that there is "substantial evidence" to suggest that today's standard facilitation process focuses largely on problem solving, perhaps even more so than in earlier years. In fact, the unique potential of facilitation to achieve moral transformation is receiving less and less emphasis in practice. This potential is therefore seldom realized, and when it is, it is generally serendipitous, rather than the result of the facilitator's conscious efforts. There is currently a crossroad facing facilitation, one reflecting the movement's two basic approaches: problem solving and transformation.

FACILITATION AT THE CROSSROAD

The problem-solving approach to destructive environmental conflict emphasizes the capacity of facilitation to find solutions that generate mutually acceptable settlements, almost always for the immediate benefit of adult humans, regardless of the effect of the settlement on children or the productive capacity of the environment. Facilitators in this approach often endeavor to influence and direct disputants toward settlement in general, and even toward the specific terms of a settlement.

As facilitation has evolved, the problem-solving approach has been increasingly emphasized, to the point where this kind of directed, settlement-oriented facilitation dominates the current movement. The premise of the problem-solving approach is that the most important goal is to maximize the greatest possible satisfaction for individuals engaged in a conflict. But as author Gail Sheehy points out, "Human institutions prepare people for continuity, not for change." To me, therefore, the limitations inherent in the problem-solving approach are precisely its narrowness in scope, rigid focus on quantifiable outcomes, and the increasing attempt to eliminate risk, all symptoms of its growing institutionalization.

Designer Milton Glaser captures well my concern with the uncritical institutionalizing of professionalism in facilitating the resolution of disputes when he says, "Professionalism really means eliminating risk. Once you become good at something, everyone wants you to repeat it over and over again. But the more you eliminate risk, the closer you come to eliminating the act of creative intervention."

In contrast to the problem-solving approach, the transformation approach emphasizes the capacity of facilitation for personal growth, which is embodied in the ability to accept risk. Transformative facilitators therefore concentrate on helping parties empower themselves to define the issues and decide the settlement in their own terms and in their own time through a better understanding of one another's perspectives.

Transformative facilitators avoid the directiveness associated with the problem-solving approach. Equally important, transformative facilitators help parties recognize and capitalize on the opportunities for personal growth inherently present in conflict. This does not mean that satisfaction and fairness are unimportant; rather, it means that transformation of human moral awareness and conduct is even more important.

The aim of transformative facilitation is to help parties become better human beings by stimulating moral growth and transforming human character, which results in parties finding genuine solutions to their real problems. In addition, the private, nonjudgmental, noncoercive character of transformative facilitation can provide disputants a safe haven in which to humanize themselves, despite their having started out as fierce adversaries. This safety helps people feel and express varying degrees of understanding and concern for one another as they grow toward greater compassion, despite their disagreement.

The most important aspect of transformative facilitation is its ability to strengthen people's moral resolve and their ability to handle adverse circumstances beyond the immediate conflict. It therefore transforms society for the better by bringing out intrinsic good in people.

I practice the transformative approach to facilitation and am deeply concerned with its philosophical foundation, because I have lived under both a ruthless dictator and a Communist regime that were, at best, indifferent to human life. From these experiences, it is clear that coercion of any kind settles no differences and lays to rest no issues. It only degrades human beings and steals hope from their souls.

A BRIEF LOOK AT THE FACILITATION I PRACTICE

In facilitation, it is not so much the procedural aspects that make the difference, but rather the nature and emphasis of facilitation's content within its context. Therefore, the only topic encompassed in this section is a brief look at the generalized procedure I follow while facilitating the resolution of a destructive environmental conflict. The rest of the book deals with the content of transformative facilitation.

As you read this chapter, remember that I am but one person, and the way I facilitate the resolution of a destructive environmental dispute, the framing of a vision statement, sustainable community development, or the entire process (from resolution of a destructive conflict through sustainable community development) is only one way. This does not make it the "right" way or even the best way. Nevertheless, while it has worked well over the years, I did not start out to become a facilitator.

In the beginning, I merely noticed that many of the destructive environmental conflicts grew out of the incompatibility of human material desires with the sustainable capacity of the environment. This situation was compounded as society's questions of value were increasingly subjected to "objective" scientific study, to derive "objective" scientific data, to provide "objective" scientific answers. Yet despite millions of dollars and thousands of person-hours devoted to such study, intrinsic cultural values and "objective" scientific data remain miles apart.

The original idea, therefore, was to help bridge this chasm by presenting participants with the ecological concepts (based on the best available data) and the social concepts (based on their expressed cultural values) within the context of systems thinking. My sole intent was to help them understand the information from an interactive, interconnected, interdependent ecological/social systems point of view, encompassing the past, present, and future. In this way, they could expand their common frame of reference in preparation for someone else to facilitate the resolution of the dispute.

It was always emphasized that the data presented were the most up to date that I knew of, but that *neither I nor anyone else knew what was "right" or had "the answer."* Over time, and much to my surprise, participants began asking me to stay with them and guide the entire facilitative process. Having no idea what I was doing, I reluctantly agreed, but limited myself to dealing with destructive environmental conflicts.

All I had in my favor was an undying belief: (1) in the inherent goodness of people; (2) that their blindness—their lack of conscious awareness—was born of ignorance, not malice; (3) that each person does the level best he or she knows how to do at all times; (4) that given a place in which to be safe, an empathetic ear with which to be heard, and the empowerment with which to overcome fear and ignorance, people could and would change for the better; (5) that there was no turning back once a person started down the path of personal growth, with its increasing sense of freedom through self-control and self-direction; and (6) that society as a whole is lifted up each time an individual grows and matures emotionally, spiritually, and intellectually.

My approach to facilitation was intuitively transformative because it seems much more important to cure the cause and eliminate the symptom than to merely alleviate the symptom without touching its cause (the problem-solving approach). The transformative approach inherently: (1) assumes that human relationships take precedence over procedural outcomes; (2) opens people to a greater compassion for one another; (3) allows people to argue for and protect one another's dignity; (4) is a meticulous practice of the best principles democracy has to offer; (5) balances intellect with intuition; (6) improves society by allowing people to grow emotionally, spiritually, and intellectually; (7) focuses on the cause of a conflict; (8) helps participants understand the consequences of their choices within the context of Nature's impartial law of cause and effect; (9) allows the outcome of a conflict to be decided solely by the participants, despite the fact that resolution may not take place until some months after facilitation is completed; and (10) inspires the possibility of sustainable community development.

I intentionally go into each facilitation with very little specific knowledge of the conflict or the participants. Although someone obviously contacts me about facilitating the resolution of a destructive environmental conflict, our conversation is kept to a minimum. Beyond that, I deal with as few participants as possible prior to the facilitation process; if interaction is necessary, I avoid discussing the conflict. In this way, I am, as much as possible, unbiased during the process and detached from the outcome.

Further, I only agree to facilitate an environmental conflict when the disputants have exhausted every other avenue of settlement and have come up empty handed. Only when they have reached "their wit's end" are they ready to listen and to change. Only now is true facilitation possible.

There are three basic parts to facilitating the resolution of a destructive environmental dispute: (1) the introduction, (2) the body, and (3) the conclusion.

Introduction

The introduction serves several purposes, which collectively set the stage for the facilitation process. The first is to establish common ground among the participants and between the participants and me. I usually use cards with the participants' names on them to arrange seating, so that participants sit next to someone not of their choosing and begin to mix. Next, we take some time to introduce ourselves and share a little about our respective backgrounds, often including interests and hobbies.

At other times, the participants may form into pairs with their neighbors, take a few moments to learn about each other, and then take turns introducing each other. In this way, preliminary communication is initiated, which simultaneously starts to bring each person "out of the closet" through mutual participation that captures and holds their attention and has within it the seeds of trust.

The introduction serves to clarify why the participants are taking part in the facilitation process and what each hopes to gain from it. At this time, we discuss whether all necessary parties are in attendance; if not, why not; and what can be done to rectify the situation. Here my task is to help the participants develop an inclusive attitude by helping them understand why all parties are necessary to the process and its outcome.

Next, I help the participants develop a receptive attitude toward the facilitation process itself. This is done by helping them understand what it may hold that is beneficial to them personally, such as learning how to use the democratic process as a tool of self-government as well as community government.

The introduction also allows the participants to learn what they can expect from me, what I expect from them, and what they can expect from one another. This is done in part by how I present myself as a person and in part by establishing the rules of conduct, such as waiting your turn to speak, being kind and polite at all times, and accepting one another's ideas without judgment.

Finally, the participants must understand that they will get as much or as little out of the facilitation process as they are committed to putting into it. After all, it is theirs, not mine.

Body

The body is the main part of the facilitation process. When possible, I use a three-day process. The first day is spent discussing what an ecosystem is, how it functions, and the reciprocal nature of how and why we treat a system as we do and how and why it responds as it does. This is done by using slide presentations. It is easier for the participants to begin shifting their thinking prior to their explaining to me what the dispute is about, because they know that under this circumstance I am as unbiased as possible.

This format works well, as evidenced by a write-up in the U.S. Forest Service *Southwestern Region News*:[2]

> Chris Maser...spoke to a group of Forest Service employees, preservationists, conservationists, and industrialists in Albuquerque [NM] August 9 [1988]....Plans called for 30 to attend. There were 74 at the session with standing room only....
>
> ...[Maser], who neither "preached" nor "put down" views of old growth, stressed repeatedly the need for rethinking positions, prior education, and conclusions concerning forests and old growth. A theme that was woven constantly through a several-hour monologue was that of discussion, definition, and consensus. The meeting and discussion of forest issues by those involved...is a necessity, he insisted....
>
> ...Maser, with patience, painted a picture of the cycles of the forest, and the vital part of old growth. With meticulous care, he led the group through a labyrinth of long-term activity in the soils, which can, he insisted, produce a truly sustainable forest.
>
> A question and answer session followed the formal presentation....It was notable that there were few pointed or conflict-prone questions. Reaction...from most participants was one of studied consideration of what had been presented, a reaction that we are convinced Maser was aiming for.

The second day, with as much of a "systems" view as possible, we put the current conflict into a social/environmental context in the field, preferably in the area of contention. Going into the field is critical because it helps to make the abstract concepts of the first day into concrete experiences of immediate relevance. Here the discussion begins by focusing on the teaching/learning of the first day, namely on what an ecosystem is, how it functions, and the reciprocal nature of how and why we treat a system as we do and how and why it responds as it does.

During this time each person in turn expresses his or her perception of the dispute from his or her understanding of how the ecosystem in question functions. The purpose is for each person to educate me about the dispute from his or her understanding of the whole and his or her perceived relation to the whole.

As each explanation unfolds, the person recounting it clarifies his or her own understanding of his or her perceptions and the other parties hear for the first time the whole of someone else's story from that person's point of view. During this story-telling, I learn what the dispute is about because I hear it from various sides and am thus able to find common ground, differences, negotiable areas, quagmires, and hidden potentials for resolution.

Because the ecological condition of the resource(s), which is the focal point of the conflict, has a historical perspective, it is necessary to help participants examine this perspective. From our examination of the concrete historical and current perspective, we progress to a more abstract, futuristic perspective. This perspective allows scrutiny of possible outcomes resulting from various kinds of decisions as each might affect the productive capacity of the environment, present and future. It is vital that participants be able to move from the concrete to the abstract, based on their concept of current knowledge, if they are to craft a shared vision of the future as a resolution of their immediate conflict.

Toward this end, it is imperative to accept people where they are in terms of their understanding, which normally means using simple examples of how two or three components of a system might function together and then gradually expanding the examples to show how a more complex system might function as a whole. This includes helping participants to understand such concepts as change in terms of a continual, creative process; self-reinforcing feedback loops; isolated pieces versus interconnected, interactive functions; the dynamic equilibrium of an ever-changing system; and so on.

By accepting people where they are in their understanding, it is possible to help them move from a known point of departure, with respect to their perceived knowledge, toward new ideas and concepts, while retaining their dignity intact. This process is greatly enhanced if one can lead people from more widely accepted ideas to those less widely held.

When I feel that I have an adequate understanding of the issue(s) and the participants seem ready (usually by the third day), we discuss the concept of a vision, goals, and objectives. Once the participants have an understanding of these concepts, they begin to work out their vision and goals (it is not yet time for objectives), crafting them carefully on flip charts. Doing it this way, the vision and goals can usually be drafted and agreed to during the third day.

Occasionally, however, this does not work. If the participants just do not agree, they are sent off by themselves (sometimes for a day or a couple of weeks) with the instruction that each party in the dispute, which usually consists of a number of individuals, is to craft its own vision and goals. When they have completed the assignment, we reconvene, at which time each party shares its vision and goals with the other(s).

The purpose of one party presenting its vision and goals to the other(s) is simply for the other people to help make sure—without judgment—that the stated vision and goals fit the agreed-upon criteria. If they do not, the wording is corrected so that the criteria are in fact satisfied. Each party in turn presents its material, and each party in turn helps the others assure that the criteria are met.

Once this process has been completed, all parties look for areas of overlap. I may help them out with questions, a powerful tool when used wisely, because questions open the door of possibility. For example, it was not possible to go to the moon until someone asked the question: "Is it possible to go to the moon?" At that moment, going to the moon became possible. To be effective, however, each question must: (1) have a specific purpose, (2) contain a single idea, (3) be clear in meaning, (4) stimulate thought, (5) require a definite answer to bring closure to the human relationship induced by the question, and (6) relate to previous information.

For example, in a discussion about going to the moon, one might ask: "Do you know what the moon is?" The specific purpose is to find out if one knows what the moon is. Knowledge of the moon is the single idea contained in the question. The meaning of the question is clear: do you or do you not know what the moon is? The question stimulates thought about what the moon is and may spark an idea of how one relates to it; if not, that can be addressed in a second question. The question as asked requires a definite answer, and the question relates to previous information.

Once the areas of agreement and/or a willingness to compromise are found, they may constitute up to eighty percent or more of a common ground, and there may be little dispute left to negotiate. Once this point has been reached, the parties are ready to conclude this phase of the facilitation process.

Conclusion

In winding down this phase of the facilitation process, the important elements of the dispute and its resolution are retraced, so the parties, having been consumed in the process, can now stand back and see in perspective how it works, which may give them a better understanding of the whole. This review both reinforces what they have learned and improves their retention of it for later reference. New ideas are not included at this time because they are likely to confuse the participants.

Finally, I must help them to determine what their next step is, usually another meeting to refine their initial draft of the vision and goals. They must decide how they want to do this and when. It is imperative, however, that they set their next meeting date and commit to it prior to adjourning.

Transformative facilitation helps the parties create a shared vision and goals for a sustainable future in which they can all somehow benefit and in which they want to share. Only now do I consider the dispute largely, but not completely, resolved. Full resolution of an environmental conflict requires putting the shared vision into action through sustainable community development.

Resolving a destructive environmental conflict depends first on understanding the cause or causes of the conflict. Such understanding must uncover the chain of events set in motion by the participants' decisions, which in turn triggered cause-and-effect relationships within a range of alternative decisions and outcomes. My perception of a conflict must be as objective as possible and not based on judgment as dictated by my standard of right or wrong.

Beyond this, there are seven "givens" that must be understood if a destructive environmental conflict is to be resolved: (1) conflict is a choice; (2) environmental principles, the need to know and the fear of knowing; (3) the human equation; (4) communication, the interpersonal element; (5) the process is the decision; (6) conflict is a learning partnership; and (7) practicing transformative facilitation.

2

CONFLICT IS A CHOICE

Conflict is a choice of behavior. We resort to destructive conflict in one way or another, at one level or another, because that is what we were taught to do as children. That is how we were taught to cope with change—those circumstances perceived as threatening to our survival.

Looking around the world today, various segments of the global community are blowing themselves to bits and in the process needlessly, recklessly squandering the natural resource base on which they and future generations depend for survival. Children are being ushered into emotionally shattered lives, where their inner poverty will compound the outer poverty they face in the spiritual/cultural/economic chaos of disrupted lives; gutted cities; corrupt, power-hungry governments; and war-torn, fragmented landscapes. These generations may well grow up thinking that hatred and destructive conflict are the norm, which continually fosters the unworkable paradigm of a black-and-white world, in which "I'm right and you're wrong" and "you're either for me or against me."

Is such a future unavoidable? Must we increasingly become a world of victims in which there is no escape from an eternal dysfunctional cycle of abuse and combat? If abuse, and the combat it engenders, are indeed the lot of humanity, then time and history will grind wearily on to the only social outcome possible, the ultimate destruction of human society, taking much of life on Earth with it. Is this the lesson human history is to continue teaching as each day's activities are recorded in the archives of eventide?

I think not. I see the world differently, and this difference is predicated largely on two things: (1) recognizing, accepting, and acting on the notion that destructive conflict is a choice, which means we can choose peaceful ways of resolving differences, and (2) understanding that the peaceful way lies in the art of transformative facilitation, where differences are resolved through inner shifts in consciousness. Such shifts alter the core perceptions out of which destructive conflict grows by increasing the social functionality of the participants and hence their tendencies toward peace. Simply put, the transformative approach to facilitation helps each person mirror his or her fears and sense of vulnerability to his or her opponent(s), thereby coaxing from deep within a sense of compassion that transcends each person's fear. As fear is transcended, perceived differences—fear's cradle—become novel approaches to the commonalities of a shared vision. In fact, they often become a vision's source of strength.

Finding no external fixes for internal fears, I must assume that the cause of destructive conflict is internal to the combatants themselves, as it always is to me. For example, I was taught by my parents' behavior that destructive conflict between people was simply a condition of life, a necessity of survival. Watching my parents, I did as a child the only thing a child knows how to do: I copied what I saw.

Finally, in my mid-forties, I began to understand that there are no "enemies out there," only frightened people who feel the need to defend themselves from potential loss of what they think they must have to survive—control of their own lives as they perceive it.

Thus, as a facilitator, it is imperative that I understand why destructive conflict is the chosen way of dealing with personal differences if I am to help the participants do anything more than temporarily alleviate the symptom which festered into open dispute. To do so, I must understand something of the underlying nature of destructive conflict, beginning with the notion of each person's "right" of survival, however that is defined.

WHAT IS A RIGHT?

In medieval literature, brave knights came from across the land to be considered for membership at the Round Table. King Arthur designed its circular shape to democratically arrange the knights and give each an equal position. When a knight was granted membership at the Round Table, he was guaranteed equal stature with everyone else at the table and a right to be heard with equal voice.

Today, one understanding of a "right" is a legalistic, human construct based on some sense of moral privilege. Although a right in a democratic system of government is created by people and defined and guaranteed by law, access to a right may not be equally distributed across society. Conversely, a right does not apply to any person outside the select group unless that group purposely confers such a right on a specifically recognized individual, such as the disenfranchised.

In a true democracy, the whole protects all of its parts and the parts give obedience to the will of the whole. Ostensibly, therefore, a right in democracy gives everyone equality by sanctifying and impartially protecting certain socially acceptable behaviors while controlling unsanctioned ones. There is, however, a price exacted for having rights, even in a true democracy.

Rights have responsibilities attached to them. Thus, whenever a law is passed to protect the rights of the majority against the transgressions of the minority, everyone pays the same price—a loss of freedom of choice, of flexibility—because every law so passed is restrictive to everyone. Put succinctly, we give up personal freedoms in order to gain personal rights.

The problem is that rights, as granted by humans to one another in daily life, including in the United States, are based not on equality but rather on access. Access is determined by some notion that one race, color, creed, sex, or age is superior to another, which means that differences and similarities are based on our subjective judgments about whatever those appearances are. In American society, for example, men are judged more capable than women in most kinds of work because society has placed more value on certain kinds of products, i.e., those demanding such masculine attributes as linear thinking and physical strength as opposed to those demanding such feminine attributes as relationship and physical gentleness.

With notable exceptions, the stereotype holds that perceived differences in outer (superficial) values become social judgments about the inherent (real) values of individual human beings. Superficial characteristics are thus translated into special rights or privileges simply because the individuals involved are different in some aspects and either perform certain actions differently or perform different actions. The greater the difference I perceive between another person and myself, the more likely I am to make black-and-white judgments about that person's real value as expressed through my notion of that person's rights.

Such judgments are made against the personal standard I use to measure how everything around me fits into my comfort zone. I thus judge people as good or bad, depending on how they conform to my standard of acceptability, a standard taught and reinforced by my parents and later by my peers and teachers. Such judgments are erroneous, however, because all I can ever judge is appearances. In addition, my standard is correct only for me; it is not validly imposed on anyone else. Nevertheless, I use socially constructed, hierarchical couplets of extrinsic differences (white male versus white female, white male versus black male, human versus Nature) as a basis for judging the equality of such things as one race versus another, men versus women, secular versus spiritual, right versus wrong, good versus evil, and so on.

The most extreme example of personal judgment is the use of superficial differences to justify a social end. One group of people thus declares itself superior to another group because it wants what the other group has. The "superior" group tells the "inferior" group that they have no rights, and through this denial of rights justifies its abuse of fellow human beings.

When, for instance, the invading Spanish conquered the Pueblo Indians, they could not accept, let alone acknowledge, that they and the Pueblos were equally human. Had they acknowledged that truth, they could never have justified the wholesale murder of the Indians and theft of their land. In turn, when the invading Anglos conquered the Spanish, they could not accept, let alone acknowledge, that they and the Spanish were equally human. Had they acknowledged that truth, they could never have justified the wholesale murder of the Spanish and theft of their land. As modern conquests continue, so does the cycle.

The same principle holds for the indigenous peoples of the South American tropical forests. If the cattle barons ever admitted that the indigenous peoples living in the forests were their equals, they could not clearcut and burn the forests to gain pasture for their beef herds. In creating the pastures, the cattle barons destroyed an ecosystem and stripped the indigenous peoples not only of their current livelihood but also of their future options and those of their children. If the cattle barons were to admit that the indigenous peoples are in every way their equals, then they would have to *treat* them as their equals. And that, in turn, means sharing control of their mutual social destiny.

It is not a question of who is better than whom. Rather, it is a question of who is more afraid of whom. It is a question of who has internalized all the assumed differences and therefore perceives another human being as an unknown entity. It is a question of who is so afraid of losing control of their perceived rights that they will do anything to keep control, regardless of social and environmental consequences. In the end, therefore, it becomes a question of the equality of differences.

THE EQUALITY OF DIFFERENCES

Notions of superiority and inferiority are based on personal, familial, and societal judgments about the intrinsic values of extrinsic differences. To illustrate, consider two questions about garbage collectors and medical doctors: Is collecting garbage as a social service of equal value to that of treating sick people? Is the social stature of a garbage collector equal to that of a medical doctor?

Most people, in my experience, seem to think that the service performed by medical doctors is of greater social value than that performed by garbage collectors and that doctors not only enjoy but also deserve a higher social status than garbage collectors. But when judging garbage collectors versus medical doctors, most people focus on differences and fail to take similarities into account, one of which is that both occupations help maintain a healthy environment for people. Both occupations also rely on each other's services. In fact, doctors probably rely on garbage collectors more than garbage collectors rely on doctors.

How much more difficult would the doctor's task be if garbage collectors stopped collecting garbage, allowing it to accumulate around houses and in streets? The outcome could be an epidemic of bubonic plague, a disease carried by rats that proliferate in human garbage and whose fleas transmit the disease. Once plague bacteria began spreading, doctors would have to marshal their numbers to treat the sick.

Garbage collectors serve society before the fact at a fundamental, collective level. Medical doctors tend to society after the fact, after someone is ill, one individual at a time. We therefore become personally acquainted with our doctors but not usually with our garbage collectors. I find that such a personal acquaintance greatly increases the value I attribute to an individual's job, because I have not only a more intimate sense of the person's intrinsic value but also a greater knowledge of how his or her profession contributes to society and my welfare.

Nevertheless, garbage collectors are as vital to human health as medical doctors, only in a different way. Why, therefore, are they not afforded equal status in society? Perhaps the reason is that they do not need to go to school for seven to eight years to become sufficiently trained to collect garbage and therefore do not have a socially coveted title before their names. Perhaps it is because few people see them at work and therefore do not ponder the value of the service they perform. Perhaps it is because we do not go to garbage collectors to make us feel better when we are ill and thus do not form a personal relationship with them as we do with our doctors. (Have you, for instance, ever thanked your garbage collector for taking away your trash as you have thanked your doctor for making you feel better?) Perhaps it is because, compared to medical doctors, garbage collectors do not make nearly as much money, so we deem them less successful in a society where affluence is the measure of success and social status. Perhaps it is because they are filthy and stink when they get off work, instead of wearing an expensive suit and tie.

The above notwithstanding, garbage collectors and medical doctors are of equal value professionally, albeit different in how they serve the health needs of society. Further, their services are not only vital but also complementary in that they accomplish far more together than either could possibly accomplish alone.

There may be a number of judgmental reasons for these discrepancies in social stature, but none of them can be applied in the context of the real value of each person. An appropriate analogy might be the spokes of a wheel. Each spoke is slightly different and seemingly independent of the others, yet each is equal in its importance to the functioning of the wheel. Each spoke is connected at the center of the wheel and at the outer rim. Leave out one spoke and the strength and function of the wheel are to that extent diminished, although the effect might not become immediately apparent.

Each person has a gift to give, and each gift is unique to that person and critical to the social whole. All gifts are equal *and* different. What is true for individual human beings is true for cultures and societies because each is equal in its service to the Earth. Each life, each culture, each society is equally important to the evolutionary success of our planet, whether we understand it or not. Each also has its own excellence and cannot be compared to any other. All differences among people, cultures, and societies are just that—differences. The hierarchies or judgmental levels of value are human constructs that have little or nothing to do with reality. Every life, culture, and society is a practice in evolution, and each is equal before the impartiality of Universal Governance.

We must therefore discard our view of the Earth as a battlefield of subjective competition, where our human "superiority" reigns over that of Nature and where my "superiority" reigns over yours. We will all be better off if we instead consider the Earth in terms of complementary efforts in which all gifts are equal and each in its own way is important to the health and well-being of the whole living system because life demands struggle and tenacity, which continually fits and refits each living thing to its function. Complementary efforts, such as those of garbage collectors and medical doctors, imply equality among people, and human equality brings us to the notion of the inalienable right of all people to environmental justice.

ENVIRONMENTAL JUSTICE IS PREDICATED ON HUMAN EQUALITY

The concept of environmental justice, from the human point of view, by its very nature asserts that we owe something to every other person sharing the planet with us, both those present and those yet unborn. "But," you may ask, "what exactly do we have to give?" The only things we have of value are the love, trust, respect, and wisdom gleaned from our experiences and embodied in the ramifications of each and every option we pass forward. And it is exactly because options embody all we have to give, to those living today and the children of tomorrow and beyond, that environmental justice as a concept must of necessity be examined within the context of human equality.

A wonderful example of perceived inequality among humans took place in my home town of Corvallis, Oregon, a number of years ago; it involved people living in the city versus those living in the country. I read in the local newspaper that a farmer had been arrested and fined for throwing garbage on somebody's lawn in town. As I read the article, it was apparent that, despite the Constitution of the United States, some people are a lot more equal than others. The story went as follows:

Joe City, who lived in Corvallis, took his garbage out to the country and dumped it on Bill Rural's property near Bill's house. Although Bill did not see Joe dump his garbage, he found an invoice in the garbage with Joe's name and address on it. So Bill picked up all of Joe's garbage and drove into Corvallis, where he dumped it onto Joe's front lawn. Joe went to the police and complained.

Even though Bill said that the people of Corvallis were continually dumping their unwanted garbage on his land and that in this case he was sure it was Joe's garbage, Joe had legal standing and Bill did not. Bill was arrested and fined, but *nothing* happened to Joe—something that sent a clear message of inequality to Joe, to Bill, and to everyone else. The message was that it is okay for city folks to dump their garbage with legal impunity on the property of rural folks, but not vice versa.

Let's look at this another way. Rural people who value clean air and quality water have a right to enjoy these amenities, especially when they purposefully live "out in the middle of nowhere." But bureaucrats hundreds of miles away give cities and industries the right to pollute air and water because of economic and political pressures. They do this despite the fact that such pollution fouls the air and contaminates the water that rural people use.

Human inequality has to do with fear and its companion, control. The person who harbors the most fear also harbors the greatest need to be in control of his or her external environment; the need to be in control is always fed by the need for the "inequality of enemies" from which one can steal "personal rights." For example, I spoke at a forestry conference in Victoria, Canada, in March 1988. While there, I listened to an eloquent speech by a hereditary chief from a community of Aboriginal Canadians on his people's right to the land on which they lived because they had never signed a peace treaty. Their traditional land had simply been wrested from them. To my complete astonishment, an indignant timber company executive wanted to know what right *they*—as Indians—had to own any land or cut any timber.

Inequality, which translates into injustice, carries over into every institution in our land, but it is perhaps clearest in those agencies whose missions are to uphold and fulfill the legal mandates of protecting environmental quality for all citizens, present and future. It is seen everywhere: in the appalling lack of evenhandedness and in the bending of people within the agencies—including the Congress of the United States—to the political pressure of special interest groups at the expense of society as a whole, present and future. There have been times, however, when equality and justice counted for something; as Thucydides said of the Athenian code, "praise is due to all who...respect justice more than their position compels them to do." And in more recent times, the founding fathers of The United States did their level best, through the Declaration of Independence, the Constitution, and the Bill of Rights, to instill equality and justice in the new nation.

Nevertheless, agencies and individuals responsible for the welfare of our nation's natural resources have functions prescribed by law but not necessarily specified by law. A wide range of administrative discretion is therefore permitted by legislative bodies. Although this is as it should be, the system lacks a guiding precept for "public service," one that in fact means serving the whole of the public with the impartiality of justice for the common good of all generations.

These agencies and individuals are most often under great political pressure from special interest groups. This pressure, exerted through elected politicians, results in dedicated public servants being captives not only of the traditions of their organization but also of the fears and political weaknesses of their superiors. This means that these same public servants are subjected to conflicting demands and receive no assurance of ethical governance from the public or any overseeing body. The result is that our system of caring for the nation's natural resources has neither an ethical standard, or ethos, nor a sense of social/environmental justice within society itself or toward the environment that nurtures and sustains society.

Ethos, a Greek word meaning character or tone, is best thought of as a set of guiding beliefs, which is sorely lacking in most state and federal land management agencies. In phrasing this guiding direction, a distinction needs to be made between ethos and policy. Policy, written in explicit terms, can be in the form of an order—the letter of the law. Ethos, on the other hand, is implicit and includes a guiding set of human values—the heart of the law—that is understood but cannot easily be written out. Yet ethos can be translated into policy should one wish to do so.

Instead of a clearly articulated ethos translated into a policy of environmental justice and human equality, however, our society is both arrogant and greedy. Arrogance arises from the ignorance that assumes present knowledge is both correct and unchanging. Greed, which fosters hoarding, is born out of the fear of loss, the fear of never having enough in the material sense. And both are justified—even hallowed—in the economic theory that underlies our capitalistic way of doing business, which is but a reflection of our social psyche, out of which arise destructive environmental conflicts.

PERCEIVED RESOURCE SCARCITY ACCENTUATES DESTRUCTIVE ENVIRONMENTAL CONFLICT

Destructive environmental conflict is born out of a perceived threat to a person's "right of survival," however that is defined. The perceived security of our right to survive is weighed against the number of choices we think are available to us as individuals and our ability to control our choices. Thus, as long as one party in a destructive conflict thinks it can win agreement with its stance, which means to defend its perceived choices, that party will neither compromise nor change its position.

Perceived choices are ultimately affected by the real supply of and demand for natural resources, the source of energy required by all life in one form or another. Perhaps with this in mind, former Soviet leader Mikhail Gorbachev asked: "If we're going to protect the planet's ecology, we're going to need to find alternatives to the consumerist dream that is attracting the world. Otherwise, how will we conserve our resources, and how will we avoid setting people against each other when resources are depleted?"[3]

The greater the supply of a particular resource, the greater the freedom of choice an individual has with respect to that resource. Conversely, the smaller the supply, the narrower the range of choices unless, of course, we steal choices from other people to augment our own. And scarcity, real or perceived, is the breeding ground of environmental injustice, which rears its ugly head each time someone steals from another rather than taking responsibility for his or her own behavior and sharing equally.

An excellent example of environmental injustice occurred in 1991, when the people of Las Vegas and Clark County (in southern Nevada) attempted to take their neighbors' water against their neighbors' will. Las Vegas not only is built in a very fragile desert where no city should exist but also is made up of many people who squander more water than people anywhere I have ever been. And they can least afford it. Nevertheless, during the two years that my wife, Zane, and I lived in Las Vegas, the gutters of the streets ran almost every morning with great streams of water, some of which extended for a quarter of a mile or more.

The squandered water came from uncontrolled irrigation used solely to keep household and corporate lawns green. In addition, water was squandered on numerous artificial lakes and ponds and countless open swimming pools. Rather than conserving its limited supply, the city and county coveted the water of their northern neighbors and tried to figure out ways to get it, very much against the wishes and the will of those to whom it "belonged."

In short, rather than accepting the limitations of the desert in which they chose to live, the people of Las Vegas and Clark County were trying to usurp the choices of others. If they succeed, then those who use water wisely and therefore have a greater number of options would be unjustly penalized for their thrift. The people of Las Vegas and Clark County, on the other hand, could continue squandering water with impunity by taking from others, thus avoiding personal restraint and accountability while squandering still more water.

The variety of available choices dictates the amount of control I feel I have. This consequently affects my sense of security about my survival. What happens when I perceive my array of choices as fading or when they have suddenly been ripped away, as would happen if the people of Las Vegas and Clark County ever manage to steal their neighbors' water? Have you ever been told that you can no longer do something you have always done and therefore have taken doing for granted? How did you feel?

How would you feel if you were suddenly plucked from whatever you are doing without warning and for no apparent reason thrown into prison without explanation or recourse and held indefinitely against your will? Are there such innocent people behind bars now? The answer is yes!

How would you feel if you were jerked out of the only life you know, smuggled into an alien country, and sold into the bonds of slavery, never again to see anyone or anything you know or to enjoy the rights you once had as a citizen of the United States? This is not a far-fetched scenario; slavery is very much alive in the world today!

How would you feel, as an average citizen with no political desires, if civil war, such as that which occurred in the now defunct Soviet Union, erupted suddenly all around you, and you had nowhere to go while your family, home, and town were being blown apart? I had a very small taste of this powerless feeling when held at gunpoint on more than one occasion in Egypt while the country was under Nasser's dictatorial fist.

I ask these questions, even though they are not specifically resource oriented, in the hope that you can imagine how you would feel deep inside if you were suddenly to lose your sense of safety and well-being—your sense of choice. I ask because I am convinced that destructive environmental conflicts arise from a deep, albeit usually unconscious, sense of potential loss—a chronic or acute fear of the future based on a socialized disaster mentality.

RESOURCE OVEREXPLOITATION: A MATTER OF PERCEIVED LOSS

According to a song popular some years ago, "freedom's just another word for nothing left to lose," which in a peculiar way speaks of an apparent human truth. When I am unconscious of a material value, I am free of its psychological grip. However, the instant I perceive a material value and anticipate possible material gain, I also perceive the psychological pain of potential loss.

The larger and more immediate the prospects for material gain, the greater the political power used to ensure and expedite exploitation, because not to exploit is perceived as losing an opportunity to someone else. And it is this notion of loss that we fight so hard to avoid. In this sense, it is more appropriate to think of resources as managing humans than of humans as managing resources.[4]

Historically, then, any newly identified resource is inevitably overexploited, often to the point of collapse or extinction. Its overexploitation is based, first, on the perceived rights or entitlement of the exploiter to get his or her share before someone else does and, second, on the right or entitlement to protect his or her economic investment. There is more to it than this, however, because the concept of a healthy capitalistic system is one that is ever growing, ever expanding, but such a system is not biologically sustainable. With renewable natural resources, such nonsustainable exploitation is a "ratchet effect," where to ratchet means to constantly, albeit unevenly, increase the rate of exploitation of a resource.[4,5]

The ratchet effect works as follows: During periods of relative economic stability, the rate of harvest of a given renewable resource, say timber or salmon, tends to stabilize at a level that economic theory predicts can be sustained through some scale of time. Such levels, however, are almost always excessive, because economists take existing unknown and unpredictable ecological variables and convert them, in theory at least, into known and predictable economic constants in order to better calculate the expected return on a given investment from a sustained harvest.

Then comes a sequence of good years in the market, or in the availability of the resource, or both, and additional capital investments are encouraged in harvesting and processing because competitive economic growth is the root of capitalism. When conditions return to normal or even below normal, however, the industry, having overinvested, appeals to the government for help because substantial economic capital, and often many jobs, are at stake. The government typically responds with direct or indirect subsidies, which only encourage continual overharvesting.

The ratchet effect is thus caused by unrestrained economic investment to increase short-term yields in good times and strong opposition to losing those yields in bad times. This opposition to losing yields means there is great resistance to using a resource in a biologically sustainable manner because there is no predictability in yields and no guarantee of yield increases in the foreseeable future. In addition, our linear economic models of ever-increasing yield are built on the assumption that we can in fact have an economically sustain*ed* yield. This contrived concept fails in the face of the biological sustain*ability* of a yield.

Then, because there is no mechanism in our linear economic models of ever-increasing yield that allows for the uncertainties of ecological cycles and variability or for the inevitable decreases in yield during bad times, the long-term outcome is a heavily subsidized industry. Such an industry continually overharvests the resource on an artificially created, sustained-yield basis that is not biologically sustainable.[5]

When the notion of sustainability arises in a destructive conflict, the parties marshal all scientific data favorable to their respective sides as "good" science and discount all unfavorable data as "bad" science. Destructive environmental conflict is thus the stage on which science is politicized, largely obfuscating its service to society.

Because the availability of choices dictates the amount of control we feel we have with respect to our sense of security, a potential loss of money is the breeding ground for environmental injustice. This is the kind of environmental injustice in which the present generation steals from all future generations by overexploiting a resource rather than facing the uncertainty of giving up potential income.

There are important lessons in all of this for anyone facilitating destructive environmental conflicts. First, history suggests that a biologically sustainable use of any resource has never been achieved without first overexploiting it, despite historical warnings and contemporary data. If history is correct, resource problems are not environmental problems but rather human ones that we have created many times, in many places, under a wide variety of social, political, and economic systems.

Second, the fundamental issues involving resources, the environment, and people are complex and process driven. The integrated knowledge of multiple disciplines is required to understand them. These underlying complexities of the physical and biological systems preclude a simplistic approach to both management and conflict resolution. In addition, the wide natural variability and the compounding, cumulative influence of continual human activity mask the results of overexploitation until they are severe and often irreversible.

Third, as long as the uncertainty of continual change is considered a condition to be avoided, nothing will be resolved. However, once the uncertainty of change is accepted as an inevitable, open-ended, creative life process, most decision making is simply common sense. For example, common sense dictates that one would favor actions having the greatest potential for reversibility, as opposed to those with little or none. Such reversibility can be ascertained by monitoring results and modifying actions and policy accordingly.

Fourth, I believe that the seed of all destructive conflict is a perceived loss of choice over our own individual destinies, which we interpret as a threat to our personal survival. The sense of loss, which usually translates into a life-long fear of loss in some degree, originates in childhood as lessons from parents.[6]

DESTRUCTIVE CONFLICT IS A MISTAKE

The result of many childhood lessons is the perceived need for control, and anything which threatens that control is an enemy onto whom we can project blame for our fears and thereby justify them. But who or what is the enemy? An enemy is one seeking to injure, overthrow, or confound an opponent; something harmful or deadly. Of course *I* am not "the enemy" because I am convinced that *my* position and *my* values are the *right* ones, and everyone knows that "the enemy" is wrong. That is what I was taught. That is the eternal verity around which destructive conflict rallies.

The problem is that when all sides feel justified in their points of view, there is little understanding that an enemy is anyone or anything opposing that view. Opposition to that view is thus perceived as a threat to survival, however it is defined. Herein lies the great irony: most destructive environmental conflicts in one way or another are the spawn of misunderstandings, miscommunication, and misperceptions. Destructive conflict is thus often a mistake, a misjudgment of appearances, or an assumption that is avoidable because it is only one choice of response to a given circumstance. Other responses are available, should one choose to accept one or more of them.

Consider war, the ultimate destructive conflict, both socially and environmentally. War, as is all destructive human conflict, is based on the personalities of the people involved (in this case the leaders) and their common feelings about fear and enemies.

Once one side or the other perceives a threat to its survival, the single most important precipitating factor in the outbreak of war is in fact misperception, which manifests itself in a leader's self-image and view of the adversary's character, of the adversary's intentions toward himself or herself, and of the adversary's capabilities and power. Once misperception is in play, miscommunication closes in and joins hands with misjudgment to foster a distorted view of the adversary's character, which helps to precipitate destructive conflict.

If a leader on the brink of war believes the adversary will attack, the chances of war are fairly high. If both leaders share this perception about each other's intent, war becomes a virtual certainty.

But it is a leader's misperception of the adversary's power, and his or her willingness to use it, that is perhaps the quintessential cause of war. It is vital to remember, however, that it is not the actual distribution of power that precipitates a war; what precipitates war is the way in which a leader *thinks* the power is distributed. Thus, on the eve of each war, at least one leader, through miscommunication, misperceives and thus misjudges the other's available power and his or her willingness to use it. In this sense, the beginning of each war is a folly of misperception. The war itself then slowly and agonizingly teaches people the terribly high cost of destructive conflict.[7]

DESTRUCTIVE CONFLICT IS USUALLY BASED ON THE MISJUDGMENT OF APPEARANCES

The lesson that war has to teach us is that destructive conflict of any kind is a cycle of attack and defense based on the fear of uncertainties and unknowns, which usually results in the *misjudgment of appearances*. Appearance is an outward aspect of something that comes into view; judgment is the process of forming an opinion or evaluation by discerning and comparing something believed or asserted. Therefore, those whom I define as enemies are those onto whom I affix blame for my perceived sense of insecurity, a perceived threat to my own survival.

My judgments are almost always incorrect, however, because things are seldom as they appear since appearance is external. If I could but understand the inner motive of my "enemy," I would likely find a mirror reflection of my fears for my own survival. In that reflection I would also find that I was mistaken about my enemy's motives, that I had made an incorrect judgment of my enemy's character or ability based on inadequate knowledge.

Well, you might ask, if we are not one another's enemies, what is the enemy? What are we really afraid of? I think we are afraid of change, loss of something we value through circumstances we perceive as a threat to our sense of survival because we cannot control them.

Yet almost very circumstance we encounter in some way evokes an unanticipated change in our participation with life. In turn, each change we are obliged to make is a compromise in our sense of control, a frightening condition of life to most people in an increasingly complex world.

Control, often used as a synonym for power, is an interesting phenomenon in our lives. We pay dearly for control, but regardless of the price, there are limitations. I cannot, for example, control the wind, but I can trim the sails on my boat. The wind is the circumstance beyond my control, but by trimming the sails I can choose how my boat responds to the wind. And in my response, I am in control of myself, which *de facto* controls the outcome of the circumstance.

Have you ever had a "bad" day, a day when nothing went right, you felt out of sorts, and every little thing that could go awry delighted in doing so, which unduly annoyed you, causing you to say, "I'm at my wit's end! If one more thing happens I'm going to explode!" We have all had days like that. Because you feel out of sorts, or not at peace with yourself, you are therefore compelled to control the environment around you. Your inner sense of survival is shaky, and the only way you can ride out the inner storm is to have outer calm.

Now think of a "good" day, a day when everything went right, you felt in tune with the world, and you had a feeling of inner control and peace—a day when you said, "Everything I touch turns to gold!" On that day, the external things that still delighted in going awry did so, but they didn't bother you.

Was it the day that was good or bad or was it how you felt about yourself and your sense of survival? The difference between the two days was simply how you responded to the circumstances based on how you were feeling about yourself.

That I cannot control circumstances is a given, although I continually try, which results in either inner or outer conflict of some magnitude. But I can control how I react to circumstances, and therein lies both my problem and its potential resolution.

My inability to control circumstances in any meaningful way translates into fear of change because every circumstance causes something to shift, and I tend to focus on the negative—be it relatively minor (such as finding a tiny nick in the fender of my new car) or catastrophic (such as Willamette River flood waters pouring through my home). I thus perceive change as a loss of control that threatens my survival. I therefore want to control circumstances whenever

I can, so that other people—my perceived enemies—will have to risk change, but not me.

There are no true enemies, only people frightened of the same kind of things that I am afraid of. These people are thus mistakenly rejected by me as enemies, which I use to justify my side of the destructive conflict in the war of survival, the war to control circumstances beyond my control.

When I focus my attention on human enemies, I am really focusing on the wrong thing. The other person is not the enemy. Rather, it is my fear that dehumanizes my soul. Destructive conflict is my attempt to place my problem onto someone or something else, to move away from my fear, away from something I do not want to happen.

3

ENVIRONMENTAL PRINCIPLES: THE NEED TO KNOW AND THE FEAR OF KNOWING

Change often occurs between need and fear. On the one hand, we know we need to do things differently, but on the other hand, we are terrified of facing the unknown and unfamiliar. To change our direction for the future, however, we must suspend our conventional notion about change and our ability to learn, because there are no problems to resolve other than those we perceive as manifestations of how we think and act. The problems we face are a matter of who we are consciously. And many people prefer to err again and again rather than let go of some cherished belief, pet notion, or deified assumption.

To resolve any dispute, the facilitation process must go beyond human valuation of a resource to disclose and examine the fundamental issue of how use of the resource will affect the long-term biological sustainability of the ecosystem of which it is a component. One must also recognize the long-term issues that need to be dealt with to resolve the long-term potential for destructive conflict. This is necessary because the environment and the sustainability of its resources are silent parties present in any dispute, which *de facto* will determine the options passed forward to future generations.

To accommodate the sustainability of the environment's favorable ecological integrity—the "silent third party"—each person must understand the environmental postulates given in this chapter as a condition for resolving a specific destructive conflict. I say this because these posits, to the best of my knowledge, are among the physical underpinnings through which Nature operates and the philosophical valuations through which we accept our participation with Nature. Understanding these posits does not connote acceptance or agreement with them. It does, however, connote acknowledging their validity as a current data set. This means that whatever decisions are made in resolving a destructive conflict, they are made consciously by those who can be held accountable for their outcome.

It is just for the participants of a destructive environmental conflict to be held accountable for the outcome of its resolution because the effects of their decisions become the consequences for all generations to come. This is particularly poignant in the face of an exploding human population and rapidly dwindling resources.

ALL RESOURCES ARE INTERCONNECTED, INTERACTIVE, INTERDEPENDENT, AND ULTIMATELY FINITE

As long as the human population was but a small fraction of its current size, Earth's resources were considered unlimited. But even then, "The history of almost every civilization," says British historian Arnold Toynbee, "furnishes examples of geographical expansion coinciding with deterioration in [environmental and, therefore, resource] quality." Today, there is much talk about "renewable" resources but no longer so much about unlimited resources.

Ultimately, however, all resources are finite. Not only can we literally run out of a resource by exhausting its earthly supply, such as the extinction of a species and its attendant ecological function, but also can we alter an existing resource so as to render it useless to us, such as poisoning our drinking water through radioactive pollution. And we are doing both.

As a burgeoning human population demands more and more material commodities from a rapidly dwindling supply of raw materials, the ratio of resources apportioned to each human must decline. Further, those resources currently deemed renewable are only renewable as long as the system that produces them remains healthy and is exploited only in a biologically sustainable manner.

Consider, for example, the following scenario. As you hike in a wilderness area or wander through a national park, no matter how far removed you seem to be from the center of civilization, you are still breathing pollution. It is everywhere and will continue to worsen as long as decisions similar to that at the Rio World Summit on the Environment are made. To placate big industry, President Bush sabotaged the global pursuit of air quality standards.

We dare not kid ourselves about the importance of air quality. Our earthly survival, and progressively that of our children and their children *ad infinitum*, depends ultimately on clean air. Air is the interactive thread connecting soil, water, biodiversity, human population density, sunlight, and climate. (Biodiversity refers to the variety of living species and their biological functions and processes.)

Yet we as society, with our myriad data bits and seemingly vast knowledge, listen to the world's economists and *assume* they are correct when they take such ecological variables as air, soil, water, sunlight, biodiversity, genetic diversity, and climate and convert them, in theory at least, into economic constants whose values are unchanging. Ecological variables are therefore omitted from consideration in our economic and planning models, and even from our thinking. Biodiversity and genetic diversity, on the other hand, are simply discounted when their consideration interferes with monetary profits. On top of it all is the nagging problem of human population growth. We talk about it and worry about it, but in the end we give only lip service to the one solution that can control it—total, real gender equality.

Finally, we, the human component of the world, must understand and accept that each of these variables is an interactive thread in the tapestry of the natural/cultural world, which must be accounted for if society is to become a sustainable partner with its environment. To enliven our understanding, let's briefly examine each variable individually and then their collective relationship.

Air: The Breath of Life—And of Death

It is late afternoon on a clear, warm, sunny September day. A tiny spider climbs a tall stalk of grass in a subalpine meadow and raises its body into the air, almost standing on its head. From spinnerets on the tip of its abdomen, it ejects a mass of silken threads into the breeze. Suddenly, without visible warning, the spider is jerked off its stalk and borne skyward to join its relatives riding the warm afternoon air flowing up the mountainside, all casting their fortunes to the wind. Like their ancestors in centuries past, they float on air currents from the far corners of the Earth, and some become the first inhabitants of newly formed South Seas islands.

Spiders are not the only things borne aloft on air currents. In 1883, Krakatoa (a small Indonesian island between Java and Sumatra) was virtually obliterated by explosive eruptions that sent volcanic ash high enough above the Earth to ride the world's airways for more than a year. This affected the climate by reducing the amount of sunlight reaching the Earth, which in turn cooled the climate and affected all life. Like the volcanic ash of Krakatoa, air also carries the reproductive spores of fungi and the pollen of various trees and grasses, as well as dust and microscopic organisms. And it carries life-giving oxygen and water and death-dealing pollution—the legacy of human society.

Air can therefore be likened to the key in a Chinese proverb: To every man is given the key to the gates of heaven, and the same key opens the gates of hell. In this case, air is the key that carries both life-giving oxygen and death-dealing pollution, and as pollution increases, the quality and utility of the air are decreased.

Soil: The Great Placenta

Soil is like an exchange membrane between the living (plant and animal) and nonliving components of the landscape. Derived from rock and organic matter, soil is built up by plants that live and die in it. It is also enriched by animals that feed on plants, void their bodily wastes, and eventually die, decay, and return to the soil as organic matter. Soil is by far the most alive and biologically diverse part of any terrestrial ecosystem. In addition, soil organisms are the regulators of most processes that translate into soil productivity.

Many cultures have emphasized in their religion and philosophy that humans must be trustees of the soil. Confucius saw in the Earth's thin mantle the sustenance of all life and the minerals treasured by human society. A century later, Aristotle viewed the soil as the central mixing pot of air, fire, and water, which formed all things.

Most people cannot grasp these intangible long-held beliefs. Thus, we pay scant attention to the soil because it is as common as air and, like air, is taken for granted. But if we pause and think about it, we see that human society is tied to the soil for reasons beyond measurable materialistic wealth.

Yet, in the name of short-term profits, people rob the soil of the very organic material necessary for its sustainable fertility. They also use artificial chemicals that poison the soil, alter the way its many hidden processes function, and pollute the water moving through it into the world's water system.

Soil is the stage on which the entire human drama is enacted. If we continue to destroy the stage on which we depend for life, we will play a progressively ebbing role in a terminal tragedy of human society.

Water: A Captive of Gravity

Water and oxygen are the most important products produced from the world's forests. Most of our usable water comes from snows high on forested mountain slopes. When snow melts, the water percolates through the soil. It is purified when flowing through healthy soil; it is poisoned when flowing through soil stripped of Nature's processes and polluted with artificial chemicals. In addition, water bearing tons of toxic effluents flows directly into streams, rivers, estuaries, and the open ocean. Because water is a captive of gravity, all the pollutants it accumulates on its downhill journey eventually end up in the oceans, where they accumulate in ever-increasing concentration.

Biodiversity: The Variety of Life

Because every ecosystem adapts in some way to changes in its environment, biodiversity acts as an ecological insurance policy for the flexibility of future human options. In turn, the degree of a system's adaptability depends on the richness of its biodiversity, which creates a redundancy—duplication or repetition of the elements of a system. Redundancy provides alternative functional channels in case of a failure and so retains the ability of a system to respond to continual change.

Each ecosystem contains redundancies that provide resilience to absorb change or to bounce back after disturbance. Biological redundancy strengthens the ability of an ecosystem to retain its integrity. This means that the loss of one or two species is not likely to result in such severe functional disruption as to cause ecosystem collapse, because other species can make up for the functional loss.

At some point, however, the loss of one or more species will tip the balance and cause an irreversible change that can lower the quality and productivity of the system. This point of irreversibility is an unknown biological threshold; we do not know which species' extinction will trigger its effects, which is why it pays to save every species possible. Hence the precautionary principle: err on the side of prudence.

Species variety is important because each species has a shape and structure that allows certain functions to take place. These functions interact with those of other species to create a viable system. All biodiversity is ultimately governed by the genetic code that builds some redundancy into each ecosystem by replicating the character traits of a species.

A stable ecosystem may respond positively to disturbances to which it is adapted, but it also may be vulnerable to the introduction of foreign disturbances to which it is not adapted. Plant and animal diversity therefore buffers an ecosystem against disturbances from which it cannot recover. When we lose species, we lose not only their combination of structural and functional diversity but also their genetic diversity, which eventually results in complex ecosystems becoming simplified and unable to sustain either themselves or us.

A forest, for example, is a living entity that often completes a cycle of interdependent processes over several centuries, spanning many human generations. Yet with grossly incomplete, short-sighted knowledge, and unquestioning faith in that knowledge, we predict the sustained-yield capability of economically designed tree plantations far into a problematic and unforeseeable future.

Based on these erroneous predictions, clearcutting the old-growth forest and converting it to a biologically simplified plantation is traditionally justified economically, completely ignoring biodiversity—especially that which sustains the infrastructure of the forest soil. Destroy the soil and the forest ceases to be! Destroy the forest and the soil becomes further impoverished and erodes, which degrades water quality and diminishes the oxygen content of the air.

Human Population: A Matter of Gender Equality

We have been warned for decades that the human species is overpopulating the Earth. Yet our population explodes and the usable portion of the Earth per individual shrinks, as does the allotted proportion of its resources, all of which become more quickly limiting when abused. We have tried many things to remedy this situation: education, birth control, feeding the hungry, shipping industrial technology to poor nations, and so on. In my opinion, however, we have not addressed the primary cause of overpopulation: the inequality between men and women.

Women have long been dominated by men. Through such domination, women are physically forced to produce most of the world's food yet are allowed to own but an infinitesimal part of the land. And women have had only one way to be uniquely valued by men—by having babies.

Regardless of where I have traveled, I have found that women who have a good education have fewer children and have them later in life. Education affords increased options and a variety of ways to be valued. I submit, therefore, that if we are serious about controlling the human population, women must have an equal voice in all decisions and unequivocal access to opportunities for self- and social valuation. On the surface, this means such things as equal opportunity for education, jobs, and pay and equal pay for equal work. At its root, this means changing the male attitude of superiority towards women—a difficult task but a vitally necessary one.

Sunlight: The Source of Global Energy

The sun has been worshipped for millennia, and the quality of its light has been taken for granted. Sunlight powers most of the Earth's processes; we harvest the sun's energy through the fruits and vegetables we eat. But what happens when air pollution— smog—reduces the intensity of sunlight before it reaches the plants? What happens when the ozone shield disappears, allowing deadly ultraviolet rays to bombard the Earth? What happens when both of these events occur simultaneously, as is now happening?

Human impacts, such as air pollution, now directly affect the quality of the sun's light and energy reaching us. Like everything else, the quality of the sun's light is an ecological variable that must be taken into account.

Climate: The Global Arbiter

Western society has developed an array of technologies on the assumption that they cannot harm the autonomous biosphere that produces the environment needed for life. The day has come, however, when the global life system itself is within reach of our technology, with its power to disarrange and destroy. No age but ours has faced such peril.

The consensus among atmospheric scientists is that global warming, at some unknown intensity, is imminent. In northwestern Ontario, Canada, for example, climatic, hydrologic, and ecological records for the Experimental Lakes Area show that temperatures of the air and the lakes have risen by 3.6 degrees Fahrenheit and that the duration of ice-free days has increased by three weeks over the last twenty years. Higher than normal evaporation and lower than average precipitation have caused a decrease in the rate of renewal of lake water. In addition to other changes within the lakes themselves, concentrations of most chemicals have increased in both lakes and streams because of decreased renewal of water and because of forest fires in the watersheds.[8] Are these observations a preview of the effects of global climate change on boreal lakes?

The increased warming is thought to be caused by an array of gases in the atmosphere that trap heat radiated outward from the Earth's surface—the "greenhouse effect." Carbon dioxide has to date received the most attention, but other gases are involved as well: water vapor, ozone, nitrous oxide, chlorofluorocarbons, and methane.

The greenhouse effect alters the average temperature of the Earth's surface, which is determined by many factors, including the amount of energy received from the sun, the properties on the Earth's surface that absorb the sun's heat, and the absorptive properties of the atmosphere. A high proportion of the energy absorbed by the lower atmosphere and by the Earth's surface is emitted as heat. Like a window in a greenhouse, the atmosphere passes some of the heat through itself into space, but the atmosphere absorbs the rest into itself and passes it back again towards Earth.

It is not known exactly how the climate will respond, but there is no doubt that "greenhouse gases" are accumulating. Atmospheric carbon dioxide began increasing in the latter part of the nineteenth century when forests were clearcut and prairies were plowed. Both actions released carbon dioxide once stored in the plant tissues and soil. Since the 1940s, fossil fuel burning and accelerated deforestation have greatly increased the accumulation of greenhouse gases.

The pre-industrial level of atmospheric concentration of carbon dioxide will be doubled some time in the next century. As a result, temperatures in the contiguous United States are predicted to increase in winter by an amount equivalent to a four- to six-degree shift southward in latitude; in summer, the increase would be equal to a five- to eleven-degree shift southward in latitude. This would be like shifting central Oregon to southern California, a difference of about ten degrees latitude.

A greater warming is predicted for summers than winters. The magnitude of warming is also predicted to vary from east to west across the United States and Canada. The greatest warming will take place in the area of the Great Plains, where North Dakota may have a climate similar to that which presently exists in Texas. In addition, models predict a warming in the mountains that will be equivalent to roughly a 2000- to 3000-foot decrease in elevation. Under this situation, most, if not all, of the subalpine and alpine areas would probably disappear from the contiguous United States.

Models are less consistent in predicting the result of the greenhouse effect on precipitation, a crucial factor in the way ecosystems will respond to climatic changes. There is, however, general agreement that warming will be greater at higher rather than at lower latitudes. The consequence will be a narrowing of the global temperature gradient, which in turn seems likely to alter global patterns of precipitation, yet what exactly these changes might be remains unclear. Nevertheless, a warming climate, even with no change in precipitation, may increase drought in the world because of a greater evaporative force brought about by generally higher temperatures.

To date, much attention has been focused on greenhouse effect problems caused by tropical deforestation, but major problems are also caused by deforestation elsewhere. Burning tropical forests gasifies about fifty percent of the nitrogen in the forest biomass, which then rises into the atmosphere. Tropical burning also causes vast amounts of smoke, which alters the internal physical structure of clouds and causes severe repercussions in the tropical water cycle.

On the other hand, clearcutting old-growth Douglas-fir forests in the Pacific Northwest results in a net release of carbon dioxide into the atmosphere. Even when the original forest is replaced with young, fast-growing trees, several centuries must pass before the carbon dioxide, which originally was stored in the stems of live old trees, can be recouped.

Some projected scenarios for global warming include increasing drought in various areas, such as the mid-continental "Great Plains." The greenhouse effect also may alter fire regimes by contributing to an increase in the frequency of forest fires in some areas. In other areas, there may be an increase in the frequency and intensity of hurricanes. In what way will change in the global climate affect the boreal forests of northern Canada and Alaska, the great Douglas-fir forests of the Pacific Northwest, or the ponderosa pine forests of the American Southwest? We do not know, because the Earth has never before undergone the effects of such abuse as society now inflicts on it.

The Key to the Gate

Humans directly affect five of the seven foundation stones of social survival: air, soil, water, biodiversity, and population density. We affect the other two, sunlight and climate, indirectly. If, for example, we choose to clean the world's air, we will automatically clean the soil and water to some extent because airborne pollutants will no longer poison them, and the sunlight that reaches the Earth will be unimpeded. If we then choose to treat the soil in such a way that we can grow what we desire without the use of artificial chemicals and if we stop using the soil as a dumping ground for toxic wastes and avoid over-intensive agriculture, the soil can once again filter and purify water. If we stop dumping waste effluents into the water, streams, rivers, estuaries, and oceans can again become clean and healthy.

With clean and healthy air, soil, and water, we can also have clear, safe sunlight with which to power the Earth and, with the eventual repair of the ozone shield, a more benign—and perhaps predictable—climate in which to live. In addition, effective population control can tailor human society to fit within the world's carrying capacity.

A population in balance with its habitat will reduce demands on the Earth's resources. With reduced competition for resources can come the cooperation and coordination that will allow our landscapes to provide the maximum possible biodiversity. Protecting biodiversity translates into the gift of choice, which in turn translates into hope and dignity for future generations.

For the sake of discussion, let's add to this scenario the end of wars and their weapons. Such a world, a wonderful place in which to live and raise families, is possible, but this possibility ultimately hinges on clean air.

If we do everything outlined here—except clean the air, we will still pollute the entire Earth, from the blue arc of its heavens to the bottom of its deepest sea, in every corner of the globe. Clean air is the absolute "bottom line" for human survival. Without clean air, there eventually will be no difference in the way we destroy ourselves, either by nuclear war or air pollution, because our biosphere is comprised of interdependent, interactive components, where one affects the whole and the whole affects the one. But there are alternatives, based on intrinsic values, and the choice is ours. To the children we bequeath the consequences.

NATURE KEEPS ITS OWN SCORECARD

Nature affixes no human-derived values to either its components or the interactive whole. Its intrinsic value is sufficient unto itself.

Humanity, on the other hand, puts its own values on some portions of the environment at the expense of others. People then compete for those items of Nature in which they find common value and waste those in which they do not.

The Pacific yew tree is a good example. A shade-tolerant tree in the understory of old-growth forests of the Pacific Northwest, it was once considered a weed species that was simply trashed after more valuable trees had been removed. But in recent years, the Pacific yew has been recognized as the sole source of one of the most promising new drugs (Taxol), which is used to treat ovarian, lung, and breast cancers in women. The new technological ability to synthesize Taxol, however, has once again relegated the yew to a weed species.

The Pacific yew was once widely distributed from the southern tip of southeastern Alaska throughout the western portions of British Columbia, Washington, Oregon, and northwestern California. Today, the Pacific yew is rapidly disappearing because of clearcut logging of the old-growth forests of which it is a component and because of once uncontrolled, commercial harvesting of its bark for medicine.

NATURE IS GOVERNED BY IMPARTIAL LAWS

Nature is governed by impartial laws that are immutable to social solicitations. Humanity, on the other hand, attempts to control Nature with laws derived by humans, which are partial to their own benefits. All parties in a destructive environmental conflict must understand that impartial Nature always wins in the end—whether we understand it or not, whether we like it or not, whether or not it is in our lifetime.

DESTRUCTIVE CONFLICT OVER A GIVEN RESOURCE LIES IN ITS PERCEIVED VALUE

Destructive conflict over a given resource lies in either (1) competition among parties seeking its tangible monetary value or (2) competition among parties split in seeking its tangible monetary versus its intangible spiritual and/or scenic values. The former is epitomized by the California gold rush or the Oklahoma land rush, in which many people from a wide variety of backgrounds all competed for a limited resource that could be turned into cash. In this sense, the real competition was for the perceived value to be obtained by taking possession of the resource for its conversion potential—its ability to produce money.

The objective in the gold rush was to find the gold, take it out of the ground, remove it from the site, and trade it for money, which could be used to purchase something else. Here, the competition was to get the most gold possible in the shortest time possible. The gold itself had no value other than its conversion potential.

In the land rush, on the other hand, the objective was to obtain a free piece of land to live on, to invest in, and to reap crops from. The crops in turn could be converted into cash, which could be used to buy something else. Here, the competition was to get the best piece of land possible because, all the land being of the same size, quality was the supreme variable. The quality determined what and how much could be grown, which determined how much money could be made and converted into other things. That someone might develop a sense of place and call a particular piece of land home was an outgrowth of time and personal investment, having little or nothing to do with the initial competition for the land itself as a commodity from which to raise subsets of commodities.

But what about competition among parties split in seeking one or more resources for their tangible value versus their intangible value, especially where one resource, such as water, contains within itself one or more additional resources, such as gold and/or fish? Consider, for example, a heretofore untouched stream of incredible scenic beauty, loaded with gold and wild trout and with the potential for irrigation if its water is diverted. What destructive conflicts can arise out of this milieu?

Let's begin with the gold. Someone finds gold in the stream and files a claim to the overriding legal right to extract the gold according to current mining laws, regardless of the damage done to the other resources, such as the stream's channel, its fish population, its scenic beauty, and so on. Next comes the water rights, which also takes precedence over the well-being of the fish and scenic beauty. Then come the politically important fish. Finally, we arrive at the stream's scenic beauty.

By now the stream's scenic beauty has been destroyed by dredging for gold, which has left great piles of rocky rubble along the stream's once-stable vegetated banks and endangered the fish population in winter for lack of suitable habitat. The water level has been lowered by the withdrawal of irrigation water, endangering the fish population in summer. The stream's banks are littered with garbage from sport fishers, and the stream itself is strewn with lost fishing gear.

In this case, as in almost every other, the commodity with the greatest perceived commercial value and/or the strongest commodity-oriented laws—the gold—takes precedence over everything else. Then comes the next highest commercial value (in this case the water) and so on, until all that is left is that which has no immediate cash value.

The paradox is that the thing of intangible value (in this case scenic beauty) is the very thing that usually gives the most enjoyment to the greatest number of people over the longest time but turns no immediate profit. Commercial value, as opposed to intrinsic value, holds our mechanistic society captive; herein lies the destructive conflict. If my past observations are correct, gold will likely prove over time to have been the thing of least value when the effects of its extraction become apparent in the ever-changing course of human consciousness and social evolution.

CHANGE: THE DYNAMIC CONSTANT

Change is the creative process that keeps the world ever novel, interesting, and evolving. It is also a messenger of uncertainty and a tester of faith, which caused Egyptian President Anwar el-Sadat to remark that "...he who cannot change the very fabric of his thought will never be able to change reality, and will never, therefore, make any progress." Sadat's concept is carried a step further by Henri Bergson, who stated that "To exist is to change; to change is to mature; to mature is to create oneself endlessly." This is the crucible into which I step each time I facilitate the resolution of a destructive environmental conflict. Armed with faith in the facilitation process as the only comfort, I stand defenseless before the unknown—continual change, which is at once uncertainty and creativity, both of which I must learn to handle with equanimity.

One of Nature's great lessons is revealed if we observe closely and participate consciously in life: knowledge represents our notion of the historical surety of the past; change flows as the ongoing current of the active present, and unpredictability is the womb of uncertainty and future possibility.

In dealing with change as an ecological given, there are three important notions: (1) Nature deals with processes and trends over variable scales of time, despite the fact that we want to deal with absolute, predictable quantities and values of products in rigid, predetermined scales of time; (2) Nature's processes are a cyclical continuum, regardless of our human desire for things to be linear in accord with our predominant thinking; and (3) Nature is always in a dynamic state of becoming something else, which means that although we have some scientific understanding of the principles governing this dynamic balance, we can only anticipate the outcome of our tinkering based on our meager knowledge of these principles.

Of the principles governing Nature's dynamic balance, three, as far as we know, are inviolate physical laws.[9] The first principle, *the law of conservation of mass*, simply states that mass can neither be created nor destroyed; therefore, materials cannot really be "produced" or "consumed." The mass of a material remains the same while its form is altered from a raw material to finished products, wastes, and residuals without a change in quantity. Thus, over time, the amount of matter moving through a stable system must equal the amount stored in it plus the amount moving out of it. The only known exception to this rule is expressed in Einstein's Theory of Relativity.

Einstein's theory states that under special conditions of a thermonuclear reaction, the energy produced (E) is equal to the amount of equivalent mass destroyed (m) times the square of the speed of light (c, or 3×10^8 m/s) or $E = mc^2$. But the thermonuclear conditions for this conversion occur naturally only in our sun and other stars or are created artificially by the detonation of nuclear weapons or controlled reaction in nuclear power plants.

The second principle, *the law of conservation of energy*, states that energy can neither be created nor destroyed, outside of a thermonuclear reaction. Thus, while energy can be changed in form and distribution, the quantity remains the same. The notion of either "energy production" or "energy consumption" is therefore a non sequitur.

Energy is neither produced nor consumed; it is only converted from one form to another. For example, when the energy stored in fossil fuels is released ("consumed"), creating thermal, mechanical, or electrical energy, only the form of the energy has changed.

The third principle, *the law of entropy*, states that in any closed system, the amount of energy in forms available to do useful work diminishes over time. Thus, over time, the loss of available energy represents a diminishing capacity to maintain "order" in any closed system, which increases disorder or entropy.

It is vital that we understand the relationship of the law of entropy to both human and nonhuman systems because the law holds that to sustain or enlarge any system requires the "expenditure" of energy. Expenditure in this sense means to convert a useful or available form of energy (that with which work can be done) to a less useful or unavailable form. The law applies to all human activities, from personal hygiene to growing a crop of corn to governing a nation.

A final lesson from the law of entropy is that, all things being equal, the larger the ordering process or the faster the rate of resource and energy use, the greater the disorder created. Further, the entropy resulting from the ordering process may occur in a location other than that where the ordering process took place. Consider the following.

The evolution of life on Earth depends on the use of available energy contained in sunlight. However, entropy has already occurred on the sun during the conversion of available hydrogen fuel to helium, a less available form of energy. Solar energy therefore represents a "free" form of energy to the biosphere because the detrimental effects of its formation are isolated by space and distance from the earthly systems that is powers.

In contrast, however, the socio-economic ordering of recent times, based largely on the conversion of nonrenewable fossil fuels to usable forms of energy, such as electricity, cannot escape the problems associated with increasing entropy (witness air pollution). In the process of converting coal to electricity, pollutants, such as sulfur dioxide, are spewed into the air and carried hundreds or thousands of miles from the coal-fired power plants that produced them in a phenomenon known as acid deposition, commonly called acid rain.

Acid rain has long been recognized as a pollution problem in Europe, where statues and gargoyles that once proudly adorned city streets and plazas and guarded centenarian buildings have had their faces dissolved over recent decades. The statues that I remember seeing as a boy, in perfect form and feature, today are often unrecognizable relics of a past era because acid rain has eaten away the marble much as leprosy eats away the flesh.

Acid rain is not confined to European cities. It is also found in forest and fen, in highland and lowland. And there, too, it is destroying the essence of life as it joins league with other forms of industrial/technological pollution and mismanagement in a phenomenon the Germans call *Waldsterben*, the dying forest.

The dying forest syndrome is not exclusively the property of Europe, however; it is owned by every industrial country, including the United States and Canada. Here, called forest dieback, it manifests itself primarily along the eastern seaboard, where declining growth rates and the dieback of red spruce and other tree species, particularly at high elevations, are attributed to atmospheric pollution, of which acid deposition is one of the most widespread components.

A primary human source of the precursors to acid deposition is coal-fired power plants, which still provide more than fifty-five percent of the electricity generated in the United States and seem to account for the largest amount of sulfur dioxide. This atmospheric pollutant is capable of a phenomenon known as long-distance transport, which simply means that it can travel great distances from its source on air currents before being deposited on agricultural fields and forests, where it affects plant growth.

Direct effects of acid deposition include a reduced functioning of plant roots. This reduction in root function may be caused by chemical changes in the soil as a result of acid deposition, by reduced translocation of carbohydrates from pollution-damaged shoots, or from excessive nitrogen. In fact, the emission of pollutants has tripled the level of nitrogen some forests are receiving.

Changes in nitrogen levels work as follows. People are used to the idea that if one puts nitrogen on a corn field, the corn grows faster, but then corn happens to be a plant that opens its stomata (pore-like entrances into the leaves) and takes up more carbon to create a balance. Thus, up to some point, the more nitrogen corn is given, the more carbon it will acquire, and the better it will grow. Unlike corn, however, most forest species will not grow any faster with additional nitrogen.

Since trees do not take up any more carbon to offset the additional nitrogen, an altered carbon–nitrogen ratio develops in the plant tissue, which means that trees are receiving three times the level of their nitrogen tolerance. It *does not* mean that they are getting three times their optimum level, but rather three times their *tolerance*. Such a shifted carbon–nitrogen ratio translates into, among other things, an alteration of the materials plants produce to resist diseases and insects, which permits pathogenic fungi (those that create rot in living trees) to enter where previously they had been excluded.

If we lose sight of the principles discussed in this chapter, we set not only ourselves but also the future adrift on a sea of continually increasing uncertainty and ultimate social destruction. (If you are interested in reading more about some of these notions, see *Global Imperative* and *Sustainable Forestry*.[5,10])

4

THE HUMAN EQUATION

In any facilitation process, people must be thought of and treated as though they are equal and deserving of love, trust, respect, and environmental justice. Environmental justice asserts that we owe something to every other person sharing the planet with us, both those present and those yet unborn.

"But," you may ask, "what exactly do we have to give?" The only things we have of value are the love, trust, respect, and wisdom gleaned from our experiences embodied in each and every option, in each and every choice we pass forward. And it is exactly because options embody all we have to give those living today and the children of tomorrow and beyond that environmental justice as a concept must fit within the context of human equality.

It must therefore be understood that the resolution of any environmental dispute will in some way affect the next generation—for good or ill. In this sense, a decision in the present always represents a circumstance in the future, and if it bodes ill, it is analogous to taxation without representation. Each party must therefore be aware of how its decision will affect future generations.

If you wonder whether we even need to be concerned about the future, remember that adults are responsible for bringing children into the world. We are thus also responsible for being their voice and for protecting their options until the time when they can speak and act responsibly for themselves.

It has been my experience, however, that many people seem not to be overly concerned about what social/environmental circumstances future generations will inherit. I have heard it asked, for example, "Why can't these changes wait until I've retired? Then someone else can worry about them."

Whether people are concerned about future generations depends very much on the way they grew up and the family values they learned. How we learned to cope with circumstances as children influences how we treat one another as adults. Society is thus as peaceful or combative as we are as individuals.

The more a person is drawn towards peace and an optimistic view of the future, the more functional (psychologically healthy) he or she is. The more a person is drawn towards debilitating, destructive conflict, cynicism, and pessimism about the future, the more dysfunctional (psychologically unhealthy) that individual is.

To change anything in society, therefore, I must first look inward to confront, understand, and change myself, especially if I am going to act as a facilitator in helping others to confront their fears and resolve their destructive conflicts. This process of self-evaluation and change puts the battle where it really belongs—within my own heart. As such, my inner struggles are the greatest learning experiences I will ever have. In addition, the greater my understanding of my own behavioral dynamics, of my own unresolved fears and pain, the easier it is for me to understand these dynamics in others and thus introduce compassion into a transformative conflict resolution and wisdom into a vision created for the future.

Facilitating the resolution of a destructive conflict requires a basic understanding of those family dynamics that shape us as individuals. I therefore discuss familial dysfunction as openly and honestly as I can, which means that I must at times tap into my own familial dysfunction while growing up. This is important, because to be a good facilitator, I must risk being an imperfect human. I must be open, honest, and vulnerable, and I must have the courage to work continuously and seriously on healing my own dysfunctions.

My experience has been that we probably never really leave our families; we take them with us wherever we go throughout the rest of our lives. We take not only our families, both emotionally and intellectually, but also our familial heritage.

Thus molded in the family template in an unknown and unknowable Universe, the most consistently pressing existential questions since the dawn of humanity have probably been: "Who am I?" and "What value do I have in the immensity of the ever-changing Unknown and Unknowable?" When I facilitate resolution of a destructive conflict in a transformative approach, these are the fundamental questions that I indirectly help the combatants to address.

First, however, I must have some understanding of family dynamics, because every destructive conflict I have ever facilitated was very much like stepping as a stranger into a family feud. Therefore, I will begin sharing what I have learned about family dynamics by looking at the gift of a child, that little person whose psychic slate is initially untouched by socialized behaviors.

A CHILD'S GIFT

Childhood, the tender age during which we are taught to compete and fight, is the age in which the need for transformative facilitation is born. Thus, as a facilitator I must understand how life, which today may seem like deadly grapple to many people, replaces childhood innocence and creative possibilities through the tutelage of parents, peers, schools, culture, and society.

To the Indian poet Rabindranath Tagore, "Every child comes with the message that God is not yet discouraged of man." And author Friedrich Holderlin finds that, "In the child is peace; it has not yet come to be at odds with itself. Wealth is in the child; it knows not its heart nor the inadequacy of life. It is immortal, for it has not heard of death....But the time of awakening is beautiful, too, if only we are not awakened unseasonably."

Each child offers his or her parents and society another chance to learn the meaning of love, to explore the boundaries of selflessness, to rediscover the possibilities of innocence, and to help us define who we are. Each child is a holy canvas on which we paint our loves and our fears, our joys and our sorrows, and a thousand other perceptions we hold to be ourselves.

Buckminster Fuller, American architect and inventor, thought that "Every child is a genius but is enslaved by the misconceptions and self-doubts of the adult world and spends much of his or her life having to unlearn that perspective." Thus, each child becomes the outward manifestation of the inner, adult self, for in the children of the world we see ourselves reflected. We who are an imprint of our parental templates have become the templates who will imprint ourselves on our children. And what can we give them? "There are only two lasting bequests," according to Hodding Carter, "[that] we can hope to give our children. One of these is roots; the other wings."

To this end, Dr. Edward Bach penned a beautiful paragraph on the ideal essence of parenthood:

> Parenthood is a sacred duty, temporary in its character and passing from generation to generation. It carries with it nothing but service and calls for no obligation in return from the young, since they must be left free to develop in their own way and become as fitted as possible to fulfill the same office in but a few years' time.[11]

As children, we are molded in the template of our parentage, our peers, and our social environment, just as our parents were similarly molded. Too often the result is that the precious gift with which each child comes into the world—innocence mirrored in spontaneous joy, aliveness, and creativity without preconceptions or limitations—is not recognized, not acceptable, and not accepted.

Our innocence, which manifests itself as unbounded imagination, is stolen from us, often quietly and unobtrusively, through all sorts of external pressures to conform, because we need to fit in rather than be something new, challenging, and exciting. Yet it still seems to me that life is intended as a process of learning, a grand adventure, rather than a terror to be survived.

Nevertheless, however we turn out as adults, we are our family. And unless we consciously choose otherwise, we take our family with us wherever we go, through our personal philosophy and through our behavior.

WE TAKE OUR FAMILIES WITH US

Taking our families with us emotionally and psychologically is an important notion to understand as a facilitator, because we are inescapably our families to some degree. It is quite likely that the clearest things participants bring to the arena of destructive environmental conflict are their familial upbringings. They are so entangled in their familial heritages that they seldom can separate their dysfunctional behaviors from the ecological and social principles over which they fight. Helping the combatants make this distinction is my task as a facilitator.

A word of caution is necessary here. While the behaviors exhibited by the disputants towards one another are often condemnable, the person acting out the behavior is doing the very best he or she is capable of at that moment and must be accepted with compassion—never condemned as a person.

It is not my intent to delve into a clinical discussion of family systems; excellent books on the subject are available. A brief overview of some dysfunctional familial dynamics will, however, be provided because, as Mother Teresa says, "In the home begins the disruption of the peace of the world." Understanding dysfunctional familial dynamics is therefore critical to good facilitation.

DYSFUNCTIONAL FAMILY DYNAMICS LEAD TO ONGOING DESTRUCTIVE CONFLICT

Dysfunctional behavior often leads to destructive conflict, and thus it is absolutely necessary for me, as a facilitator, to understand dysfunction, since the more dysfunctional a person is, the more inclined he or she is towards destructive conflict. Facilitation is therefore a process whereby I help the combatants to consciously break their dysfunctional cycle of destructive conflict. To be a good facilitator, however, I must work seriously on resolving *my own dysfunctional behaviors*.

Only when I am free of my own dysfunctional familial patterns can I really be open to the humility, spontaneity, and creativity demanded by the transformative facilitation process. Only then can I offer the understanding, insight, and empathy necessary to lead and communicate effectively. Each person's story is the same in principle but differs in detail.

We are the strengths and the weaknesses of our upbringings, because we all go through similar dynamics in various forms as we come into, grow up, and leave our families. We thus tend to repeat the patterns—whether they are functional or dysfunctional—over and over again unless we consciously break an unwanted cycle. To break a dysfunctional cycle, however, one must first understand homeostasis.

HOMEOSTASIS IS DESIGNED TO HIDE DYSFUNCTION

It is critical that I, as a facilitator, understand homeostasis and homeostatic mechanisms because, just as each dysfunctional family has its own set of mechanisms, each party of combatants within a given conflict has its own. And each party's set is fashioned through an unconscious forging of the individual members' familial patterns into one collective pattern—that of the combatant party.

Homeostasis is the maintenance of a dynamic equilibrium within a system, such as a family. A family is a system governed by a set of rules that determine and control the interaction of its members in organized, established patterns. The family rules are a set of directives concerning what shall and shall not occur within and outside of the family. Homeostatic mechanisms maintain the ongoing arrangement among family members by activating the rules defining each member's relationship to the whole.

My father, for instance, could not control the imperfections in his family no matter how hard he tried, because they were really the imperfections he perceived within himself, which he transferred or projected onto us. In turn, his perception of our imperfections triggered his abusive behavior, and his abusive behavior was the secret skeleton in our family closet.

My family probably appeared to be quite "normal" on the surface. Seen through knowledgeable eyes, however, which could have interpreted the symptoms I acted out as a child away from home, the red flag of abuse would have been readily apparent.

Dysfunction and homeostasis are therefore a self-perpetuating, self-reinforcing cycle founded on coercion and fear. My father was abusive, and that would have drawn criticism. To avoid the criticism, we were all assigned roles to play, which kept the dynamic equilibrium in the family within acceptable bounds; this in turn kept the dysfunction within the family while giving the outward appearance of normalcy.

The roles we were assigned were to be the perfect son, daughter, wife, and mother—according to my father's definitions. This was particularly important where his public image was concerned. If the homeostasis began to crumble, so would his perception of other people's perceptions of the family image, of his image, and that was an unacceptable threat to my father's sense of survival.

At this same juncture stand the combatants in every environmental dispute, feeling an unacceptable threat to their survival. As prisoners of their familial upbringing, they are searching, albeit often unknowingly, for appropriate behavioral boundaries within which to feel safe.

BOUNDARIES, THE SILENT LANGUAGE

Boundaries are those lines of silent language that allow a person to communicate with others while simultaneously protecting the integrity of one's own personal space as well as the personal spaces of those with whom one interacts.

The language of boundaries transcends individual space to include familial space, cultural space, and even national space. Understanding personal boundaries during facilitation among individuals of the same culture is difficult enough, but expanding that concept into a fluid working ability among different cultures is most difficult to accomplish. This is especially true in other countries, where facilitation may be done through a translator in a language I can neither understand nor speak.

A simple way of looking at boundaries is the adage "good fences make good neighbors." As an example, consider cliff swallows, which attach their mud nests to such surfaces as the faces of cliffs, the sides of buildings, and under bridges. These enclosed, globular nests share common walls, which not only strengthen the nests but also keep the peace by preventing the inhabitants from peeking into each other's abodes. If, however, a hole is made in the common wall and the swallows can see each other, they bicker and squabble until the hole is repaired, which immediately restores tranquillity.

A more complicated way of dealing with physical boundaries is to compare them to the home ranges and territories of animals. A home range is that area of an animal's habitat in which it ranges freely throughout the course of its normal activity and in which it is free to mingle with others of its own kind. A territory, in contrast, is that part of an animal's home range that it defends, for whatever reason, against others of its own kind. This defensive behavior is most exaggerated and noticeable during an animal's breeding season.

How does this concept apply to us? Suppose it is Saturday morning and you leave your home to go take care of a few errands. You simply go about your business without paying much attention to what is going on around you or to the people you pass, unless you happen to meet someone you know. In general, you are simply engrossed in what you are doing. When you have finished your errands, you start home.

The closer you get to your neighborhood, the more alert you unconsciously become to changes around you, such as the new people moving in two blocks away. This "protective feeling" becomes even more acute as you approach the area of your own home and notice a car with an out-of-state license plate parked in your neighbor's driveway. You get out of your car and immediately notice, perhaps with some irritation, that the neighbor's dog has visited your lawn again while you were gone. If your neighbor's dog had anointed someone else's yard with its leavings, you probably would have paid no attention.

The same general pattern extends into your home. Inside your home, how well you know someone and how comfortable you feel around them determines the freedom with which they may interact with you and your family and use your house. You are the most particular about your ultimate private space, your physical being.

For example, an unwanted salesperson may not be allowed inside your home. A casual acquaintance, on the other hand, may be allowed in the living room and use of the guest bathroom, but he or she is not allowed to wander about the house without permission. If one of your children's friends comes over, he or she may be allowed into the living room, kitchen, family room, guest bathroom, and your children's rooms (but only with both your and their permission), but is not allowed into your room or your bathroom. At times, even your children may not be allowed in your room without your permission, or perhaps you in theirs.

As you return home after a Saturday morning of errands, the closer you get to your home, the more you notice what is going on and the more observant and protective you become. Inside your home, the closer you get to your own room, and beyond that to your physical person, which represents your ultimate territory, the more clearly and carefully you define your boundaries. The reverse is in effect, however, as you leave your room and go into the rest of your house or your neighborhood, which represents your home range.

Although the above dynamic may function in a "normal" manner for strangers, it often becomes so blurred among the members of a dysfunctional family that personal boundaries, including the physical body itself, are violated. In some families, appropriate personal boundaries are all but absent. This dysfunctional trait is usually carried into the arena of destructive environmental conflict.

It is therefore my task both to set the behavioral boundaries as rules of conduct, which not only are the infrastructure of society but also make the facilitation process work, and to make sure that all participants understand and respect them. Understanding and respecting boundaries helps to build and maintain trust. This is critically important because interpersonal boundaries are an absolute social necessity of communication.

Let's look at a few concrete examples, beginning with me as a facilitator. The most important interpersonal boundary for me to maintain is that of a guest at all times, because I am serving at the participants' behest. By staying within "guest boundaries," I am nonthreatening and can create and maintain a safe environment within which the participants can struggle to communicate. This means that I must never crack a joke or allow anyone else to do so, because every joke is at the expense of someone or something, which can only be insulting.

One of the more important behavioral contracts that I make with the participants is to listen to one another without interrupting. If necessary, a "talking stick" is passed from person to person as he or she speaks. The talking stick signifies the right of the holder to speak and the obligation of everyone else to listen in silence. This is imperative because waiting one's turn is part and parcel of civility and equality, both of which are prerequisites for a safe environment.

Although these examples may sound fairly simple, learning to understand boundaries is often complicated by the various "coping mechanisms" through which we as children learn to survive and with which combatants attempt to quell their fears while dealing with one another. These mechanisms comprise a part of everyone's personality characteristics and as such are important for me to understand because they are often the key to unlocking the stubborn discord of destructive conflict.

COPING MECHANISMS: UNCONSCIOUS THOUGHTS THAT MANIFEST AS RECOGNIZABLE BEHAVIORS

Coping mechanisms, first deciphered and named "defense mechanisms" by Sigmund Freud, who developed psychoanalysis, begin as thought processes we devise to protect ourselves from that which we deem dangerous to our well-being. What begins as a thought manifests as a behavior when we are confronted with the perceived life-threatening circumstance from which the thought process was originally devised to protect us. If the combination of thought and action is successful, then we have devised a functional mechanism of survival, a "coping mechanism," which is reinforced by a feedback loop every time it works as we expect it to. As we automatically use it, the thought process is relegated to our subconscious, and only the behavioral pattern is manifested.

Coping mechanisms therefore become the unconscious, behavioral devices we learn to use to help us retain or regain control in uncomfortable situations. This really means we are trying to cope with a Universe in constant change.

Coping mechanisms as a strategy for survival are often functional, positive, and entirely appropriate for a given circumstance when we develop them, but they eventually can and often do become outmoded and dysfunctional as circumstances change. Clinging to dysfunctional coping mechanisms when they fail to meet current or new situations in life can lead to a hardening of attitudes, a hardening of the heart, and create a rigidity that leads to destructive conflict.

Because dysfunctional coping mechanisms involve self-deception and a distortion of reality, they do not resolve problems; they only alleviate symptoms. Moreover, since they operate on a relatively unconscious level, they are not subject to the normal checks and balances of conscious awareness.

Although there is a vast array of coping mechanisms, only a few of the more common ones will be discussed here. They will not be dealt with in the "clinical" sense, but rather as I see them operating in life.

Keep in mind that the point of this discussion is *not* that coping mechanisms are bad or that we need to rid ourselves of our particular tactics for coping with life. Coping mechanisms are not clearly defined, separable behavioral patterns, but rather are overlapping behaviors, which grade into and out of one another almost at will. It is thus the awareness, the consciousness, with which I observe my behavior and that of others that is at issue. Therefore, I must ask myself with compassion and forthrightness: Does this behavior and its underlying motivation best serve my present needs in life?

I will not dwell on the coping mechanisms per se, but rather give brief examples to illustrate how they are used, because they form the backbone of conflict's thrust and parry. As such, it is absolutely necessary for me to understand coping mechanisms because the more functional a person is, the more inclined she or he is towards peace; conversely, the more dysfunctional a person is, the more inclined he or she is towards destructive conflict.

Recognizing and understanding the language of coping mechanisms, especially dysfunctional ones, is a vital clue in understanding a person's family dynamics and how that person deals with life. It is thus a critical step in understanding the dynamics of a destructive conflict and how to help the combatants resolve their differences with dignity. As you read the following descriptions, you might think of examples from your own life and family upbringing.

Anger and Aggression

Anger and aggression are discussed together because anger is the emotion that triggers aggression as the act. Anger is a feeling of extreme displeasure, hostility, indignation, or exasperation toward someone or something. I see anger as extreme fear and/or frustration violently projected outward. Anger is synonymous with being upset, feeling a minor irritation, or an intense rage. It is a temporary insanity that isolates us from the facts, from ourselves, and from one another.

In addition, I am not angry for the reason or at the person or thing I think I am. I am always angry at myself for being afraid of circumstances and therefore feeling out of control, which has nothing to do with the person or thing at which I level my anger.

Unfortunately, this realization all too often follows my anger, which I have attempted to project onto someone or something else. I also find that a minor irritation is of the same genera as intense rage, because the dynamic is the same; it is only a less intense reaction on the same continuum. I feel internal disharmony, which is fear of a circumstance in which I feel a loss of control, and I am angry about feeling afraid of the circumstance.

Unless I fully understand the above dynamic, I think I am really angry for the reason and at the person or thing at which I level my anger. I therefore use my anger as a means of *not* having to deal with the circumstance that I am really afraid of. This often happens at meetings between agency representatives and the public. The latter often hear things with which they disagree and over which they have no control. Instead of calmly listening, they get angry and start yelling. I have, in fact, facilitated meetings where participants have been so charged with emotion that they became red in the face, yelled, cursed, and physically shook with rage.

In the intensity of the emotion, they often feel that they are right in projecting their anger onto those who seem to be in control, those who have "taken" control away from them. In the grip of their anger, they do not perceive that they have a choice because they feel a loss of control, which they find terrifying.

Anger usually translates into aggression, which, as it is used here, is the habit of launching attacks, of being hostile. If I show enough aggression toward a person or persons at whom I think I am angry, then I am coping with my fear by causing the person or persons to back away from the threatening energy.

Through aggression, I think I can avoid having to deal with the circumstance over which I have no control and of which I am frightened.

All I have really accomplished, however, is to isolate myself from any understanding of the data and from the people who are presenting it. If, on the other hand, I am patient, open-minded, and gently ask questions, then I might be able to overcome my fear, and in so doing realize that there are no enemies out there—only other people who, like myself, are frightened of the unknown.

Appraisal

Appraisal is the act of evaluating something; of estimating its quality, amount, size, and other features; of judging its merits. As such, appraisal is an interesting coping mechanism in that it can effectively prevent forward motion. It is like being the traveler on the platform at the train station who is so afraid of missing the train that he spends all his time checking and rechecking the schedule. He is so preoccupied with appraising the schedule that he does not even see the train come and go.

Another example of an over-appraiser is the shopper who goes to the grocery store to buy three items and has to read every comparative label in minute detail and then weigh and reweigh the data before making a choice. Thus, what would take most people five minutes to buy takes such an appraiser forty-five minutes.

Appraisers cope with their fear of criticism by checking, rechecking, and further rechecking the data; they are seldom willing to make a decision for which they may be held accountable. When in doubt, they conduct another study, but refrain, at any cost, from *saying* or *doing* anything until all the data are collected and have been carefully and properly analyzed. This, of course, will never happen, because even if all the data could be collected, the appraiser would still continue the analysis indefinitely.

Over the years, I have met many people who appraise their life away. Although I find them exceedingly difficult to work with when decisions need to be made, I feel deep compassion for them, because I remember times in my boyhood when I also was too terrified to make a decision, knowing I would be humiliated, or beaten, or both, no matter what I did.

Defensiveness

To be defensive means to protect that which already is; to resist a new view, to resist the possibility of change, and to resist the truth about oneself. Defensiveness limits my growth in that I argue for my old self rather than taking a new look and embracing a new possibility. I defend the rut in which my old belief, my old behavioral pattern, is stuck. I become defensive because at some level I know that what is being said is at least partly true. And I am afraid to listen to the truth, because I will have to act on it, and that means changing my stance, something I am afraid to do. I thus feel obliged to defend the old groove. After all, it is a comfortable, known entity, like home.

Defense as a coping mechanism takes planning. I have often watched my mind plan its defense against change. A planned life can perhaps be tolerated, but cannot be fully lived.

> The mind engaged in planning for itself is occupied in setting up control of future happenings. It does not think that it will be provided for, unless it makes its own provisions. Time becomes a future emphasis, to be controlled by learning and experience obtained from past events and previous beliefs. It overlooks the present, for it rests on the idea the past has taught enough to let the mind direct its future course.
>
> The mind that plans is thus refusing to allow for change. What it has learned before becomes the basis for its future goals. Its past experience directs its choice of what will happen. And it does not see that here and now is everything it needs to guarantee a future quite unlike the past, without a continuity of any old ideas and sick beliefs. Anticipation plays no part at all, for present confidence directs the way.
>
> Defenses are the plans you undertake to make against the truth. Their aim is to select what you approve, and disregard what you consider incompatible with your beliefs of your reality. Yet what remains is meaningless indeed. For it is your reality that is the "threat" which your defenses would attack, obscure, and take apart and crucify.[12]

Denial

Denial is a refusal to recognize the truth of a situation; it is a contradiction, a rejection of what is. Although denial as a coping mechanism is part and parcel of almost all other coping mechanisms, it is also an entity unto itself.

Think, for example, of your mind as the honeycomb in a beehive, and visualize yourself stuffing your unwanted feelings into an empty comb and sealing it so you will not have to deal with them—out of sight, out of mind. You are now effectively in denial of your feelings. The rest of your mind seems to be cleared of your discomfort. You are free to live, but only so long as you can continually mend the comb already filled and continually create more comb to accommodate future discomfort.

Denial is one of the most pervasive coping mechanisms in the world. It is such a simple device that it is probably the great, great grandparent of all coping mechanisms. The following is a typical example of denial. Speaking intently and quickly, the dark-haired, green-eyed young woman explained she had been sexually abused by a relative from the time she was five years old until she was fourteen. Although she had two miscarriages, her parents still refused to believe her, which means they were denying that anything improper had taken place.[13]

Displacement

Displacement as a coping mechanism is used to shift the focus from that which is uncomfortable to that which is safe; it is often referred to as a "smoke screen." I have had attorneys for the federal government try to distract me with this tactic while I was under oath as an expert witness; they did not want me to complete my answer to a question they had asked because they were afraid of what I was saying, so they interrupted and asked a totally unrelated question. Recognizing this tactic, however, I always completed my answer to the first question and then answered the displacement question.

Another way to cope with fear of losing control is to displace the real reason with the use of time. Some people have their lives so tightly scheduled that they do not have a minute to waste. They confuse motion and time constraints with productivity. In this way, they control what they do, who they see, and how long they see them without ever having to take responsibility for saying: "I don't want to see you, because you make me uncomfortable," or "I don't want to see so and so, because I am afraid that I might fail, which I cannot handle right now."

I use time to control which circumstances I wish to deal with and to see those people I wish to see for as long as I want to see them. At the same time, I am pleading a case for being innocently out of time—out of control—for those circumstances or those people with which I do not want to deal.

One retired man was so afraid of dying that he displaced his fear onto time; consequently, he had no time to waste. The sad thing was that he was so conscious of his time running out that he did not enjoy what he did because he never had time to do it. He always had to get on to the next thing. He raced time around his prison cell—his fear of dying—and literally wore himself out before his time might have been up. His coping mechanism had became his unconscious agent of indirect suicide.

Filters

A filter is a device through which a substance (such as light, water, or thought) is passed to remove "unwanted impurities." In the sense of a coping mechanism, I filter out unwanted material, so that way I can "accept" and "understand" whatever I want to. For example, have you ever tried explaining something to someone and had them hear only part of it, the part they *wanted* to hear?

I often find this to be the case when I speak to a group of people comprised of the timber industry, environmental organizations, and land management agencies. They each hear what they want to hear in what I say, and they each address these different aspects of my presentation during the question and answer period. The more polarized the audience is, the more predictable are the questions they are likely to ask and the responses they are likely to hear and accept.

At times, people live as though they are in a giant "safe" with filters to control what they see, what they hear, and what they feel. They thus hear only what they want to hear, see only what they want to see, and feel only what they want to feel. They can accept and understand that which they choose and do not have to move out of their comfort zone and be accountable in the world. This is what it means to "look at life through rose-colored glasses." Filtering is a common coping mechanism to "selectively" hear and see, as exemplified in two of the three monkeys—hear no evil and see no evil.

Filters can be very frustrating for the person who is trying to communicate with someone who does not want to hear what is being said. Yet we all filter information simply because we have different frames of reference. Speaking for myself, I always endeavor (and often fail) to lay aside my filters so I may become educated in the sense that the poet Robert Frost meant when he wrote: "Education is the ability to listen to almost anything without losing your temper or your self-confidence."

Projection

Projection is a casting forward or outward of something. As a coping mechanism, it means the externalization of an inner thought or motive and its subsequent behavior, which is then attributed to someone else.

> ...and Aaron shall lay both his hands upon the head of the live goat, and confess over him all the iniquities of the people of Israel, and all their transgressions, and all their sins; and he shall put them upon the head of the goat, and send him away into the wilderness....The

goat shall bear all their iniquities upon him to a solitary land; and he shall let the goat go in the wilderness.[14]

In biblical times, on the Jewish day of atonement, Yom Kippur, all the transgressions of the Jewish people were heaped (projected) onto the back of a "scapegoat," which was then driven away into the wilderness, "taking" all the people's transgressions with it. Projection as a coping mechanism thus has a long-recognized history.

Just as an empty movie projector casts only light, I can project onto other people only what I think about myself, because without thought, there is nothing to project. Thus, I see in others what I both consciously and unconsciously see in myself—nothing more, nothing less.

As such, judgment, the projection of that which I see in myself, is the projectile I cast outward in the word "should" (You should do this; you should do that). "You should" is thus a common attitude of the opposing sides in a conflict.

In reality, however, should is the stuff of someone else's standard of operation, of someone else's concept of right and wrong, of what I should or should not be or do. Someone else's "should" is only mine if I choose to accept it. On the other hand, I can choose to ignore another person's "should," and then it has no effect.

Projection is a very common coping mechanism. When understood as such, projections can be very enlightening. I can, for example, tell almost immediately how a participant feels about herself or himself by the kinds of projection she or he levels at her or his opponent.

Rationalization

To rationalize in the sense of a coping mechanism is to devise self-satisfying but inauthentic reasons for one's own behavior. For example, suppose I have been told to do something in my job with which I do not agree ethically. If I do not comply, however, I will lose my job—a real possibility in these days of corporate/political administrations. I therefore rationalize that I can do more good working for change on the inside of the agency or company, by compromising my beliefs, than I can by getting myself fired for sticking to my beliefs. In so doing, I intellectually rationalize acceptance of the order and comply with it, but I have simultaneously committed the honesty of my feelings to the prison of repression. Thus, I have murdered a vital, creative part of myself.

The most commonly used rationalization is lack of control: "I can't." Can't means that whatever it is, it is beyond my control. Therefore, I am not responsible for my behavior. What I am really saying when I say "can't" is: "I will not, I choose not to, I am afraid to," or some similar declaration.

This rationalization probably came about because not knowing the answer to a question is not acceptable in our society. "I don't know" is reinforced as an unacceptable answer from grade school through college, the military, the workplace, and life in general. In fact, when you think about it, the statement "Ignorance is no excuse under the law" is saying the same thing. Not knowing is not okay!

Repression

Repression can be thought of as a one-way, spring-loaded valve into the unconscious. Any thought or emotion that causes me anxiety passes through this one-way valve, building tension in the coiled spring as it does so. Once trapped in the unconscious, neither the thought nor the emotion is allowed to reappear in my awareness. It might be expressed as follows: Homer really wanted to slug his brother for having offended Alice, but that would not have been acceptable at the party. So he clamped his jaws together and clenched his fists as he stalked from the room, tamping down his anger—putting a lid on it—so it would not erupt unacceptably. He repressed his emotions. Without an acceptable "safety valve" for releasing tension, energy continually builds in the spring until one day Homer will unexpectedly "blow up" and badly hurt his brother over some trivial matter.

I have seen this coping mechanism in agency personnel. On being ordered to do things for the good of the agency, things that violated their moral sense of what was right, they repressed their emotions to keep their jobs rather than maintaining the integrity of their beliefs, even if it meant resigning. The moment they retired, however, they attacked the agency with all the pent-up vehemence and bitterness of those long-repressed emotions.

Resistance

To resist is to work against, to fight off, to actively oppose. Resistance in and of itself is not bad. It is simply a conservative, stabilizing tendency, which keeps an individual from overstepping limitations too quickly and rashly.

Problems arise when my resistance to change becomes overreactive, obsolete, or maladaptive—in a word, dysfunctional. Then I am unable to express my potential or to meet my goals. Resistance, in the dysfunctional sense, is one of the most commonly used coping mechanisms to ward off change, to avoid the responsibility of moving forward, of participating in life.

Resistance is like swimming directly against the current of a large, swift river. The swimmer, in such circumstances, despite maximum effort, becomes worn out, is carried down river by the overwhelming, persistent strength of the current, and sometimes drowns. If, perchance, the swimmer is strong enough and determined enough just to stay even with the current, it soon becomes apparent that while the current does not tire from the effort of flowing, the swimmer tires from the effort of swimming. Thus, the swimmer is ultimately carried away by the current—the tired carried away by the tireless.

Circumstances are the river of life, and change is its current. The individual swimmer can choose to resist the current, become fatigued and perhaps drown, or can choose to flow with the current and, with patience, learn the skill necessary to cross the river easily. Herein lies the secret of the statement "to be in control, one must give up the desire to control." Only when I give up trying to control life can I master navigating its current.

That which I resist persists in the degree to which I resist it, and I become like that which I resist. It cannot be otherwise. What I resist is a lesson in life not learned, and life seems to persist in its lessons until I learn them.

Social psychologist Marsha Sinetar said in essence that resistance is a subtle inner device urging us to "back away" from the difficulties and demands of life. Psychoanalyst Carl G. Jung stated it a little differently: resistance "begets meaninglessness."

I find, however, that resistance serves two purposes in life, one positive and one negative. A feeling of resistance is positive when it is my inner voice telling me that what I have been asked to do really goes against my deepest sense of principles. In this case, I can feel good honoring my own resistance.

On the other hand, there are times when I simply do not want to do something that needs doing. Then my resistance works against me. I may end up with a terrible headache, because my resistance is like driving a car by stepping on the gas pedal and the brakes at the same time with equal pressure.

Standards and Judgment

A standard is an acknowledged measure of comparison for qualitative and quantitative value, a criterion or a norm. We each have a standard against which we measure how things around us fit into our comfort zone. Our standard is therefore our basis for judging a person, situation, or thing as right or wrong, good or bad. It is not necessarily an accepted standard of social morality, however, because each person's standard is only his or her mental landscape of acceptability and has no validity for anyone else.

My standard of judgment can be so narrow and biased, however, that it is self-defeating, because it blinds me to the truth. Consider the twelve-member committee for admission to a prestigious prep school in New York, which voted unanimously to exclude a particular thirteen-year-old boy. The rejection was not surprising, because the boy's academic record contained marks from failing to barely passing in almost every subject except English. In addition, his teachers' comments about his behavior ranged from "lazy" to "rebellious." After its decision, the committee learned that it had just passed judgment on the scholastic record of young Winston Churchill![15]

I believe everyone—myself included—does the level best he or she knows how to do at all times, and I seriously doubt any of us live up to our own standards for ourselves. If this is true, where is *the* standard as a true basis for judgment?

> Judgment, like other devices by which the world of illusions is maintained, is totally misunderstood by the world. It is actually confused with wisdom, and substitutes for truth. As the world uses the term, an individual is capable of "good" and "bad" judgment, and his education aims at strengthening the former and minimizing the latter. There is, however, considerable confusion about what these categories mean. What is "good" judgment to one is "bad" judgment to another. Further, even the same person classified the same action as showing "good" judgment at one time and "bad" judgment at another time. Nor can any consistent criteria for determining what these categories are be really taught. At any time the student may disagree with what his would-be teacher says about them, and the teacher himself may well be inconsistent in what he believes. "Good" judgment, in these terms, does not mean anything. No more does "bad."[16]

All I can judge is *appearances*. There is nothing else. An appearance is an outward aspect or an outward indication. Judgment is the process of forming an opinion or evaluation by discerning and comparing.

Because I am afraid of deviations from my standard, I cope with my fears by remaining the same while trying to control circumstances so other people will have to risk change. If the "other" people are unwilling to change, they become my enemies, whom I judge as not being okay, even inferior, because they do not live up to my standard. There are no enemies out there, only people frightened of change, of losing control, of being powerless, and who therefore are mistakenly rejected by their fellow human beings.

I was a bachelor in the mid-1970s, and everything in my house was just so. Everything had a place and was in its place—always! I was so rigid with my standard of housekeeping that I was often uncomfortable with someone else's.

One day a friend of mine called and said he needed a place to live and asked if I knew of any. Without thinking, I said, "Yes. I have an extra room. Come and live with me." That was the beginning of the end! I did not know that I was about to get an education. He moved in with his dog, horse blankets, bridles, saddles, tools, rifles, and even his periodic girlfriends. My nice, neat, orderly, quiet, simple life was an instant shambles, because in those days my friend seemed to be utter chaos looking for a place to happen.

Yet this was one of the best things that ever happened to me. I could not "correct" my friend, no matter how hard I tried (and believe me, I tried!), so I eventually joined him. He in his mid-twenties taught me, at the age of forty, how to play. He helped me to relax my standards and live a little. He became my personal counselor in overcoming my workaholism and my perfectionism. He gave me an irreplaceable gift, the ability to seize the moment and live it to the full.

Victim

Feeling like a victim of anything is a helpless, hopeless feeling, a feeling of being somehow violated. Being a victim of abuse is a violent, confusing, and overwhelming experience. One of the major aspects of being a victim is the experience of having little or no control over events. Something happens to me, and I feel powerless to do anything about it. In fact, implicit in the word "victim" is to be at the mercy of events or of a circumstance or person, essentially to be in a position in which I have no control over what happens to me.

To use being a victim as a coping mechanism, therefore, is difficult at best for a facilitator to deal with, because it is usually an unconscious act that is readily denied. After all, who would be a victim by choice? Although the following definitions seem to be relatively clear-cut, they are intellectual and leave much unsaid.

There are many definitions of victim, but three general ones will suffice for our discussion of victim as a coping mechanism: (1) one who is harmed by or made to suffer from an act, circumstance, agency, or condition; (2) a person who accidentally suffers injury, loss, or death as a result of a voluntary undertaking—a victim of his or her own behavior; and (3) a person who is tricked, swindled, duped, or taken advantage of.

One thing to notice about these definitions is that the victim suffers from a loss of control and is dealt a cruel blow by life. This image of having lost control makes playing a victim an easy way to get out of having to accept responsibility for having made the choice that put one in the circumstance of being the victim in the first place. I think most of us play the victim at some point in life to cope with the feeling of being humiliated for not possessing control. What our society is telling us, in our own minds at least, is that it is not okay to be human, to err, that loss of control is somehow a terrible weakness.

To understand and accept the transformative premise of facilitation requires not only an understanding of coping mechanisms but also acknowledging each person's capacity for rational thought.

THE CAPACITY FOR RATIONAL THOUGHT

It is critical that I, as a facilitator, work from the premise that all people possess the potential for rational thought (rational logic). To attain it, however, they must first work their way through the barriers of existing irrational thoughts (emotions that give rise to a sense of logic that is irrational).

It is thus necessary to understand the meaning and relationship of two words: emotion and logic. As used here, emotion is a state of feeling, such as joy, anger, or fear, which is centered in the individual's sense of self. Emotion, which produces an irrational sense of logic, is the energy that drives us, that gives us values and feelings. Logic is the mechanism that allows us to understand the emotions contained in our values. Logic allows an individual's understanding that he or she is part of an interconnected, interactive system in which the governing principle of cause and effect is impartial.

Because the Universal Laws are rational, Nature, which obeys these laws, is rational. We as a part of Nature must therefore possess the potential for rational thought, but we also possess irrational thought and so imperfectly understand Nature's rationality.

That notwithstanding, unless I believe that the people with whom I work possess the potential for rational thought, I am powerless to bring about peace short of total human annihilation, because I cannot negotiate with another person as long as I am convinced that my counterpart's thinking is irrational. A cardinal principle of facilitation, negotiation, and the power to act with confidence is the belief that the people with whom one works possess the potential for rational logic. This means one must believe that people have the potential to honor their feelings while thinking clearly, accept their individual power, and possess the desire for peace. Only then is it possible to reach accord with them.

When thinking is rational, based on the impartial principle of cause and effect, the group one is facilitating can become dedicated to the proposition that no person shall abuse another, that all members shall defend the rights of each member, and that each member shall defend the rights of all members. This is possible because a rational person tends to seek peace, which in turn can lead to the organized enactment of a shared vision for the future.

Rational thought can be tested through its converse. Namely, if one does not believe in the rational nature of another person, then one believes it is impossible to negotiate with him or her. If one does not believe that rational people ultimately desire peace, then one cannot negotiate confidently toward peace with one's opponent. If one cannot negotiate with one's opponent, one is powerless to create peace, and if one cannot organize around rational thought, then the principles of peace cannot move from the minds of people into the actions of society.

By the time I am asked to facilitate the resolution of a destructive conflict, however, the people involved have usually reached a place of such psychological pain, such feelings of fear and rage, that a sense of hopelessness prevails. Under such circumstances, it is difficult for them to think clearly and therefore direct much attention to dealing with the real causes of their emotions.

Although emotion and logic appear to be mutually exclusive, both are valid because they are different and not substitutable. For example, emotions—either negative (such as pain, fear, and despair) or positive (such as love and compassion)—must be validated and transcended before the impartial logic of the whole systemic picture can be accepted. Thus, negative emotions can be brought to logic only when all parties feel safe enough to be open and honest—where love, trust, and respect can eventually prevail, when "a gentle answer turns away wrath."[17]

A major problem in the world today is the apparently irreconcilable split between faulty logic based on repressed emotions[6] and rational logic based on the impartial outworking of cause and effect, which is reached when the emotions are accepted, validated, understood, incorporated, and transcended. If not transcended, the faulty logic of unbridled emotions can become violence and moral chaos.

Only when emotions are transcended can they give the insight, the inner vision necessary to reach rational thought, that which allows one to perceive the world as an impartial system based on cause and effect. If I, as a facilitator, choose to accept my own inner struggle toward rational thought, I can help others to do the same just because I had the courage to make that choice.

EVERYONE IS RIGHT FROM HIS OR HER POINT OF VIEW

We now come to the notion of right versus wrong, again based on perceived similarities and differences. Society is composed of individual human beings much as the compound eye of an insect is composed of individual facets, each of which is slightly different in structure but equally important to the total vision of the eye. Each facet has its own light-sensitive element; each has its own refractive system, and each forms but a portion of the image.

As there are as many points of view in the compound eye of an insect as there are facets, so too there are as many points of view in a society as there are people. Although everyone is right from her or his point of view, no one person has the complete image, and no one is totally right.

We all sense things differently when we see, hear, touch, taste, and smell; because we sense things differently, we understand them differently. In addition, our senses are variously effective under ever-changing circumstances. Our individual brains coordinate and integrate our individual sensing, producing an individual awareness. Through communication, our manyfold individual awarenesses are coordinated and integrated into a collective awareness. And it is through our senses that we become aware of the complementary nature of the "otherness."

It is precisely because we each have our point of view, established after we have considered the data and have reached a conclusion, that I cannot convince you of anything. But from a point of communication, I must accept what you think you heard, and you must accept what I think I said. Such acceptance is important because for me to convince you that I am right, I must simultaneously convince you that you are wrong. You will resist, of course, first because I have assaulted your dignity and second because you *are* correct from your interpretation of "your" data just as I am from my interpretation of mine.

Although I cannot convince you that you are wrong without somehow attacking your dignity, I can give you new data, which *raises the value* of your making a new decision based on new information. In this way, I can be patient and give you the space that allows you to change your mind if you so choose while maintaining your dignity intact.

The question is then, who is right when we are all right from our own points of view? If everyone is right, then who is wrong? Because no one is wrong, we cannot argue any case based on "right" or "wrong." Right or wrong is always a human judgment dealing with appearances, not reality, which means that if I think I am right, I must "win," and if I win, I must be right. You, on the other hand, are clearly wrong because you "lost," and you lost because you are clearly wrong. Thus, each side becomes committed to winning agreement with its outlook and is not even in a position to contemplate another possibility under the competitive illusion of winners and losers.

Everyone loses, however, when issues are "settled" by judgments of right or wrong because everyone appears to be right from his or her own point of view. This really is no different than a world at war in which each nation, each army, each person is sure God is on its side.

The duality of right versus wrong does not have to exist. There can instead be a continuum of "rightness" in which some are a little more right than others. Such a continuum is predicated on our individual lack of knowledge owing to our own limited perception of possible outcomes. Since I do not know for sure who is more right than whom, I must in fairness accept that everyone is right from her or his own point of view, and each point of view is different—not wrong, only different, regardless of what the discussion is about. The notion of "wrong" is therefore unacceptable in resolving a conflict.

If we are to survive the present upheavals of social evolution, we must be willing to accept the notion of right, right, and different. Wrongness in the classical, combative, human sense must become a relic of the past if we are to treat others as we ourselves would like to be treated. Only then can any issue be *resolved* in such a way that each side retains its dignity and society can progress with some semblance of order into the future.

I find the duality of "rightness" or "wrongness" of almost everything to be so pervasive that the notion of *right, right, and different* is exceedingly difficult to get across in a society that stresses judgmental values as the wisdom of its norm. If we insist on the duality of "right" versus "wrong," we will always be in competition with one another. If, on the other hand, we can agree that everyone is right from his or her own point of view and that each point of view is only a different perception along the same continuum, we will be able to coordinate and cooperate with one another and hold our society together.

ACCEPTANCE OF CIRCUMSTANCES OFFERS THE CHOICES OF WHAT MIGHT BE

Choice equals hope. Choice and hope are the ingredients of human dignity. Dignity means living in peace, free of fear. My most important choice in overcoming fear and violence is learning to accept a circumstance, whatever it is, as it is. In talking about acceptance, Mother Teresa says that if God puts us in a palace, to accept being in the palace; if God puts us in the street, to accept being in the street. But she says that we are not to put ourselves either in a palace or in the street; we are simply to accept whatever God gives us at the present moment.

Unconditional acceptance of circumstances is perhaps the most difficult lesson with which I daily struggle. I cannot, for example, control a circumstance, but I can choose to control how I respond to it and what my attitude will be. In that choice lies my freedom from fear, because I recognize that I have a choice, and I have it now. Thus, by giving up trying to control things outside of myself, I am in better control *of* myself and can choose how I want to respond to any given circumstance.

In the last analysis, I have a choice. I always have a choice, and I must choose, much as I might wish it otherwise. If I do not like the outcome or if I err in my choice, I can choose to choose again. I am not, therefore, a victim of my circumstances but rather a product of my choices and my decisions based on those choices.

What in a conflict is one's choice? One's choice is to control one's attitudes, as manifested through one's behavior. One is thus responsible for one's behavior, and therein lies the potential resolution of any dispute—to raise the value of changing one's attitude and thus one's behavior for the common good.

My task as facilitator is to help the parties understand that attitudinal and behavioral change is the key to the resolution of their dispute. If one or both of the parties want something, it is up to them to decide how they must behave in order to enhance the possibility of achieving their goals.

The more people are able to choose love and peace over fear and violence, the more they gain in wisdom and the more we all live in harmony. This is true because what we choose to think about determines how we choose to act, and our thoughts and actions set up a self-reinforcing feedback loop, a self-fulfilling prophecy that becomes our reality and our truth.

Choice is the tool with which we make ourselves who we are. It is here that we must recognize, amidst the myriad choices daily confronting us, that as we think so we create and so we become, either on the material plane or on the spiritual plane. And we are either freed by our creations (those born of love) or imprisoned by them (those born of fear).

The choice is ours, for we have free will, which means that each day, with pen in hand, we write and rewrite, edit and re-edit our autobiographies. Choice is thus the clay with which we daily mold and remold our character until the day we look into the mirror of our souls and see the cumulative reflection of our many choices. But for now, we can still choose what we might be in that future time.

5

COMMUNICATION: THE INTERPERSONAL ELEMENT

Transformative facilitation revolves around understanding and sharing emotions and knowledge, both of which grow from and are a reflection of social experience. Emotions and knowledge are shared through communication, which is the very heart of transformative facilitation and must be treated with the utmost respect. Just as dishonest or careless communication tells much about the people we are listening to, so too does good communication. Good communication means respect for both listener and speaker, because one must first listen to understand and then speak to be understood.

Communication is perhaps one of the most difficult things we do as human beings, and yet it is simultaneously one of the most important things we do. We are creatures who must share feelings, senses, abstractions, and concrete experiences in order to know and value our existence in relation with one another. Communication, or language, is the way we share the very core of our relationships. Our existence revolves around it, and without it, we have nothing of value.

LANGUAGE AS A TOOL

Although communication involves far more than mere words, we are only concerned with words here. Words are symbols for the things we experience;

therefore, the more accurately a chosen word builds a bridge to our common ground, the easier it is to get in touch with one another, stay in touch, build trust, and ask for and receive help.

In this sense, semantics is more than quibbling over words; it reveals both our thought patterns and our consciousness of cause and effect. It is the conveyance of concepts, perceptions, personal truths, trust, and a shared vision for the future. Like every linguistic creation, language can empower or limit, depending on whether we see it as a set of labels describing some pre-existing, unchangeable reality or as a medium with which to articulate a new reality—a sustainable way of living together on and with the Earth.

My task as a facilitator is to create a safe place in which common bonds can be built, maintained, and strengthened through good communication, or a clear, concise use of language. Just as any relationship requires sensitive, honest, and open communication to be healthy and grow, so too are relationships in the facilitation process forged, maintained, and improved when feelings and information are shared accurately, freely, and with tact.

The quality of communication is thus enhanced if simple rather than complex words are used. Picturesque slang and free-and-easy colloquialisms, if they are appropriate to the subject and if they do not offend the sensibilities of the participants, can add variety and vividness to the facilitation process. But substandard English, such as grammatical errors and vulgarisms, not only detracts from my dignity as facilitator but also reflects my attitude towards the participants' intelligence.

If the subject under discussion includes technical terms, I must be sure to define each term clearly and concisely so that all participants know exactly what is meant by it. It is also best to use specific rather than general words. In addition, to ensure clarity, I use sentences of short to medium length because, for most people, the spoken word is often more difficult to grasp than the written word, which can be read over and over and studied.

Quality communication requires constant, consistent practice. It is thus imperative that I continually monitor my words, their meanings, and their usage in my everyday speaking and writing. Every word must be valued, and every word that does not carry its weight must be discarded. I must practice all day every day because good communication comes first and foremost from good thoughts. By our thoughts we privately define and by our speech and actions we publicly declare who and what we are. British author James Allen stated this beautifully:

> A man's [woman's] mind may be likened to a garden, which may be intelligently cultivated or allowed to run wild; but whether

cultivated or neglected, it must, and will, bring forth. If no useful seeds are put into it, then an abundance of useless weed seeds will fall therein, and will continue to produce their kind.

Just as a gardener cultivates his plot, keeping it free from weeds, and growing the flowers and fruits which he requires, so may a man tend the garden of his mind, weeding out all the wrong, useless, and impure thoughts, and cultivating toward perfection the flowers and fruits of right, useful, and pure thoughts. By pursuing this process, a man sooner or later discovers that he is the master gardener of his soul, the director of his life. He also reveals, within himself, the laws of thought, and understanding, with ever-increasing accuracy, how the thought forces and mind elements operate in the shaping of his character, circumstances, and destiny.[18]

A word spoken is thus the manifestation of a thought, whether positive or negative. Once spoken, it can never be withdrawn, despite an apology, because words are the public extensions of our private selves.

Good communication, a prerequisite for both teaching and learning, clears the way for shared, participative ownership of ideas as a means of building relationships within the facilitation process. There are, however, a number of obligations that accompany good communication.

Because the right to know is basic in the facilitation process, all parties must have equal access to pertinent information if a conflict is to be resolved. Here, I believe, it is better to err on the side of sharing too much information rather than risking someone being left in the dark. I say this because hoarded information subverts the facilitation process through misrepresentation.

Everyone has a right to simplicity and clarity in communication and an obligation to communicate simply and clearly. If I cannot be simple and clear in what I say, then I do not understand the topic well enough to discuss it. Sometimes, for example, I have trouble expressing a concept either while writing a book, giving a speech, or during the facilitation process. When this happens, I write an essay on the topic in a maximum of five double-spaced pages. And I work on it until I've got it down as pat as I can. From that point on, it is clearly in mind and flows easily whenever I need to discuss the subject.

I go to this length because I owe everyone truth and courtesy, although truth is often uncomfortable and at times a real constraint, and courtesy may be an inconvenience. Nevertheless, it is these qualities that allow communication to educate and liberate us.

I am obliged to practice discrimination in both what I say and what I hear, which means that I must respect my own language through its careful usage.

I must acknowledge and accept that muddy language means muddy thinking, and muddy thinking means muddy language. I must therefore always remember that my audience (the parties in the dispute) may need something special from me, such as an extraordinary amount of patience and clarity while they struggle to communicate.

Language is the most profound tool I have because it both educates and liberates. Teaching and learning underlie facilitation literacy and action. Facilitation literacy is the "why" the process does what it does, and action is the "what" it does. With this in mind, I can use language to help the parties engaged in transformative facilitation to free themselves from their bonds of conflict. To allow the parties to liberate themselves, however, my communication must be based on sound reasoning, compassion, detachment, and sometimes on silence.

THE USE OF SILENCE IN COMMUNICATION

I must learn to appreciate the power of silence in communication. Most people are profoundly uncomfortable with silence and feel compelled to speak, including many facilitators who possess the need to direct, control, and intervene in the facilitation process and so destroy it. Silence, when allowed to flow unimpeded through indeterminate seconds and minutes, draws people out, causing them to engage both uncomfortable circumstances and one another.

For example, some years ago a small group of ranchers in central Oregon asked me to help them articulate a vision statement for grazing livestock on public lands, one that would allow them to continue using public lands if they lived up to it. I agreed, but said that I could only help them if they could tell my why they wanted to be ranchers. Silence. They had no answer. They had never thought about it. So I took out the book I was reading, sat down, and became engrossed in it.

After agonizing over the question for a couple of hours, one of the ranchers approached me and said: "Ahh..., Chris, ahh..., I guess it's the way of life that I love."

"Okay," I replied, "let's call it lifestyle. What's it worth to you? How much are you willing to change your attitude and behavior concerning your use of public lands to maintain your chosen lifestyle?"

With these questions answered, the ranchers drafted their vision statement. Now, years later, they are not only grazing their livestock on public lands but also are model ranchers. One of them travels around the United States speaking to other ranchers about what he learned.

It was their agony in the two-hour silence that finally drew out the answer they needed to find, and the answer was theirs—not mine. Had I in any way helped them with the answer because I was uncomfortable with the silence, it would have been my answer—not theirs—and it would have been useless to them. As it turned out, the answer raised the value of being ranchers. They felt like the first-class citizens they are, and because they act accordingly, people listen when they speak.

THE NEED TO BE HEARD

Although one may not think of it as such, listening is the other half of communication. Communication is a gift of ideas; therefore, the other person can give me a gift of ideas through speaking only if I accept the gift through listening. The spoken word that falls on consciously "deaf ears" is like a drop of rain evaporating before it reaches the Earth. Intolerance of another's ideas belies faith in one's cause.

The watchword of listening is *empathy*, which means imaginative identification with, as opposed to judgment of, the person's thoughts, feelings, life situation, and so on. The more I can empathize with a person, the more she or he feels heard, the greater the bond of trust, and the better I understand the situation. This means, however, actively, consciously listening with a quiet, open mind, without forming a rebuttal while the other person is speaking. Such listening is an act of love, and anything short of it is an act of passive violence.

Some years ago, I was on a television program in which the intent was to discuss the issue of ancient forests in the Pacific Northwest. An elderly lady on the program tried in vain to be heard, but the moderator consistently ignored her. Even after we were off the air, she tried again to tell the moderator how she was feeling, but he continued to ignore her. In the end, just to be heard, perhaps only by herself, she spoke out loud to no one; she spoke into space. She may as well have been alone in the world.

Not listening is an act of violence because it is a purposeful way of invalidating the feelings—the very existence—of another person. Everyone needs to be heard and validated as a human being because sharing is the bond of relationship that makes us "real" to ourselves and gives us meaning in the greater context of the Universe. We simply cannot find meaning out of relationship with one another. Therefore, only when I have first validated another person through listening as an act of love can that person really *hear* what I am saying. Only then can I share another's truth. Only then can my gift of ideas touch receptive ears.

All we have in the world as human beings is one another, and all we have to give one another is one another. We are each our own gift to one another and to the world; we have nothing else of value to give. I cannot give my gift, however, if there is no one to receive it, if there is no one to hear. Therefore, if we listen—really listen—to one another and validate one another's feelings, even if we don't agree, we can begin to resolve our differences before they become disputes. But to listen well and to speak well, it is important to consider the basic elements of communication.

THE BASIC ELEMENTS OF COMMUNICATION

Communication occurs when one person transmits ideas or feelings to another or to a group of people. Its effectiveness depends on the similarity between the information transmitted and that received, a common frame of reference.

The communication process is composed of at least three elements: (1) the sender—someone speaking, writing, signing, or emitting the silent language of attitude or movement; (2) the symbols used in creating and transmitting the message—sounds of a particular and repetitive form called spoken words, particular and repetitive hand-crafted signs called written words, a particular arrangement of musical notes called melody, and facial expression and "body language"; and (3) the receiver—someone listening to, reading, or observing the symbols. These elements are dynamically interrelated, and that which affects one influences all.

Suppose I have something in my mind that I want to convey to you. I try sending my thoughts through the air as intelligent noise for you to pick up with your receivers, your ears. You must then translate the sounds back into your thoughts that simulate my thoughts as you understand them. And you think you know what I said? I cannot even accurately tell you what I meant because there are seldom words with which to express clearly the nuances of my thoughts. How, for example, can I really say "I love you?" What does that mean? I can feel it, but there simply are no words to describe the feeling.

Communication is thus a complicated, two-way process that is not only dynamic amongst its elements but also reciprocal. If, for instance, a receiver has difficulty understanding the symbols and indicates confusion, the sender may become uncertain and timid, losing confidence in being able to convey ideas. The effectiveness of the communication is thus diminished. On the other hand, when a receiver reacts positively, a sender is encouraged and adds strength and confidence to the message. Let's examine how the three elements work.

Sender

A sender's effectiveness in communication is related to at least three factors. First is facility in using language, which influences the ability to select those symbols that are graphic and meaningful to the receiver.

Second, senders, both consciously and unconsciously, reveal their attitudes towards themselves, towards the ideas they are transmitting, and towards the receivers. These attitudes must be positive if the communication is to be effective. Senders must indicate that they believe their message is important and that there is a need to know the ideas presented.

Third, a successful sender draws on a broad background of personal, accurate, up-to-date, stimulating, and relevant information. A sender must make certain that the ideas and feelings being transmitted are relevant to the receiver. The symbols used must be simple, direct, and to the point. Too often, however, a sender uses imprecise language and/or technical jargon that is nonsense to the receiver and thus impedes effective communication.

Symbols

The most basic level of communication is achieved through simple oral and visual codes. The letters of the alphabet, both spoken and written, constitute such a basic code when translated into words, as do common gestures and facial expressions. But words and gestures only communicate ideas when combined in meaningful wholes: speeches, sign language, sentences, paragraphs, or chapters. Each part is critical to the meaning of the whole.

Ideas must be carefully selected if they are to convey messages that receivers can understand and react to. Ideas must be analyzed to determine which are best suited for starting, carrying, and concluding the communication and which clarify, emphasize, define, limit, or explain the context—all of which form the basis of effective transmission of ideas from the sender to the receiver.

Finally, the development of ideas from simple symbols culminates in the selection of the medium (such as hearing or seeing) best suited for their transmission. In the facilitation process, however, a variety of media (hearing, seeing, touching, and at times smelling and tasting) makes for the most effective communication because it relates to the widest range of experiences.

Receiver

A basic rule of facilitation is that it is my responsibility as a facilitator to be clear, concise, and relevant, and because communication is a shared responsibility, the receiver must do his or her best to understand. I know communication has occurred when receivers react with an understanding that allows them to change their behavior.

To understand the communication process, it helps to appreciate at least three aspects of receivers: their abilities, attitudes, and experiences, which often and in many hidden ways relate to their familial upbringings. First, it is important to discern a receiver's ability to question and comprehend the ideas transmitted. I can encourage a receiver's ability to question and comprehend by providing a safe atmosphere that welcomes such participation.

Second, a receiver's attitude may be one of resistance, willingness, or passivity. Whatever the attitude, I must gain the receiver's attention and retain it. The more varied, interesting, and relevant I am, the more successful I will be in this respect.

Third, a receiver's background, experience, and education (often extremely diverse in a group situation) constitute the frame of reference towards which the communication must be aimed. I assume the obligation of assessing the receiver's knowledge and of using it as the fundamental guide for effective communication. For me to get a receiver's reaction, however, I must first reach him or her, and it is in this area that the major barriers to communication are usually found.

COMMUNICATION BARRIERS

The nature of language and the way in which it is used often lead to misunderstandings and conflict. These misunderstandings stem primarily from three barriers to effective communication: (1) the lack of a common experience or frame of reference, (2) how one approaches life, and (3) the use of abstractions.

Lack of a Common Experience or Frame of Reference

The lack of a common experience or frame of reference is probably the greatest barrier to effective communication. Although many people believe that words carry meaning in much the same way as a person transports an armful of wood or a pail of water from one place to another, words *never* carry precisely the same meaning from the mind of the sender to that of the receiver. Words are vehicles of perceptive meaning. They may or may not supply emotional meaning as well. The nature of the response is determined by the receiver's past experiences surrounding the word and the feelings it evokes.

Feelings grant a word its meaning, which is in the receiver's mind and not in the word itself. Since a common frame of reference is basic to communication, words in and of themselves are meaningless. Meaning is engendered when words are somehow linked to one or more shared experiences between the sender and the receiver, albeit the experiences may be interpreted differently. Words are thus merely symbolic representations that correspond to anything people apply the symbol to—objects, experiences, or feelings.

Thus, a sender must differentiate carefully between the symbols and the things they represent, keeping both in as true a perspective as possible. The truth of a perspective (the interpretation of an experience) is based on the degree to which a person is functional or dysfunctional, which is largely determined by the functionality of one's family of origin. It is also based on the degree to which a person has grown not only beyond his or her own dysfunction but also in the breadth and depth of his or her individual life experiences. Taken altogether, this translates into generalized personality traits.

General Personality Traits

In a sense, generalized personality traits are an amalgamation of the dominant coping mechanisms with which one navigates life. They thus become the essence of one's interpretation of life experiences and the springboard of one's personal capabilities. These traits, which we each possess to a greater or lesser degree, are not cut and dried, but rather are overlapping tendencies with varying shades of gray. Nevertheless, they can be substantial barriers to communication.

For example, some people can take ideas seemingly at **random** from any part of a thought system and integrate them; these people have mental processes that instantly change direction, arriving at the desired destination in a nonlinear, intuitive fashion. Others can think only in a **linear sequence,** like the cars of a train; these people have mental processes that crawl along in a plodding fashion, exploring this avenue and that, without assurance of ever reaching a definite conclusion. If the random thinker is also at ease with **abstractions** but the linear-sequence thinker requires **concrete** examples, their attempts to communicate may well be like two ships passing in a dense fog.

Then there is the **introverted** person, who appears self-possessed, even aloof, processes things internally, navigates life's path more or less alone, and has few friends over a lifetime. An **extroverted** person, on the other hand, is outgoing, mingles easily with other people, requires the presence of people to be happy, processes things through mutual discussion, and has a constant string of friends. An introvert works well alone behind the scenes, whereas an extrovert works well with people out front. In addition, there are four other traits, which can be summed as fatalist, exasperator, appraiser, and relator.

A **fatalist** is the consummate victim who feels powerless in the face of an all-powerful system or life itself and is forever suffering a loss of control. To this person, the operational word is "can't." A fatalist, resigned to his or her lot in life, is often barely functional and requires a tremendous amount of energy, sucked from whomever will give it, to even reach zero on the scale of enthusiasm. Just as soon as the person stops propping up the fatalist, however, he or she plunges below zero again.

Although the fatalist wants to be rescued, he or she will resist any attempt to be rescued at any cost. Here I must be wary. The only one who can rescue a person is the person himself or herself. And only he or she knows when he or she is ready for self-rescuing.

I think of fatalists as good technicians. They tend to be most comfortable with simple, clear instructions about which they do not have to think. Having said this, it is critical to understand that fatalists are usually paralyzed by having to bear responsibility. They work well behind the scenes, are usually patient with details, and may even accept monitoring the progress of an activity, provided they do not have to accept any responsibility for its outcome.

An **exasperator**, on the other hand, must be the center of attention and is deeply invested in so being. Here the watchword is control. Some exasperators go to great lengths to command attention and be in control of whatever they are involved in. They tend, for instance, to be good at "one liners," know "all" the jokes, be the life of the party, and will argue any and every side of an issue, even changing sides in midstream rather than acquiesce.

Exasperator personalities are as persistent as a bulldog. Rather than agree, they will say, "Yes, but..." just as long as someone will try to show them another way of thinking about something or another possible outcome.

I have found it best to openly and freely acknowledge the exasperator's point of view, the supposed position of power, which does not mean that I necessarily agree with it. Once exasperators feel they have exerted their power and have been appropriately recognized, they can relax and everyone can get on with the process of facilitation.

Once an exasperator has an idea in mind, however, he or she gets impatient for action and, throwing caution to the wind, often barges ahead without getting adequate data and/or listening to other sides of an argument. On the flip side, if I want to get something done, done well, and completed on time, I give it to an exasperator because he or she will move heaven and earth to show off his or her prowess.

While an exasperator often "knows it all," an **appraiser** wants facts, facts, and more facts! An appraiser seems to be uncertain in the world and wants to make sure that all the data are in, examined, weighed, reexamined, and re-weighed before any decision is made. Such caution demands much patience on my part because an appraiser often seems to hold the forward motion of the process in abeyance, regardless of how much data is at hand.

Here I find it prudent to refer constantly to such data as are available and to relate such data to the process and its potential outcome. If data are needed, I ask an appraiser to obtain it, and I will likely get the best there is—and lots of it.

Then there is the **relator**, the person who is vitally concerned with what others will think and will go wherever the political wind blows. The relator seldom seems to know who he or she is and seems to have ideas only in relation to their acceptability to others. Such a person changes his or her mind often and gives away her or his power to whoever asks for it.

Since success or failure is not an event, but rather the interpretation of an event, successes or failures of relators are determined by what everyone else thinks, because they are constantly comparing themselves to those around them and internalizing what they are told by others. Unfortunately, we usually lose in the end when we compare ourselves to others because we tend to select someone we admire and then find our differences to be deficiencies, even liabilities.

Relators, in my experience, are subject to getting their feelings hurt easily and often. This is perhaps the major way in which they try to control uncomfortable circumstances because it causes most people around them to "walk on egg shells."

In working with relators, I have found it best to refuse to accept their power, even when it is offered. I instead ask them what they think and how they feel in an effort to draw them out. Done gently and patiently, this can work quite well.

Relators are generally excellent with public relations because they are sensitive to how others feel and work very hard to win approval. They thus have a good sense of how to market an idea.

There are also **piece thinkers**, the people who tend to focus on individual pieces of a system, or its perceived products, in isolation of the system itself. **Systems thinkers**, on the other hand, tend more toward a systems approach to thinking. A person oriented to seeing only the economically desirable pieces of a system seldom accepts that removing a perceived desirable or undesirable piece can or will negatively affect the productive capacity of the system as a whole. This person's response typically is: "Show me; I'll believe it when I see it." To such a person, facilitation is usually seen as an immediate problem-solving exercise.

In contrast, a systems thinker sees the whole in each piece and is therefore concerned about tinkering willy-nilly with the pieces because he or she knows such tinkering might inadvertently upset the desirable function of the system as a whole. A systems thinker is also likely to see himself or herself as an inseparable part of the system, whereas a piece thinker normally sets himself or herself apart from and above the system. A systems thinker is willing to focus on transcending the issue in whatever way is necessary to frame a vision for the good of the future.

In my experience as a facilitator, the more a person is a piece thinker, the more reticent he or she is to change. This type of individual sees change as a condition to be avoided because he or she feels a greater sense of security in the known elements of the status quo, especially when money is involved. But, as Helen Keller once said: "Security is mostly a superstition. It does not exist in Nature. Life is either a daring adventure or nothing." Conversely, the more of a systems thinker a person is, the more likely he or she is to agree with Helen Keller and risk change on the strength of its unseen possibilities.

A piece thinker is likely to be a rural resident who is very much concerned with land ownership and property rights and wants as much free rein as possible to do as he or she pleases on his or her property, at times without regard for the consequences for future generations. The more of a piece thinker a person is, the greater the tendency to place primacy on people of one's own race, creed, or religion, as well as on one's own personal needs, however they are perceived. The more of a piece thinker a person is, the greater the tendency to disregard other races, creeds, or religions, as well as nonhumans and the sustainable capacity of the land. Also, the more of a piece thinker a person is, the more black and white one's thinking tends to be, as illustrated in the following example:

> The wimpy [sic] comments by Mike Mitchel in Sunday's "Rural Issues" were disturbing. As the head "honcho" and decision-maker for a BLM [Bureau of Land Management] office, he said things like, "We just follow the regulations and enforce them...." Also, "We have our regulations and have no choice."
>
> That's typical bureaucratic arrogance, and a cop-out. Those regulations didn't come down the mountain on stone tablets. They are the product of a well-funded lobby in Washington, DC, that represents those who are "saving us" from the horrible ranchers, miners and farmers of Nevada.

He says the land will restore itself in 15 or 20 years if we change grazing practices. Restore itself for what? So some manicured marshmallow-butt from Washington can start up a cattle ranch on abandoned land? Get real! Nevada ranchers are on the land now! The BLM should help them do what they do best, or get the hell out of the way. I'm not to [sic] smart, but I recognize typical Sierra Club rhetoric when I hear it.

As the song goes: When will they ever learn?[19]

A systems thinker, on the other hand, is most often an urban dweller who is likely to be concerned about the welfare of others, including those of the future and their nonhuman counterparts. Systems thinkers also tend to be concerned with the health and welfare of planet Earth in the present for the future. And they more readily accept shades of gray in their thinking than do piece thinkers.

And there are still other generalizations that can be made, such as people who are visually oriented as opposed to those who respond to sound or touch. In addition, these traits come in a variety of combinations, which indicates how different and complex people can be in response to their life experiences. These differences and complexities naturally carry over into people's patterns of communication. None of these patterns is better than any other as far as the facilitation process is concerned; each is only different and needs to be understood.

In the end, having in one way or another incorporated all of the familial pieces within ourselves—both functional and dysfunctional—we go out into the world and take our families with us. How we grow up thus determines how we approach life.

As I finally broke the cycle of dysfunction within myself, I learned something that is critical to resolving conflicts of any kind:

> The more a person is drawn towards peace and an optimistic view of the future, the more functional (psychologically healthy) an individual is. Conversely, the more a person is drawn towards debilitating destructive conflict, cynicism, and pessimism about the future, the more dysfunctional (psychologically unhealthy) an individual is.

Recognizing and understanding the language of coping mechanisms is thus a vital clue to one's personality dynamics. Such understanding is critical in altering the dynamics of a destructive conflict and in helping combatants to resolve their differences with dignity.

Use of Abstractions

Concrete words refer to objects a person can directly experience. Abstract words, on the other hand, represent ideas that cannot be experienced directly. They are shorthand symbols used to sum up vast areas of experience or concepts that reach into the trackless time of the future. Albeit they are convenient and useful, abstractions can lead to misunderstandings.

The danger of using abstractions is that they may evoke an amorphous generality in the receiver's mind and not the specific item of experience the sender intended. The receiver has no way of knowing what experiences the sender intends an abstraction to include. For example, it is common practice to use such abstract terms as "proper method" or "shorter than," but these terms alone fail to convey the sender's intent. What exactly is the "proper method?" "Shorter than" what?

When abstractions are used in facilitation, they must be linked to specific experiences through examples, analogies, and illustrations. It is even better to use, as much as possible, simple, concrete words with specific meanings. In this way, the facilitator gains greater control of the images produced in the receiver's mind, and language becomes a more effective tool.

Since I facilitate the resolution of destructive environmental conflicts, I endeavor to get the participants physically out of the comfortable conference room and into the field, where we can wander through the area of conflict and discuss it. I can thus transform the abstractions of the conference room into concrete examples of the field, which one can see, touch, smell, hear, and, if necessary, taste.

For example, I was asked to facilitate a better understanding between a local mill owner/logger and the personnel of the U.S. Forest Service in the state of Colorado. The mill owner/logger had recently purchased a large, very expensive piece of logging equipment that was more efficient in harvesting trees than were the men who used to work for him, which the machine had replaced. The problem was that the huge piece of equipment was severely compacting the fragile soils of the mountainous forest, to the ecological detriment of the sustainable productive future of the forest. But the mill owner did not understand the ecological effects he was causing.

I spent two days with the Forest Service folks and the mill owner/logger. The first day was spent in the conference room, where I showed slides of how forest ecologists at that time thought a forest functioned both above- and belowground. The audience was asked to explore the consequences of long-term management decisions on both the native forest ecosystems and their human culture. Much of the first day's discussion was a maze of abstractions to the mill owner/logger, no matter how simply I explained the data, because he had no frame of reference for what happened belowground.

The second day was spent in the forest in the area where the logging was taking place. We discussed the concepts and data from the first day as we examined and discussed the actual soil condition in the uncut forest and compared it to the area just logged. Throughout the discussion, which included digging in and examining the soil to establish a common frame of reference, I related our observations to the abstract notions of the day before.

By mid-afternoon, yesterday's abstractions became today's concrete examples to the mill owner/logger, and he began to understand what the Forest Service folks had been trying to tell him. Finally, much to my surprise, he turned to the forest supervisor and said that he had never really understood the consequences of his actions on the forest and on his young son's options to log if he so chose. He said that while the piece of equipment was more efficient and cost effective than the men who used to work for him, it was compacting the soil so much that the forest may have trouble coming back. He said he realized that by making a little more money now, he might be costing his son the opportunity to log in the future, and he owed his son that chance. Thus, he decided to sell the piece of equipment and rehire the men.

In another case, I was asked by a forest supervisor in Minnesota to conduct a two-day workshop on the ecological value of the old-growth forest. The supervisor had one district ranger who saw only dollar signs when he looked at the big old trees and resisted anything that prevented cutting them as fast as possible. The problem was that the forest supervisor had established an old-growth committee throughout the entire forest to create a long-term, forest-wide management plan for the old-growth component of the ecosystem. For the committee to be effective, however, it had to include a representative from every district, but this particular ranger refused to assign anyone from his district to the committee.

Folks from throughout the forest and I spent the first day in a conference room, where I showed slides of how a forest functions above- and belowground. I emphasized the role of large woody material, such as whole fallen old-growth trees, on the forest floor and in the forest soil. Again, this was a day of general discussion of people's perceptions and frames of reference. As such, it was riddled with abstractions for some of the people, including the ranger.

Knowing this, I took the group into the field on the next day, where we explored the first day's abstractions in the concreteness of touchable examples. The ranger was quiet most of the time, appearing skeptical at best. Part way through the afternoon, however, he went up to the forest supervisor and said: "I never thought about a forest like this. I still don't understand everything I've heard, but I want to be on the old-growth committee myself."

This, again, was for me a totally unexpected outcome, but it illustrates the power of the transformative approach to facilitation.

INABILITY TO TRANSFER EXPERIENCES FROM ONE SITUATION TO ANOTHER

Another major barrier to communication is the inability to transfer the outcomes of experience from one kind of situation to another. The potential ability to transfer results of experiences from here to there is influenced by the breadth of one's experiences. Every group represents a vast array of experiences, some broad, others narrow.

Experiential transfer, however, is critical to understanding how ecosystems and their interconnected, interactive components function, including the bridge between a community and its surrounding environment. It is also a necessary ability in resolving destructive environmental conflicts, whereby potential outcomes can be projected to a variety of possible future conditions.

When a participant cannot make such transfers for lack of the necessary frame of reference, he or she will find the ideas to be abstractions, whereas others with the required experience will feel them to be concrete examples, based on their accumulated knowledge. This is where analogies are useful.

To make sure that my analogy will be understood, I ask the participant if he or she is familiar with the concrete example I propose to use in helping to extend the participant's frame of reference to include the abstraction. If I am talking about the value of understanding how the various components of an ecosystem interact as a basis for the system's apparent stability, I may use the following examples:

1. What happens when just one part is removed? A helicopter crashed in Nepal some years ago, killing two people. A helicopter has a great variety of pieces with a wide range of sizes. The particular problem here was with the engine, which is held together by many nuts and bolts. Each has a small sideways hole through it so that a tiny "safety wire" can be inserted; the ends are twisted together to prevent the tremendous vibration created by a running engine from loosening and working the nut off the bolt. The helicopter crashed because a mechanic forgot to replace one tiny safety wire that kept the lateral control assembly together. A nut vibrated off its bolt, the helicopter lost its stability, and the pilot lost control. All this was caused by one missing piece that altered the entire functional dynamics of the aircraft. The engine had been "simplified" by one piece—a small length of wire.

Which piece was the most important part in the helicopter? The point is that each part (structural diversity) has a corresponding relationship (functional diversity) with every other part. They provide stability only by working together within the limits of their designed purpose.

2. What happens when a process is "simplified"? A newly elected mayor of a city whose budget is overspent guarantees to balance the budget; all that is necessary, in a simplistic sense, is to eliminate some services whose total budgets add up to the overexpenditure. In a "simplistic sense" is used here because it is not quite that simple. What would happen, for example, if all police and fire services were eliminated? Would it make a difference, if the price were the same and the budget could still be balanced, if garbage collection were eliminated instead?

The trouble with such a simplistic view is in looking only at the cost of and not at the function performed by the service. The diversity of the city is being simplified by removing one or two pieces or services, without paying attention to the functions performed by those services. To remove a piece of the whole may be acceptable, provided we know which piece is being removed, what it does, and what effect the loss of its function will have on the stability of the system as a whole.

Once I am sure that the participant is following the analogy, then I can help him or her transfer the concept to the abstraction. As the principle of transfer becomes clear, the abstraction begins to take on the qualities of a concrete idea, and the barrier to communication is dissolved. Removing such barriers to communication is important if the facilitation process is to fulfill its greatest transformative potential.

6

THE PROCESS IS THE DECISION

The process of facilitating the resolution of a destructive conflict is the *decision* for the combatants. For this statement to be valid, however, facilitation must be freely sought and accepted, and I as facilitator must be mutually acceptable to all parties. In addition, because people change their positions most easily when their dignity is intact, it is my task to make the process as gentle and dignified as possible.

Further, for the process to work, everyone involved must understand and accept that the primary responsibility for the resolution of a conflict lies with the parties themselves. They must voluntarily reach agreement, which means that I must protect, to the extent possible, each party from any pressure that may jeopardize a voluntary decision to resolve the disagreement.

There is yet another ingredient in the milieu of facilitation that must be accounted for prior to reaching agreement between or among parties. Namely, I must earn the respect and trust of the people involved and simultaneously help them find faith in themselves, which enables them to forgive themselves and one another for the mistakes we all make while growing up. Through such forgiveness, we free one another to perform in the present for both the present and the future through the environment of trust. In addition, I, through my behavior, foster faith in the process itself, which is a major step towards success.

FAITH IN THE PROCESS IS BELIEF IN THE OUTCOME

Faith, which is belief without evidence, keeps the dreamers dreaming, the doers doing, and the process flowing. If I have faith in the outcome of the facilitation process, I foster the participant's faith in it as well. That notwithstanding, however, I must have faith in the process because I never know what is going to happen or what the outcome may be. "Faith," says Tagore, "is the bird that knows dawn and sings while it is still dark."

Virtually all the Christian church's greatest thinkers adopted faith as a principle, which first appeared in the writing of St. Augustine:

> ...*Understanding follows faith.* We do not believe what we are already able to understand, but attempt to understand that in which we have faith....The fact that knowledge, or understanding, does not come before faith means inevitably that faith entails risk. The risk entailed in faith is of a very special sort; it involves no calculation....The emphasis in faith is on the willingness to risk, not on the chances of losing your wager.[20]

I learned faith while planting peas as a young child. After I planted my peas, I immediately began wondering if they were growing, so I would dig some of them up to see. Sometimes I even dug them up more than once a day. Those that I dug up too often died, but those I left alone long enough or those I failed to find germinated and grew. I could then see them coming up through the soil. I did not know what went on in the soil because I could not see, but I learned that if I was patient, the seeds would grow and that each pea seed would grow only a pea plant—a profound lesson in faith.

Most of us, without even thinking about it, place an extraordinary amount of faith in taxicab drivers to get us safely where we are going. I have had many and varied experiences in taxis in such different places as New York City; Washington, D.C.; Cairo, Egypt; New Delhi, India; Tokyo, Japan; and Paris, France. I have actually gone through Cairo and Tokyo with my eyes closed, and in Paris, my wife, Zane, dug holes in my hand with her fingernails as the driver wove in and out of howling, bumper-to-bumper traffic at kamikaze speed. Yet I have never been in an accident in a taxi.

I also fly a lot, and I have faith in the whole concept of an airplane. That huge gadget actually gets off the ground, stays in the air, and lands in some predictable manner. In addition, it usually ends up where I am told it will. What is even more amazing is that it most often gets to the appointed destination on or about the time I am told it will, and I have not had a pilot run out of fuel yet. I have, however, had some interesting experiences flying.

In another vein, have you ever looked closely at leaf buds on a tree in winter? I am still awed that inside the frozen buds are miniature leaves just waiting for spring to release them from bondage. I find the same miracle in the seeds of a flower. Each seed has already present, hidden within its coat, all the flower's radiant colors, like an artist's paint stored in tubes, and I can imagine what the flower will look like when it blooms. Yet if my lack of faith causes me to break open either bud or seed, I destroy the miracle.

In all these instances, I had faith in the outcome. I have risked my life in taxis and airplanes based on faith in the outcome of my venture. I also have faith that trees will continue to leaf out each spring and that flowers will continue to bloom, each in its own time.

We do a thousand things each day armored with our past experience of their having worked but with no direct evidence that they will work again, although we have faith that they will work as before. Yet how often have you heard someone say, "I'll believe it when I see it," rather than "I'll believe it until I see it, and then I'll know it."

We live by faith all the time. Even the practice of science is based on faith: faith in the questions posed, faith in the procedures used, faith in the data collected, and faith in the interpretation of the data. I remember, for example, testifying before an Administrative Tribunal in Toronto, Canada, in 1991, regarding forestry practices in the Province of Ontario.

I spent two days explaining my interpretation of forested ecosystems and how they function based on more than twenty years of research. On the third day, my cross-examination began by a criminal lawyer hired by the timber industry. At one point, she wanted to challenge my data with a number of other studies, which she contended would refute my findings.

"My data are my truth," I said, "and I will not allow it to be compared to other data. My truth needs no defense, but it might need explanation."

At that point she hissed, "You mean to tell me that you expect the Tribunal to accept your data on faith?"

"But of course," I replied. "They either accept my data on faith or they accept someone else's on faith. I don't know what the correct answer is, nor does anyone else. Whatever data the Tribunal accepts will of necessity be accepted on faith."

"Yes, but," began the lawyer, I still think…"

The chairwoman of the Tribunal interrupted. "I agree with Mr. Maser," she said. "You have made your point, now please proceed."

Someone once said that it is not the load that wears you down; it is the way you carry it. The way we each carry our load depends on our understanding and acceptance of faith as the guiding principle of life. We must have faith in something greater than ourselves because self-knowledge comes through struggle with things unseen, things that help us understand not only ourselves but also the struggles of others. Life, after all, is a matter of faith, not of sight.

The same is true of the facilitation process. It only works with active participation in and faith in the primacy of the process.

THE PRIMACY OF PROCESS

A process is the functional interaction of two or more components and is the necessary sequence of steps toward a desired outcome—the product. But first, I need to know what outcome I want. Then I need to focus on the process with a consistent, constant, disciplined effort. If I focus only on the outcome, I destroy the process, as clearly stated in Thomas Merton's[21] translation of Chuang Tzu's classical poem:

> When an archer is shooting for nothing he has all his skills.
> If he shoots for a brass buckle, he is already nervous...
> The prize divides him.
> He cares.
> He thinks more of winning than of shooting—and the need to win
> Drains him of power.

The story of the brass buckle is often applicable in life. My grades in college, for example, were mediocre, including my first term in graduate school, for which I barely qualified. I was so worried about maintaining a B-average grade point (the brass buckle) that I could not study (shoot my arrows well). I was so worried about the outcome that it was all I could focus on.

One day I decided that I was not going to make it in graduate school anyway, so I decided to forget about grades. I would just go to school while my money lasted, and concentrate on learning what I wanted to know. It was only then that learning became an exciting process. Once I became focused on the process of learning and forgot about the grades, I never got below a B average again.

Years later, I had another poignant lesson about the relationship between process and product. While working in the U.S. Department of the Interior, Bureau of Land Management (BLM, as it is usually called), I was ordered to go to Washington, D.C., to brief the director's staff of the BLM about the results of our research. I was being given an opportunity to speak, and I wanted my audience to hear what I had to say. Therein lay the problem.

I was single in those days, and I thought of myself as a "wildlife biologist," which meant I had to uphold the image of an underpaid martyr for the cause. Since I had never been in the "big time" or gone to Washington, D.C., as I was now suddenly ordered to do, I asked my friend Jack Thomas about the "big city."

Toward the end of our discussion, Jack asked, "What are you going to wear when you speak to the director's staff? Do you have a $200 suit?"

"No," I snapped, "I don't have a $200 suit, and what's more I'm not going to get one. I'm going to wear my biologist clothes. After all, I'm going there to talk to them, not to put on a fashion show!"

"Do you really want them to hear you," Jack asked, "or just look at you?"

"To hear me, of course," I growled in righteous indignation. "How I look has nothing to do with what I say."

"True," he said, "but they have to get past how you look before they can hear what you say."

At some level in my being, I knew he was right, but I didn't know why. Yet I couldn't just give in, so I said, "I'll think about it," and left his office.

That evening I grudgingly took stock of my clothes. Except for a few drab, almost worn-out shirts from Sears, the rest of my clothes were from the Salvation Army, where I had figured out that I could get $250 worth of clothing for $17.50. Besides, what difference would it make if I wore a blue denim shirt with green and brown plaid pants that were three inches too short as long as I was clean and sounded intelligent? Furthermore, I had my good army shoes. True, they were twenty-five years old, but no one would notice the holes in the soles if I kept my feet on the floor.

As soon as Jack got to the lab the next day, he called down to my office. "Maser, come up here."

I went upstairs to his office.

"Have you thought over what you're going to wear to D.C.?" he demanded.

"Yes," I answered.

"Well, what have you decided?" he asked indignantly. "Do you want to be heard or just stared at?"

"Heard," I said flatly.

Jack, who was in charge of the La Grande Lab (and is now Chief of the U.S. Forest Service), picked up his telephone and rang Marion's number. Marion, our head secretary and business manager, was a wonderful, understanding woman.

"Marion," said Jack, "Maser's going to fun city next week, and he needs a $200 suit. Will you please take him to town and get him some D.C. clothes?"

"I'd love to!" she replied.

Because two people cared enough to take the time and had the patience to walk me through one of my blind spots, I was in fact heard in Washington, D.C. The director's staff might not have liked what I had to say, but I was heard.

Jack taught me a very important lesson. If I want a particular outcome, such as being heard, I must go through whatever process or take whatever steps are necessary to achieve that outcome. In this case, it meant wearing the appropriate clothing, even if I did not agree with it or even like it. It meant that I had to make a choice and that I had to accept the outcome of that choice. Thus, the clothing I wore in Washington, D.C. determined the staff's perception of me. My appearance became their truth not only about me as a person but also about what I said. It was, after all, my choice—and my outcome.

PERCEPTION IS TRUTH; FACTS ARE RELATIVE

The Indian spiritual leader Mahatma Gandhi said: "A votary of truth is often obliged to grope in the dark." Our challenge therefore lies in our blind spots, not in our vision. Unlike correcting a blind spot in the rear view of an automobile, which can be rectified simply by adding a different kind of mirror or a supplemental one, we cannot correct our personal blind spots so easily. To correct them, we must grow in our perception and in our acceptance of what is. Perceive means to seize wholly, to see all the way through. Perception, therefore, is the act of seeing in the mind, of understanding.

For Socrates, true knowledge was more than a simple inspection of facts, although the latter can provide important information. Rather, true knowledge was the power of the mind to understand the enduring elements that remained after the facts disappeared. While our perceptions grow and change as we mature, not everyone's perceptions mature at the same rate, which accounts for the widely differing degrees of consciousness with respect to cause-and-effect relationships. This disparity is neither good nor bad; it simply means that each of us has different gifts to give at different times in our lives as we see truth differently.

Truth is absolute; perceptions of truth are relative. Therefore, facts, which are perceptions of truth, are relative. Consider the following statement: The world functions perfectly; our perception of how the world functions is imperfect. We assume this statement to be true because it accepts Universal Laws as absolute truth. But what are those laws? How do they work? We do not know because our perception is constantly changing as we increase the scope of our knowledge.

Trying to understand the Universal Laws is the essence of science. Yet even having worked as a scientist for more than twenty years, I would not know a "scientific truth" if I stepped on one, because my perception of how Universal Laws work is constantly changing. A "scientific fact" is therefore a fact only by consensus of the scientists, which means that a scientific fact or "truth" is only an approximation of what is. It represents our best understanding of reality at a particular moment and is constantly subject to change as we learn.

Perception *is* learning, because cause and effect are always connected. Gandhi reached this conclusion when he said:

> At the time of writing I never think of what I have said before. My aim is not to be consistent with my previous statements on a given question, but to be consistent with truth as it may present itself to me at a given moment. The result has been that I have grown from truth to truth; I have saved my memory an undue strain; and what is more, whenever I have been obliged to compare my writing even of fifty years ago with the latest, I have discovered no inconsistency between the two.[22]

Gandhi was consistent in his changing perceptions of what "the truth" was at different stages in his life. He grew from truth to truth as his vision cleared and he could see greater and greater vistas. He said that if one found an "inconsistency" between any two things he wrote, the reader "would do well to choose the latter of the two on the same subject."

As I have grown, I am increasingly struck by the way my perception of "what is" continues to unfold. I see the world anew; I perceive it differently. My reality is therefore different, and I am increasingly capable of responding to what is without making a value judgment, because, as British physician Edward Bach said: "The knowledge of Truth also gives to us the certainty that, however tragic some of the events of the world may appear to be, they form but a temporary stage in the evolution of man...."

The accepted definitions of truth are only modifications of the definitions of perception. Truth as a human understanding resides in everyone's heart, and it is there one must search for it. Although we must each be guided by truth as we see it, no one has a right to coerce others to act according to his or her own view of truth. In the end, our "detector of truth" is our inner voice. Thus, there is no magic in the perfection of hindsight; it only points out that we did not listen to our inner voice when it spoke the first time.

The truth of the human mind is relative and therefore but a perception of that which is true. If our perception of a truth were in fact *the truth*, we would find no such thing as a half-truth.

Truth is perfect understanding of that which is. It is neither the spoken nor the written word, although these may have a ring of truth to them. Truth cannot be defined; it can only be experienced and lived. A case in point:

Environmentalists and native Indians have banded together to launch an unprecedented attack on the industry's forest practices.

Their campaigns against MacMillan Bloedel [Company] in Moresby Island in the Queen Charlottes and against B.C. Forest Products in the Stein Valley in southwestern British Columbia, among others, have focused much unwanted attention on forestry.

The industry [mainly MacMillan Bloedel] launched a multimillion-dollar public relations campaign last year to counter the lobby by environmentalists and Indians.

Ray Smith, MacMillan Bloedel's president, says the industry began its campaign, which includes television commercials stressing his company's commitment to the environment, because "the Industry's side of the story wasn't being told."

Smith says he, like the environmentalists, feels sad when stately 400-year-old trees are felled.

"But they serve a magnificent purpose too."[23]

I have been in British Columbia, and I have seen mile after mile of back-to-back clearcuts made by the MacMillan Bloedel Company. (You can see it too in a book titled *Clearcut: The Tragedy of Industrial Forestry*.[24]) Understand that what I see is what I experience, and what I experience becomes my truth. What you see is what you experience, and what you experience becomes your truth.

The environmentalists and the Aboriginal Canadians are upset by what the company has done to the forest—through their own experience of what the company has done, not by what they *think* it has done. What the company says in its multimillion-dollar public relations campaign cannot alter what the people experience.

Much of British Columbia has been deforested, and the evidence is clearly visible. Nevertheless, the company is trying to tell the people that what they experience on the landscape is not what they really experience when they look at mile after mile of often unstable logging roads and square mile after square mile of back-to-back clearcuts. No amount of defense on the company's part can hide the evidence.

When I defend something, it is because I feel attacked, and I feel attacked because at some level I am dealing with a personal untruth. All my defense does is call attention to my untruth, uneasiness, and lack of harmony, because truth ignored becomes a predator.

In British Columbia, therefore, it is the citizens' perceptions of MacMillan Bloedel's *motives*, as expressed across the landscape through its deeds and the attitude with which those deeds were performed, that are being called into question. No public relations campaign can change that. Thus, while the company may have succeeded within the realm of its motives, it failed in the public's perception of land trusteeship, in part because the visible effects of such massive clearcut logging cannot, to the public, be reframed in positive environmental terms.

REFRAMING THE ISSUE

Although our educational systems in the United States—beginning with parents and ending with universities—stress the positive, they usually teach in terms of the negative. What does this statement mean?

Suppose your neighbor lives along a busy street and has a little boy named Jimmy. Your neighbor is concerned about Jimmy because of the increasing automobile traffic in the neighborhood.

One day Jimmy's mother says to him: "Jimmy, *don't go* into the *street.*" The directive words (those telling Jimmy what to do) are "don't go" (a confusing contradiction), and the last word Jimmy hears is "street"; he thus goes into the street and gets hit by a car.

What Jimmy's mother really meant and needed to have said was: "Jimmy, *stay* in the *yard.*" Then the directive word (the one telling Jimmy what to do) would have been "stay" (singularly clear and concise), and the last word Jimmy would have heard was "yard." He would have remained in the yard and would still be alive.

This example illustrates that, having been raised trying to make positive statements out of negative ones, we spend most of our lives trying to move away from the negative—and we cannot. We can only move *towards* a positive.

Let's look at an example from the Northwest Territories of Canada. A couple of years ago, I was asked to help a band of Aboriginal Canadians create a vision for some 800 square kilometers of forest for which they had to draft a management plan that was acceptable not only to them but also to the Canadian Territorial and Federal Governments.

After we had gone through the educational part of the workshop (how forests, streams, and rivers function and how humans can fit into the processes), we went into the forest, where I instructed the participants to sit down and be silent for twenty minutes. I told them to listen to the forest and feel its heartbeat, something they acknowledged never having done. Afterward, we discussed how they were feeling, what they were thinking, and what the experience had meant to them. Then, with a much heightened awareness of their forest and its cultural significance, we went back to the conference room, where I asked them what their vision of the future was, what they wanted their forest to look like.

"We don't want it to look like B.C.," was the answer. (B.C. is the abbreviation for British Columbia, which in the northern part, just south of the border with the Northwest Territories, is laced with gigantic clearcuts to which the Aboriginal Canadians objected. Although I did not, on this occasion, ask them why they did not like the clearcuts, questions about participants' negative feelings are often instructive. They can help both a facilitator and the participants themselves more fully understand the emotions behind a particular point of view.)

"I appreciate what you're saying," I replied. "So, what *do* you want your forest to look like?" I queried again.

"We *don't* want it to look like it does south of the border," was the reply.

After two or three more such exchanges, I realized that the participants did not know how to frame their vision, their desire for the future, in a positive statement. All they could do was try to move away from the perceived negative.

I thus spent considerable time helping them reframe the negative into a positive by asking a series of questions.

"What is your staple diet?"

"Moose" was the reply.

"What kind of habitat do moose need?"

"Willow and birch thickets."

"When do you hunt moose?"

"In the late summer and autumn."

"Do you have any medicinal plants that are important to you?"

"Yes, such and such."

"Where do they grow?"

"In this kind of place and that kind of place."

"I notice that birch bark is used to make various domestic objects. Are birch trees important to you?"

"Yes."

The exchange continued. Finally, I asked if anything had been omitted or forgotten. A few things came to mind.

While I was asking these questions and the participants were responding, someone was writing both questions and answers on a large flip chart. The filled sheets were then fastened to the walls of the room. After completing this initial phase of reframing, the participants forgot about the clearcuts in British

Columbia and began focusing on the cultural requirements that needed to be translated into their forest plan.

After taking the ideas from the sheets on the walls and crafting an outline, then sentences and paragraphs, the final prose was distilled into a vision statement and a series of goals (to be discussed at length in Chapter 9). Through the simple process of questions and answers, the participants' negative fears were translated, by the participants themselves, into a shared vision and goals for the positive future of their forest and hence their culture.

To further the translation process and help the Aboriginal Canadians learn how to do it, I asked a member of their community (whom they selected) to sit next to me in front of the group. His purpose was twofold: (1) he was my "cultural attaché," the person I relied on to make sure that I did not inadvertently breach cultural etiquette, and (2) it was his responsibility to learn the process of helping the community reframe negatives into positives.

As the process continued, I increasingly gave the responsibility to him until, in the end, all he needed was a little gentle coaching here or there. In this way, the focus was taken off of me and placed on him as he learned how to lead his people through the process. This gave him an indispensable skill for the community while making me dispensable. The outcome was an acceptable management plan of the people, by the people, and for the people—present and future.

There is great power in learning to reframe negatives into positives. In so doing, the participants not only understand the conflict from another vantage point but also understand that much of the confusion in communication comes from trying to move away from negatives. Trying to move away from a negative precludes people from saying what they really mean because they are focused on what they do not want. As long as people express what they do not want, it is virtually impossible to figure out what they do want. It is thus my continual task to aid the parties in reframing their negatives into positives, which helps them begin to see conflict as a learning partnership.

7

CONFLICT IS A LEARNING PARTNERSHIP

When combatants can perceive and understand conflict as a learning partnership, it is much easier for them to ask their perceived adversary: "Will you please help me to sort out this problem?" And when they get the answer, it is rarely threatening. Through asking for help, they often find some terrified, repressed part of themselves looking back at themselves through their "adversary's" eyes.

In a sense, therefore, facilitating the resolution of an environmental dispute is much like being a therapeutic counselor. To understand what this means, I recommend reading Chapter 14 in Corey,[25] from which the following quote is taken: "Since counselors are asking people to take an honest look at themselves and to make choices concerning how they want to change, it is critical that counselors themselves be searchers who hold their own lives open to the same kind of scrutiny."

It therefore falls on me to treat the facilitation process as a learning partnership, which means that I must also be open to learning. If I am not willing to learn, I cannot teach because teacher and student are one and the same. Transformative facilitation is thus an assembly of students and teachers who agree to learn with and from one another, with the facilitator acting as an invited guide throughout the process.

I AM AT ALL TIMES A GUEST AND A LEADER SIMULTANEOUSLY

I am a guest at all times in the facilitation process, but I am also the leader. As such, I must learn to lead. Before I can learn to lead, however, I must learn to follow. The act of leadership demands humility, whereas the outcome of leadership demands grace. This is one way of saying that I am responsible for my conscience and everyone else is responsible for theirs. Thus, while I may, through transformative facilitation, help people to change their views, I shall not judge the way in which they do so.

Leadership: The Art of Being a Servant

True leadership is concerned primarily with facilitating someone else's ability to reach his or her potential as a human being. Leadership comes from the heart and deals intimately with human values and human dignity. I must lead by example, as Francis Bacon noted when he said: "He that gives good advice, builds with one hand; he that gives good counsel and example, builds with both."

A leader knows and does what is right from moral conviction, usually expressed as enthusiasm, which causes people to want to follow with action. Essentially, a leader is one who values people and helps them transcend their fears so they might be able to act in a manner other than they were capable of doing on their own.

Leadership has to do with authority, which is control, or the right or power to command, enforce laws, exact obedience, determine, or judge. Two kinds of authority are embodied in this definition: that of a person and that of a position.

The authority of a person begins as an inner phenomenon. It comes from one's belief in one's higher consciousness, which acts as a guide in life when one listens to it: "As a man thinketh in his heart, so is he."[18] In contrast, a person who has only the authority of position may have a socially accepted seat of power over other people, but *power can exist only if people agree to submit their obedience to authority*. A person who holds a position of authority, yet does not live from the authority within, can only manage or rule as a dictator—through coercion and fear—but cannot lead.

A leader's power to inspire followership comes from a sense of authenticity, because he or she has a vision that is other-centered rather than self-centered. Such a vision springs from strength, those Universal Principles governing all life with justice and equity, as opposed to the relatively weak foundation of selfish desire. It is the authenticity that people respond to, and in responding, they validate their leader's authority.

Managerialship, on the other hand, is of the intellect and pays minute attention to detail, to the letter of the law, and to doing the thing "right" even if it is not the "right" thing to do. A manager relies on the external, intellectual promise of new techniques to solve problems and is concerned that all the procedural pieces are properly accounted for; hence the epithet "bean counter."

Good managers are thus placed at a disadvantage when put in positions of leadership, because all such people can do is rise to their level of incompetency and there remain, in which case an ounce of image is worth a pound of performance. Similarly, a leader placed in the position of managerialship is equally inept because the two positions require vastly different skills.

A good facilitator, however, must be both an effective leader who guides the facilitation process and an effective manager who keeps it running smoothly. By way of example, think of driving a herd composed of a hundred head of cattle.

There are three basic positions in driving cattle: point, flank, and drag. The person riding point is the leader, the one out front guiding the herd. The flankers, or people riding along the sides of the herd, manage the herd by keeping it moving in the desired direction while preventing individuals from leaving the herd. Riding drag means bringing up the rear or keeping the cattle moving at a given speed while preventing individuals from dropping out of the herd. Being a facilitator is like being a single person who simultaneously must ride point, flank, and drag because he or she is responsible for moving the whole herd safely from one place to another.

As the leader of the facilitation process, I must be the servant of the parties involved. Servant leadership offers a unique mix of idealism and pragmatism.

The idealism comes from having chosen to serve one another and some Higher purpose, appealing to a deeply held belief in the dignity of all people and the democratic principle that a leader's power flows from commitment to the well-being of the people. Leaders do not inflict pain, although they often must help their followers to bear it in uncomfortable circumstances, such as compromise. Such leadership is also practical, however, because it has been proven over and over that the only leader whom soldiers will reliably follow when risking their lives in battle is the one who they feel is both competent and committed to their safety.

My first responsibility, therefore, is to help the participants examine their senses of reality and my last responsibility is to say thank you. In between, I not only must provide and maintain momentum but also must be effective. Beware! Most people confuse effectiveness with efficiency. Effectiveness is doing the right thing, whereas efficiency is doing the thing right, although at times it may not be the right thing to do.

When the difference between effectiveness and efficiency is understood, it is clear that efficiency can be delegated but effectiveness cannot. To me, effectiveness is enabling others to reach toward their personal potential through the facilitation process. In so doing, I leave behind a legacy of assets invested in other people.

I am also responsible for developing, expressing, and defending the participants' civility and values. Paramount in a transformative facilitation process are good manners, respect for one another, and an appreciation of the way in which we serve one another. In this sense, civility has to do with identifying values as opposed to following some predisposed process formula.

For a participant to lose sight of hope, opportunity, the right to feel needed, and the beauty and novelty of ideas is to die a little each day. For me to ignore the dignity of the facilitation process, the elegance of simplicity and truth, and the essential responsibility of serving one another is also to die a little each day. In a time when so much energy seems to be spent on mindless conflict, to be a facilitator is to enjoy the special privileges of complexity, ambiguity, diversity, and challenge.

As auto manufacturer Henry Ford once said: "Coming together is a beginning; keeping together is progress; working together is success." In the end, it is the collective heart of the people that counts; without people, there is no need for either leaders who facilitate or facilitators who lead. Lao Tzu, the Chinese philosopher, said of a good leader (facilitator): "When his work is done, his aim fulfilled, they will all say, 'We did this ourselves.'" Such is servant leadership, and such is my goal. To achieve my goal, I must make the facilitation process safe enough for people to trust it and willingly give up their hidden agendas.

Hidden Agendas

It is my responsibility as a facilitator to make the process safe enough that all hidden agendas are placed on the table; otherwise, they can destroy the essence of transformative facilitation. A hidden agenda occurs when a person holds back the information about what he or she really hopes to gain from a facilitation process or from arbitration. Hidden agendas vary, and only two will be discussed here as examples. The first has to do with the hidden agenda of a facilitator and the second with that of a participant.

Facilitator

I was recently part of a national committee dealing with grazing fees on public lands. Our charge was to advise the secretaries of both the Department of the

Interior and the Department of Agriculture on how to structure the grazing-fee incentive program.

Fairly early in the two-and-a-half-day meeting, the Interior Secretary joined us for most of a day. It soon became clear that he wanted a particular outcome and that he had a definite timetable. This was bad enough in and of itself, but what was worse was that the two facilitators knew what he wanted and were doing their level best to covertly push us in that direction. I had the distinct feeling, as did others, that they were trying first and foremost to please the Interior Secretary by getting as close as possible to what he wanted, as quickly as possible.

The facilitators' hidden agenda became clear on the first day. Whenever someone expressed his or her feelings about the issue of grazing and range condition in general, a necessary part of the process, the facilitators' did their best to cut that person off and return to the strictly structured, carefully controlled facilitation format. We were not allowed to deal with our senses of value, either individually or collectively. There were thirty of us who, for the most part, were complete strangers when the meeting was first called to order; thus we never really got to know one another.

I, as a participant, ended up not trusting the facilitators' intentions and not liking the way I was treated. Consequently, I would not choose to work with them again. They appeared to be strictly product oriented in a self-serving way. Although I do not know what they hoped to gain, my intuition at the time told me it was further employment.

Participant

Some years ago, I was asked to participate as an independent observer in a consensus group. At least thirty points of view were represented, because at least thirty people, in addition to myself and the facilitator, were present. During the two-day meeting, I interpreted three general "collective" views, two of which represented a long-standing battle over whether or not to cut a particular city's watershed. Because I knew nothing about the conflict, even though it had been alive for some years, I had no vested interest in it and could therefore see the collective views. Let's examine my interpretations of them, one at a time.

View 1: A most sincere elderly lady, who had lived in this city all her life, had been told in the third grade that the city's watershed, covered with virgin old-growth forest, was her national heritage and would never be cut. Now she finds people from a land management agency clearcutting "her watershed," and she feels betrayed. Where her third-grade teacher got the notion of an inviolate national heritage is moot. The lady, joined by her son, thought the land management agency should cease and desist all cutting and road building in the watershed forever. On this she was emphatic.

View 2: The conservation groups that were represented were unanimously opposed to further logging and roading of the watershed because the virgin old-growth forest created and protected the pure quality of the city's water supply.

View 3: The people from the land management agency saw the old-growth as an economic commodity that had to be cut and milled or there would be an irreparable economic loss because the old-growth forest would fall down and rot—for them an unthinkable economic waste.

All three views, each with a stake in the watershed, played the consensus game with a hidden agenda. The hidden agenda each side was trying to conceal from the others while acting innocently open-minded became obvious as the facilitation process unfolded. Although the hidden agendas were never admitted, much less openly laid on the table, they were covertly defended whenever someone got too close to the truth—a sure sign that all was not as it appeared. Let's examine each hidden agenda.

View 1: The elderly lady and her son had become rather prominent as distributors of a small newsletter to the group of conservationists interested in saving the watershed's old-growth forest. If the lady and her son won their point of view, they would disappear into the oblivion from which they came; with the issue resolved, the other folks would turn to new issues. Thus, whenever reconciliation seemed possible, the son categorically refused to accept anything that had the appearance of moving the problem toward solution. His hidden agenda seemed to be to keep the issue alive and thereby forestall the feeling of rejection through loss of importance and loss of identity.

View 2: The conservationists were committed to saving the old-growth forest (trees). Each time the people from the land management agency conceded a point that would benefit water quality but not save the trees, the conservationists had to find a new point from which to argue, one that sounded valid with respect to clean water and did not mention trees.

View 3: The people from the land management agency were committed to cutting the timber for economic reasons. They thus submitted to the procedure, but with the knowledge of the authoritative position and final decision on their side.

So where do we go from here? First, each person was right from his or her point of view, from his or her interpretation of the data. Second, no one in the room really understood consensus. Consensus does not mean something will be enacted; it means that the parties agree to agree on something. And the agreement the participants ended up with was that something needed to be done, which is where they started.

The mission was doomed to failure because *no one* disclosed her or his real agenda. Why not? Because there was a lack of trust in the facilitation process. After all, the facilitator was an employee of the land management agency represented in the dispute, in addition to which the agency both paid for and hosted the session. Without being an impartial third party who had earned the participants' trust, the facilitator could neither lead nor teach, even by example.

Facilitator as Teacher

Whether one realizes it or not, a facilitator is a teacher in that learning is a change in behavior as a result of an experience, which is the purpose of transformative facilitation. Most people who seek facilitation have fairly definite ideas about what they want out of the process, and they will learn from any activity that tends to further their purposes. Because previous experience conditions a person to respond to some things and to ignore others, it is imperative that the facilitation experience is made relevant to the desired outcome, namely that the parties learn to reconcile their differences and work cooperatively with one another. To accomplish this, some elements of learning must be understood.

The Foundation of Learning

If an experience challenges the learner; if it requires involvement with feelings, thoughts, and memory of past experience; and if it necessitates physical activity, it is more effective than an experience in which all a person has to do is deal with abstractions or commit something to memory. Each person approaches a task with preconceived ideas and feelings and may have these ideas changed for a variety of reasons as a result of experience. The learning process may therefore simultaneously include the following elements: verbal, conceptual, perceptual, emotional, and problem solving.

Learning is multifaceted in still another way. While learning a subject at hand, people learn other things as well. They develop good or bad attitudes about facilitation, depending on their experience with the process. They may, for example, learn greater self-reliance under the guidance of a skillful facilitator. Such incidental learning may have a great effect on a person's total development; hence the transformative nature of facilitation.

The effectiveness of learning is based on a person's emotional reaction in that learning is strengthened when accompanied by a pleasant feeling and diminished when associated with an unpleasant one. It is thus better to tell the parties involved in the facilitation process that their problem, although difficult, is within their capability to understand and resolve. Having said this, however, it is incumbent on me to keep my word. Therefore, whatever learning situation is encountered in the facilitation process, it must contain elements that affect the parties positively and produce such feelings as self-worth, success, freedom, clarification, and empowerment, all of which enhance learning.

Part of the foundation of learning is primacy, the state of being first, which often creates a strong, almost unshakable, impression. This means that what I teach through the facilitation process must be right the first time. For the parties, it means that the learning must be right the first time, because "unteaching" and "unlearning" is far more difficult than teaching and learning. It is thus critical that the first experience be positive and functional, for everything that follows is predicated on this first experience. Part and parcel of this first experience is the notion of intensity, because a vivid, dramatic, or exciting experience teaches more than a routine or boring one.

How People Learn

Learning comes initially from perceptions directed to the brain by one or more of the five senses: sight, hearing, touch, smell, and taste. Psychologists have determined experimentally that "normal" individuals acquire about seventy-five percent of their knowledge through sight, thirteen percent through hearing, six percent through touch, three percent through smell, and three percent through taste. Learning occurs most rapidly, however, when information is received through more than one sense.

Nevertheless, real meaning can only come from within a person, even though the sensations evoking these meanings result from external stimuli. People therefore base their actions on the way they believe things to be.

Factors Affecting Perception

Learning is a psychological problem, not a logical one. Therefore, I must organize the facilitation process to fit the psychology of the participants. As long as a person feels capable of coping with a situation, each new experience can be accepted as a challenge; if, on the other hand, a situation seems overwhelming, the person feels unable to deal with it and perceives a threat. Facilitation is thus consistently effective only when those factors influencing perceptions are recognized and taken into account as positively as possible.

Among the factors affecting perception are: (1) basic necessity; (2) self-concept; (3) timing, opportunity, and time; and (4) recognizing an element of threat. **Basic necessity** is a person's need to maintain and enhance the organized self. The self is complete in that it is a physical and psychological combination of a person's past and present experiences and future hopes and fears. A person's most fundamental, pressing necessity is perceived to be perpetuating this self, which in turn affects all perceptions.

Just as the food one eats and the air one breathes become part of the physical self, so the sights one sees and the sounds one hears become part of the psychological self. We are psychologically what we perceive.

As a person has physical barriers that prevent dangerous things from harming the physical being, such as flinching from a hot stove, so a person has perceptual barriers that block those sights, sounds, and feelings thought to pose a psychological threat. Helping people to learn thus requires finding ways to aid them in developing different perceptions in spite of their dysfunctional coping mechanisms. Since a person's basic necessity is felt to be self-maintenance, I must recognize that anything asked of a party that may be interpreted as imperiling the self will be resisted and denied.

Self-concept, or how one pictures oneself, is a powerful determinant in learning. A person's self-image, described in such terms as "confident" or "insecure," has much influence on one's total perceptual process. If a person's experiences in the facilitation process tend to support a favorable self-image, one is more likely to remain open to subsequent experiences. If, on the other hand, a person has negative experiences, which threaten one's self-concept, there is a tendency to reject additional participation.

Those persons in the facilitation process who view themselves positively are less defensive and more readily internalize and assimilate their experiences. Those with negative self-concepts, on the other hand, activate their psychological barriers, which tend to keep them from perceiving and may actually inhibit their ability to implement in a functional manner that which is perceived.

Timing, opportunity, and time are necessary to perceive and learn. Learning may depend on perceptions, which precede those perceptions to be learned; timing is thus important because a person may not be ready to learn certain things without prior experience. Assuming the timing is right, one requires both the opportunity and the time to experience that which is to be learned. In addition, the amount of time necessary to learn a given thing differs from person to person.

Finally, fear, or an **element of threat**, adversely affects one's perception by narrowing the perceptual field. People confronted with a threat tend to focus their attention on the perceived danger, which reduces their field of vision to a fraction of its potential. Anything I do that is interpreted as threatening makes the already frightened person less able to accept a new experience by adversely affecting his or her physical, emotional, and mental faculties.

Insights

Insights involve grouping perceptions into meaningful wholes, or systems thinking. *Evoking insights is my main task*; therefore, it is essential to keep each person constantly receptive to new experiences and to help each person realize and understand how a given piece relates to all others in the formation of patterns. Understanding the way in which each piece may affect the others and knowing the way in which a change in any one may affect changes in all others is imperative to true learning. Although insights almost always occur eventually, effective facilitation can speed the process by teaching the relationship of perceptions as they occur, thus promoting the development of transformative insights in the facilitation process.

Motivation

People in a facilitation process are like all other workers in that they want a tangible return for their efforts. If such motivation is to be effective, they must believe that their efforts will be positively rewarded. Such rewards, whether they are the furtherance of self-interest or group recognition, must be constantly apparent during the facilitation process.

Although many lessons with obscure objectives will pay off handsomely later on, a person may not appreciate this immediately. If motivation is to be maintained, therefore, it is important for me to make the participants aware of applications that are not immediately apparent.

The desire for personal security and comfort is often inadequately appreciated by facilitators. All participants want secure, pleasant conditions and states of being, even under the most trying of circumstances. If they recognize that what they are learning may promote this goal, their interest is easier to attract and hold.

Along these lines, psychologist Abraham Maslow's hierarchy of needs is helpful in understanding this point.[26] Although Maslow's hierarchy of needs is given in the shape of a pyramid, we can visualize the same concept by picturing a stepladder with a very wide base and a narrow top. Beginning with the first rung from the bottom are the basic physiological survival needs, such as air, water, food, and shelter. On the second rung are the needs for safety, security, stability, structure, order, limits, and law. The third rung deals with belongingness and love, which express themselves in the need for roots, origin, being part of a social group, and having a family and friends. The fourth rung encompasses self-esteem, which manifests itself in the need for strength, mastery, competence, self-confidence, prestige, status, and dignity. The fifth and highest rung is self-actualization, which is the inner driving need to become all that one can be by knowing truth, justice, beauty, simplicity, and perfection.

Notice how far up the ladder (the fourth rung) one must go before dignity is mentioned. Notice also how many external product-oriented needs must be met before a person feels enough in control of life's conditions to "afford" a sense of dignity.

Fortunately, there is within each person engaged in a task the belief, however small, that success is possible under the right conditions. This belief can be a most powerful motivating force. I can best foster such motivation by introducing perceptions based solidly on experiences that are easily recognized as achievements in learning.

A majority of people seem to have trouble transferring abstract concepts from one situation to another, as previously discussed. Therefore, concrete examples are important and can be supplied through the use of appropriate analogies, which help participants transfer a commonly understood experience to a foreign situation. For example, a human community can be used to explain how an ecosystem functions. Once the basic principles are understood in a human context, they can be transferred to a forest, a grassland, or an ocean, always coming back to the human community as a touchstone. In addition to using good analogies, I constantly relate the lesson's objective to the participants' intentions and necessities and in so doing build on the participants' natural enthusiasm.

The relationship between facilitator and participants has a profound effect on how much the participants learn and change. I must create as safe and gentle an environment as possible through my own demeanor in order to enable participants to help themselves.

The following generalizations about the motivation underlying human behavior may be helpful:[27]

1. Work is as natural to people as are play and rest. Work that is a source of satisfaction will be voluntarily performed, but that which is perceived as a form of drudgery or punishment will be avoided if possible.

2. A person will exercise self-direction and self-control in the pursuit of goals to which she or he is committed.

3. A person's commitment to her or his goals is directly related to the perceived reward associated with their achievement.

4. A reasonably functional person learns, under the right conditions, to both accept and seek responsibility. Ambivalence and shirking responsibility are not inherent in human nature, but rather are usually consequences of dysfunctional experiences during childhood and negative, unsafe experiences in life.

5. The capacity to exercise a relatively high degree of imagination, ingenuity, and creativity in the resolution of common problems is a widely distributed human trait.

6. Under the conditions of modern life, the intellectual potentialities of the "average" person are only partially used.

I accept these assumptions and see vast, untapped potentialities in participants. The raw material lies waiting; its release is partly in my hands and partly in those of the participants.

The Fallacy of Rescuing

Over the years, I have been in many situations where either an individual person, such as the previously discussed fatalist, or a whole group have wanted to be rescued. When someone wants to be rescued, he or she wants a quick fix, with me doing all of the work.

I have experienced two major problems with this notion. First, the person who ostensibly wants to be rescued will continually fight any effort to be rescued. To this person, wanting help to change sounds good, but he or she is not ready to give up the long investment in his or her current situation. He or she is getting something of value out of it, even if unconsciously.

The second problem is that even if I could and would rescue someone, my efforts would be of no value. For example, while in Japan in 1992, I spent much time looking at forestry problems and discussing what I saw with Japanese foresters, prefecture mayors, and others. It was clear that the plantations of larch trees, put in by the Americans following World War II, not only were a mistake but also were sick and needed to be replaced with native forest.

After I got home, a Japanese gentleman wrote to me and asked me to plan a forest for a particular area that could be grown for a thousand years. I told him no. I said that if I, an American, were to plan a forest for the Japanese, I would be giving the Japanese an American forest planned in America by an American; it would be of no value to them culturally because it would be my forest, planned for me, and based on my own sensibilities. I did say, however, that I would *help* the Japanese plan a forest in Japan for themselves. Then it would be Japanese planning their own forest, with their own species, for their own culture. Only then would the forest be of any value to them.

The point is that each person or group of people must struggle with and through their own processes if they are to derive anything of value for themselves. Even if I could rescue someone (go through their growth process for them), I would not. To do so would be stealing their struggle to grow and whatever value they would have derived from it. Besides, that which is not earned is casually tossed aside because the person, not having earned it, finds in it no value. It is thus my ever-present responsibility to define my relationship with the participants while facilitating the resolution of a dispute.

My Role in Participant Relationships

Helping achieve good human relations is one of my basic responsibilities. To achieve such relations, I must consider the following points:

1. People gain more from wanting to resolve their own issues and learning in the process than from being forced to participate through such means as court directives.

2. Participants tend to feel secure when they know what to expect or what is going to happen. When they understand the benefits of what is taking place, they are more willing to move forward.

3. Each individual within a group of participants has a unique personality, which I must constantly consider. If, however, I limit my thinking to the group as a whole, without considering the participants as individuals, my efforts are directed toward an average personality that fits no one.

4. If I give sincere praise or credit when due, I provide an incentive to strive harder. By the same token, insincere praise given too freely on my part is valueless.

5. If a participant is gently briefed, in private, on erroneous assumptions and told how he or she might correct them, progress and accomplishment follow.

6. It is vital that my philosophy and actions be consistent. If a situation, such as being allowed to interrupt and speak out of turn, is acceptable one day but not another, participants become confused.

7. No one, including participants, expects me to be perfect. Nevertheless, the best way for me to win the trust and respect of participants is to honestly admit mistakes. If I try, even once, to bluff or cover up, the

participants sense it quickly, and my behavior destroys their confidence in both me and the facilitation process. Therefore, if in doubt about some point, I must freely admit it.

These are but a few of the many attitudes and reactions that help establish the kind of facilitator/participant relations that promote resolving conflicts through effective learning. To accomplish this kind of learning, however, one must be present in the moment, every moment.

Facilitation Means Total Participation

Being present—here and now—is the only way to participate in life, and effective, transformative facilitation *requires* total participation. But I cannot be present if I am thinking about either the past or the future. It is therefore critical that I be totally focused on the present and keep the parties focused totally on the present during the entire facilitation process.

What is so important about being present? Have you ever noticed that for most people the present is seldom quite right or seldom seems good enough? Yesterday is past and gone; you cannot change it—opportunities foregone are opportunities lost. Tomorrow is not here, and you have no idea, despite your aspirations, hopes, expectations, and predictions, what it will bring. In reality, tomorrow is something that is always coming and never arrives. The present, the here and now, is all anyone really has.

Being present, in the sense of being mentally here, now, is a difficult concept, because there is no word that means mental presence as opposed to simple physical presence. Let's examine what being present means.

Suppose that while driving, you are thinking about (remembering) the past, say last year's vacation. It was your first trip to the Bahamas, and you had a very rough flight. The unexpected storm really frightened you, but once in the Bahamas, you had a marvelous time. You are flying to the Bahamas next month for your long-anticipated vacation, and you begin thinking about how much fun you had last year and you expect to have this year. Suddenly, out of nowhere, you have a vivid flash of last year's flight and become afraid that next month's flight might be the same. In all of your reverie, you are either in the past or in the future, and now you are jerked into the present as your car sputters and you coast to the side of the road out of gas. You were so busy thinking about the flight that you missed the gas station!

Being fully conscious in the present is important, because fear is a projection of a past experience into the future. I cannot, therefore, be afraid in the present, in the here and now, because the present moment cannot be projected into the future; only the past can be projected into the future. What I really fear is the future, the fear of the unknown, the fear of being afraid—the fear of fear! Struggling to keep myself in the present is thus a conscious choice I must make each time fear raises its ugly head.

Another reason for being in the present is to allow someone else to be in the present with me. I often think, for example, that I know what someone is going to say or how he or she is going to say it, whatever it is. I find this especially true if I do not want to hear either the answer or the tone of voice I "know" I will get. If I do not keep myself in the present, I expect the person's old pattern of response, and *I limit* his or her ability to respond differently in the here and now, because I simply do not hear it. I hear what I expect to hear, which justifies my expectation and imprisons both the other person and our relationship somewhere in the past. It also imprisons me in the past, because all I accept and therefore all I hear is old business.

If we are not present with one another, our attempts to communicate can become frustrating experiences of talking either at or past one another, because the present, the here and now, is all we have. It is thus my responsibility to bring the parties back to the present whenever they stray unnecessarily into either the past or the future. Such presence in the moment is a prerequisite for detachment and equanimity throughout the facilitation process.

Detachment and Equanimity

Detachment from an outcome is total acceptance of what is without any desire to have something else, which is a critical concept in transformative facilitation. Detachment is checking my ego at the door as I come into the room. This is, at best, difficult to learn, and I have consciously struggled with it for over two decades.

When I was younger, I was deeply upset by the clearcut logging of the old-growth forests in the Pacific Northwest, where I grew up. I would argue long and loudly about the need to save them and the greed and stupidity of those who wished to liquidate them. I tried to convince anyone and everyone that the forests needed to be saved. I was so rabid about my point of view being the right one that few people cared to listen, unless they already agreed with me. Consequently, I became frustrated, cynical, and self-righteous, all of which only made matters worse. I became enraged at the "greedy bastards who were clearcutting *my* forest," but I never thought to ask them how they felt about the forests they were liquidating.

One day, as I was giving a passionate speech on the need to "preserve" the ancient forests of the Pacific Northwest, I suddenly felt the sword taken from my hand and a sense of peace come over me, a sense that was immediately reflected in the audience. Several people came up to me later and said they had never thought about it that way, and that what I said made sense. It was then I realized that to speak for the forests or for anything else, I had to change—not the people in the audience, but me! If I wanted people to listen, it was incumbent upon me to change, to say what I had to say in a way that would allow them to hear. But how? I did not know how.

A few weeks later, I saw the movie *Gandhi*. Then I read a couple of biographies about Gandhi in which he was often quoted, and through his writings, he gave me the answer. I had to detach myself from the outcome, a truly difficult task.

If Gandhi was correct, in detachment lay acceptance of the outcome. Expectation is the attachment, the vested interest in the outcome, because the person with the expectation sees himself or herself as the one possessing the means of achieving the right and justifiable result. If, on the other hand, one acts willingly out of duty to a Higher Authority, one can act with detachment, because the Higher Authority is acknowledged as the only one with the wisdom to justly govern the outcome.

If I am detached, I have no vested interest in the results of a given process, and I can treat all sides, all points of view, and all possible outcomes with equanimity. Equanimity is the kernel of peace in detachment just as surely as anxiety is the kernel of agitation in attachment.

For example, a person who has worked passionately for a cause may suddenly have the insight that passion placed before principle is a house divided against itself that cannot long stand. Because of this new understanding, he or she now becomes focused on the principle as a process and becomes detached from the passion—the desired result. The reaction of his or her peers most often is: "How can you give up the cause? We've believed in it for so long."

Attachment to the cause has for these people become life itself, their very identity, as discussed under "Hidden Agendas." Therefore, even as they ostensibly fight to "win," they cannot afford to win because if they were to actually resolve the issue at the heart of their cause, they would have to find a new identity, something most people are loath to do.

If I, as a facilitator, am truly detached from the outcome, I will find equanimity to be my touchstone. Equanimity, the outworking of detachment, is reflected in the calm, even-tempered, and serene personality of one who is simply open to accepting what is. Such a person can perform facilitation without either the need for or the expectations of approval or a predetermined outcome. Such a person acts out of peace.

In turn, the peaceful action allows others to see an alternative way of perceiving something, because no one is trying to convince them of anything.

They are given the ideas and the space to consider them. Then, if they so choose, they can change their minds in privacy while retaining their dignity intact.

The one who is detached is part of the principle and is therefore part of the resolution or the transcendence of the problem. On the other hand, one becomes part of the problem when one is attached to a point of view and its necessary outcome. My detachment and equanimity serve to make the facilitation process safe enough to permit the expression of anger, which I can defuse by keeping it focused on me, where it has no effect.

I Am a Sieve, Not a Sponge

Anger, as previously stated, is fear violently projected outward from a person onto another person or an object. But I am *not* angry for the reason or at the person or thing I think I am. I am angry at myself for being afraid of circumstances and therefore feeling a loss of control, which has nothing to do with the person or thing at which I level my anger.

That notwithstanding, people must be able to vent their anger in safety during the facilitation process because the anger is there, and it will go somewhere. It is therefore important that I keep the anger focused on myself, but as though I am a sieve through which the anger simply passes because it is nothing personal.

For example, when a participant aims his or her anger at another participant, I redirect that person's anger at myself by saying, "Excuse me, but I believe you were talking to me." The person can thus dissipate his or her energy, feel he or she has been heard, have his or her fears validated, and become more receptive to other data and ideas. At the same time, I keep the facilitation environment as safe as possible by preventing another participant from being directly attacked in front of everyone else. Because I know the individual is not angry at me, his or her anger has no effect on me.

I remember meeting with the radical environmental group Earth First! in Arcata, California, some years ago. They had asked me to speak about old-growth forests and sustainable forestry. During my presentation, I pointed out that one must be careful not to become what one is against in confronting a perceived injustice with civil disobedience.

Some of the people did not understand what I meant, so I gave the example of combating violence with violence. "If I am treated with violence," I said, "and I therefore respond with violence, how am I any different than my opponent? I am not. I have in attitude, behavior, and tactics become what I am against; I have become as my opponent."

At this point, the most militant individuals arose, yelling and swearing at me with such anger that my wife, who was in the audience, became terrified for my safety. Their rage was electrifying. Had I stopped any of it, taken any of it personally, or in any way defended myself against it, the situation would easily have gotten out of hand and become dangerous. Instead, I let it pass through untouched, and the militants all stormed harmlessly out of the room, and did not return.

Because I did not respond to the anger, a number of people came up to me after I was through speaking. To a person, they said that they had not thought of violence in the way I had presented it and would reconsider their stance. To me, if but one person had said that, it would have been worth the blast of rage leveled in my direction.

If I ever make the mistake of taking someone's anger personally, of internalizing it, I will become like a sponge soaking it all up. Being a sponge for another's anger is not only detrimental to me emotionally but also causes me to become a major problem in the facilitation process. At this point, I can no longer function as a facilitator because I now have a vested interest in (can no longer be detached from) the outcome.

As the facilitation leader, I must bear, unflinchingly, all the abuses that the parties normally hurl at one another. In effect, a person, such as a facilitator, who serves the people must pass the tests described in the eulogy that Senator William Pitt Fessenden of Maine delivered on the death of Senator Foot of Vermont in 1866:

> When, Mr. President, a man becomes a member of this body he cannot even dream of the ordeal to which he cannot fail to be exposed;
> of how much courage he must possess to resist the temptations which daily beset him;
> of that sensitive shrinking from undeserved censure which he must learn to control;
> of the ever-recurring contest between a natural desire for public approbation and a sense of public duty;
> of the load of injustice he must be content to bear, even from those who should be his friends; the imputations of his motives; the sneers and sarcasms of ignorance and malice; all the manifold injuries which partisan or private malignity, disappointed of its objects, may shower upon his unprotected head.
> All this, Mr. President, if he would retain his integrity, he must learn to bear unmoved, and walk steadily onward in the path of duty, sustained only by the reflection that time may do him justice,

or if not, that after all his individual hopes and aspirations, and even his name among men, should be of little account to him when weighed in the balance against the welfare of a people of whose destiny he is a constituted guardian and defender.[28]

Such is the price of leadership—to be the keeper of everyone else's dignity.

I Am the Keeper of Each Participant's Dignity

As I understand dignity, its emotional foundation rests on the perceived ability to make choices, which in turn provides a sense of hope. As facilitator, I am the keeper of each participant's dignity, which means I will protect their dignity so they can protect mine. Protecting one another's dignity is tantamount to making and keeping transformative facilitation as safe and gentle as possible. Being the keeper of the participants' dignity means there is no blame or guilt, only an opportunity to think differently.

I spoke some years ago at an annual banquet for the Florida Audubon Society in Tallahassee. The day after I spoke, I was on a panel with the supervisor of one of the national forests in the southeastern United States. His opening story exemplifies dignity as the ability to make choices and having some things of value from which to choose.

"I am concerned about what we are doing to our forests," he began. "I am concerned about what we are saying to one another. I think about it all the time. My nine-year-old son came home from school the other day in tears. 'What's wrong?' I asked."

"Dad," he replied, "my teacher said you're destroying the forest. You're cutting it all down. What's going to be left for me when I grow up?"

The forest supervisor was trembling with emotion. I could feel his terrible pain, and because of his pain, I am not sure he was even aware of the audience as he spoke.

"I'm concerned," he said, "about what we're teaching our children in school. I'm concerned about what we're telling them about their future. I think about it all the time...."

The forest supervisor's young son was asking his father: Where is my choice? Where is my hope? What will be left for me? What will give me a sense of well-being, of dignity, when I grow up?

Our subjective feelings and human values govern our choices. They are not governed by our so-called rational, objective intellect or our scientific knowledge or technological advances. Remove the sense of choice that has to do with one's determination of one's own destiny and you remove hope as well, and human dignity withers.

Because dignity is closely tied to being in control, humiliation is dignity's greatest enemy. Let's return to the government meeting I spoke about in the discussion of hidden agendas. As I said, the facilitators were intent on meeting the Interior Secretary's agenda for grazing on public lands. To meet that agenda, they had to control the length of time each person spoke, especially on the last day. To do this, they made a big red paper flag with large yellow letters on it: BS (bullshit). Then, when they thought someone had spoken long enough and wanted to hurry the meeting along, one of them would wave the BS flag from the front of the room, in an attempt to humiliate the speaker into silence. What kind of example did they set? Was it a safe place for people with different values to come together? What did they do to the participants' trust and dignity?

Mahatma Gandhi once said: "It has always been a mystery to me how men can feel themselves honoured by the humiliation of their fellow beings." I have been humiliated in my life. I never felt that my loss contributed to anyone else's honor. I always felt robbed by humiliation, because the person who humiliated me was trying to extract my obedience, which means my submissiveness to his or her control. And I do not want to be controlled; I want to be respected. I, like everyone else, need love and help, not criticism, judgment, and humiliation.

A young man taught me a wonderful lesson about humility and human dignity, a lesson I will always remember. It was a cold winter, and most of us kept fires going in our wood-burning stoves when at home. One day, this young man's wife cleaned the ashes out of their stove. She put them into a paper bag and put the bag in the back of their pickup truck. What she did not know, however, was that some of the ashes were still hot. In fact, they were hot enough to catch the bag and other things in the back of the truck on fire and severely damaged the interior of the pickup's canopy.

"What did you say to your wife about burning up your truck?" I asked, as if it were any of my business in the first place.

"Nothing," he said. "She was already humiliated. Why should I add to it? After all, she didn't do it on purpose."

That was not the response I had anticipated. People often get a lot of mileage out of other people's mistakes and proceed to flog them with embarrassment.

What would the world be like if we were all as kind and thoughtful as that young man? What would the world be like if we were all the caretakers of one another's dignity? Do you think we could resolve the problems for which the lack of human dignity is an obstacle in the healing of our global society? As a facilitator, I have a chance to begin doing just that, healing society, but to see the oft-hidden opportunities, I must have a beginner's mind.

Having a Beginner's Mind

To approach life with a beginner's mind, a mind simply open to the wonders and mysteries of the Universe, is a gift of Zen. A beginner, unfettered by rules of having to be something special, sees only what the answers might be and knows not what they should be. The one who thinks of himself or herself as an expert, on the other hand, is bounded by the rules that govern being an expert. Such a person considers himself or herself as something special, the one who knows what the "correct" answers should be, yet is too often blind to what other answers might be. The beginner is free to explore and to discover while the self-appointed expert grows rigid in a self-created prison.

Two women and one man on three different occasions, years apart, are excellent examples of the beginner's mind. I often use a simple, fun exercise, which requires nothing more than six wooden matches or six toothpicks, to help people understand that their imagination is as bounded as their blind acceptance of social convention and as free as their willingness to reach beyond such convention in seeking their soul's creative eye.

The instructions are simple: sit at the table and make four equilateral triangles out of the six matches or toothpicks *without* crossing one over another. Rarely does a person succeed because to accomplish this feat on the single dimension of a table's flat surface seems impossible, which their mind quickly tells them, even as they struggle not to accept it. They think it must be possible because I told them to do it, but they can't figure out how and eventually give up. There are, however, at least two ways to solve this problem, one of which had been unknown to me.

The way I had learned to solve the problem was to make one triangle on the table's flat surface and then stand the other three upright within the one, thus encompassing more than a single dimension. The other way is to break a match or toothpick and arrange them appropriately on the table's surface.

The first time I saw the problem solved this way was at a workshop I was conducting to help wildlife biologists look beyond professional convention for answers to their management problems. During the workshop, one of the biologists came to me and said that his wife, who had accompanied him to the meeting, was interested in what I was talking about and asked if she could join us. "But of course," I said.

With the lady sitting at the table, I gave my usual instructions and then simply watched what happened. While all the men arranged and rearranged their matches to no avail, she put hers on the table and sat looking at them. Suddenly, a tiny smile crept over her face. Picking up the matches, she laid one down at an angle. Then she deftly broke one in two, laying each half across from the other on each side of the middle of the first match. Finally, she arranged the remaining four in a square to close the exposed sides. Although not perfect, she had four triangles!

"Well I'll be damned," was all I could say as she beamed at me from across the table.

Over the years, I continued giving my original instructions, wondering if anyone else would break a match. Finally, after more than two decades, a sixth-grade teacher looked at her matches for about thirty seconds, then looked up at me and asked: "Can I break the matches?"

"Yes," I answered and then asked her, "How did you figure that out so fast?"

"Well," she said, "any time I'm given limits, the first thing I do is check them to see if there's an alternative."

What a marvelous answer! How fortunate are her students! They have a rare teacher, one with a beginner's mind.

Even more recently I learned of yet a third way to solve the problem. I gave six toothpicks to a district ranger of the USDA Forest Service, with the usual instructions. Seated at his kitchen table, he laid the toothpicks on the table's top, looked at them for a few seconds, while his young son watched, and then broke each toothpick in two.

The boy turned to me with a questioning voice and said: "He broke them."

"He didn't tell me I couldn't," replied his father as he made four equilateral triangles on the tabletop, with one piece left over.

What does breaking matches have to do with facilitation? First, it demonstrates that most socialized individuals become stuck within their self-imposed limitations. Second, it shows that it is a rare socialized individual who has managed to retain a childlike beginner's mind.

Breaking matches is to me like going into each facilitation with little specific knowledge of the conflict with which I am about to deal. I am as detached and unbiased as possible because I have only minimal, general information about the dispute prior to my entering the arena. It is thus difficult for me to form opinions about who has done what or why, because I do not know. I therefore remain open to possibilities—a beginner's mind.

Once into the facilitation process, I have each party in turn tell me its perceptions of the dispute. The purpose is for each party to educate me about the dispute from its understanding of the whole. As each explanation unfolds, the side recounting it not only clarifies its own understanding of its perceptions but also the other party (or parties) hears for the first time the whole of the other's story from the other's point of view. During this storytelling, I learn what the dispute is about because I hear it from different sides and am thus able to find common ground, differences, negotiable areas, quagmires, and hidden potential for resolution.

With a beginner's mind, it is easier for my intuition to preside equally with my intellect and open my creative space. This open space, which allows intuition the freedom to exercise its creative powers, is perhaps the greatest value of having a beginner's mind.

Because intuition is so important to the beginner's mind, it is necessary to examine it, albeit briefly.[29] Intuition, the knowing beyond knowledge, has been widely accepted since ancient times as the forerunner of deep inner truth and creativity. It is generally characterized as an instantaneous, direct grasping of reality, the source of our deepest truths, those unquestionable knowings that we call "axiomatic." Even John Stuart Mill, the pillar of the empirical method, stated that "the truths known by intuition are the original premises from which all others are inferred."

It is well known, for example, that Niels Bohr, Albert Einstein, Sir Arthur Eddington, Eugene Wigner, and Erwin Schrödinger intuited the principles of quantum physics, where it is understood that the concepts of time, space, and the conservation of forces are based on intuitive insight, if not on faith. Intuition, says Russian revolutionary thinker Pitirim A. Sorokin, is more than a guide to truth; it seems also to be the ultimate foundation for our understanding of beauty and good because our aesthetic and moral judgments are based on deep subjective feelings.

But intuition has been clouded by ambiguity and controversy for the last century or so and regarded as a meaningless by-product of unconscious processes. At best, modern academia often assumes it to be lucky guesses based on gut hunches, creative flashes, momentary insights. At worst, academic scholars, who pride themselves on discovering logical, scientific solutions to difficult problems, see intuition as irrational concoctions of the unconscious mind, based on memories, habits of thought, social conditioning, or emotional predispositions.

Intuition is therefore implied to be unreliable, unscientific, irrational, and purely subjective with no foundation in measurable reality, which is a very different view from ancient times when it was considered "the source of deep inner truth." It is, nevertheless, this latter meaning of intuition to which I subscribe. I say this advisedly, based on years of unerring experience.

There is yet another value to having a beginner's mind: the freedom to be authentically myself, which the intuitive/creative edge brings out and to which people respond.

Being Myself

When all is said and done, it is most important to just be myself, be authentically me. Being authentically myself has two components: authenticity and being. Authenticity is the condition or quality of being trustworthy or genuine. Beyond any dictionary definition, authenticity to me is the harmony between what I think, say, and do and what I really feel—the motive in the deepest recesses of my heart. I am authentic only when my motives, words, and deeds are in harmony with my attitude—freedom from guile.

As Ralph Waldo Emerson noted: "Your attitude thunders so loudly that I can't hear what you say." My attitude is the visible part of my behavior, but my motives are hidden from view. When my visible behavior is out of harmony with my motives, my attitude points to a hidden agenda.

Being is more difficult to explain to the Western mind. According to Tao Te Ching, "In the pursuit of learning one knows more every day. In the pursuit of the way one does less every day. Less and less until one does nothing at all. And when one does nothing there is nothing that's left undone." Being is to flow with life, and in so doing, my life's mission is effortlessly accomplished.

When Zane, my wife, and I took our morning walks in Las Vegas, Nevada, we saw spadefoot toads on the lawns, bunnies in the undeveloped lots, and occasionally a roadrunner, which is a marvelous bird in the cuckoo family. None of these animals went out of its way to please us, and yet we thrilled each day just to see them and to wish them well. They were just "being," and in their "beingness" they brought us great joy. They did not have to do anything or be anything other than what they were doing and being.

My mission as a facilitator is simply to act as myself and to give what I can to the best of my ability, one facilitation at a time—no more and no less. To fully understand what I mean, I recommend that you see the movie called *It's a Wonderful Life*.

In the small town of Bedford Falls, so the story goes, lives a young man, George Bailey, who cannot wait to leave his home town to see and conquer the world. But for one reason or another, he never leaves. Being altruistic in his outlook on life, he is other-centered and keeps passing by his chances to go to college and beyond.

Finally, however, facing bankruptcy just before Christmas, through no fault of his own, George decides that he is worth more to his family dead than alive because of his life insurance policy. He therefore tries to kill himself by jumping off a bridge into the river, but an angel, Clarence Oddbody, is sent to save him. Clarence, however, cannot convince George that his life has any value. Adamant that his life is worthless, George wishes he had never been born, and Clarence grants his wish.

To the townspeople, George never existed, so while he knows everyone, no one knows him. He sees how the town would have developed and how the people would have fared had he never been born. George finally sees and understands just how many lives the ripples of his actions have affected by his just being who he is—a simple man who never left his home town, who never conquered the world. He was perfectly himself, and that was all God asked of him—just to act as himself and to give what he could to the best of his ability, one day at a time.

So I relax and be myself. In turn, my example allows the participants to be themselves and to respond to what I have to offer them even as I respond to what they have to offer me, which means that I am always learning.

THE CONTINUAL LEARNING CURVE

I, as a facilitator, am always in school, with much to learn and no hope of learning it all. Nevertheless, I have a full and continuing responsibility to study disciplines involved in the disputes I facilitate in order to improve my awareness, skills, and abilities. Above all, I must work diligently on my own personal, unresolved familial matters. I will always have a need for personal growth to free myself from unwanted psychological and emotional baggage.

The freer I am of my own dysfunctional baggage, the closer I am to having the all-important detachment and creativity of a beginner's mind. Along the way, I find that I do not and cannot have all the answers. This not only is okay in and of itself but also is a blessing that perpetuates the wonder of discovery, especially for the parties with whom I am working.

Not Knowing an Answer Is Okay

Although ignorance is thought of as the lack of knowledge, there is more to it than that. Our sense of the world and our place in it is couched in terms of what we are sure we know and what we think we know. Our universities and laboratories are filled with searching minds, and our libraries are bulging with the fruits of our exploding knowledge, yet where is there an accounting of our ignorance?

Ignorance is not okay in our fast-moving world. We are chastised from the time we are infants until we die for not knowing an answer someone else thinks we should know. If we do not know the correct answer, we may be labeled as stupid, which is not the same as being ignorant about something. Being stupid is usually thought of as being mentally slow to grasp an idea, but being ignorant is simply not knowing the acceptable answer to a particular question.

My favorite answer to a question from an audience member is a purposeful "I don't know," which not only allows me to discover some heretofore hidden secret but also affirms that I neither am nor must I be in charge of the Universe. In my ignorance, I find the incredible freedom to accept the frailty of what it means to be human, to be simply what I am.

Society's preoccupation with building a shining tower of knowledge blinds us to the ever-present, dull luster of ignorance underlying the foundation of the tower, from which all questions must arise and over which the tower of knowledge must stand. Each new brick in the tower of knowledge is born of a question that illuminates our ignorance. Yet ignorance, which often is seen as negative, is but a point along the continuum of consciousness, as are knowledge and the knowing beyond.

The quest for knowledge in the material world is a never-ending pursuit, but the quest does not mean that a thoroughly schooled person is an educated person or that an educated person is a wise person. I say this because we are too often blinded by our ignorance of our ignorance, and our pursuit of knowledge is no guarantee of wisdom. Hence, we are prone to becoming the blind leading the blind, because our overemphasis on competition in nearly everything makes looking good more important than being good. The resultant fear of looking bad is one of the greatest enemies of learning.

Although our ignorance is undeniably vast, it is from the vastness of this selfsame ignorance that our sense of wonder grows. But when we do not know we are ignorant, we do not know enough to even question, let alone investigate, our ignorance.

I cannot, however, teach anyone anything. All I can do with and for someone else is to facilitate learning by helping a person to discover the wonder of his or her ignorance. By asking an appropriate question in an appropriate way, I may be able to help a person become aware of his or her ignorance in a given area without stealing his or her dignity.

A teacher is but a "midwife," as the Greek philosopher Socrates said, because once a person realizes his or her ignorance and begins in earnest to search for understanding, that person slowly comes to see that such understanding can only be drawn out from within. Understanding, after all, is the unique perspective of each and every person.

Success or Failure Is the Interpretation of an Event

It is critical for me, as a facilitator, to understand that success or failure is the interpretation of an event and not the event itself. The Greek philosopher Epictetus hit the mark when he wrote: "Men are disturbed not by things, but by the view which they take of them."

Success and failure are opposites of the same dynamic. They are merely degrees of magnitude along a continuum. The interpretation may be somewhat influenced, however, by who does the interpreting. Knowing what I want to get out of an event, I may interpret the outcome as a huge success, whereas others, whose perceptions of success demand a different outcome, may interpret the same event as a dismal failure.

How, then, do I measure success in transformative facilitation when I may not see a tangible outcome of the process? Were I to either hope for or expect a certain outcome, I may not see anything that even closely resembles it. By seeking a certain outcome, however, I would have an attachment to the result and therefore bias it. So how do I succeed? I succeed by having no expectations and letting the process guide itself to the necessary conclusion.

The following are three examples of letting the process guide itself to the necessary conclusion. In 1988, I facilitated two different groups, one in January in southeastern Washington State and one in April in eastern Oregon, and in June 1992, I facilitated a group in Slovakia. I left each facilitation with absolutely no idea of the outcome.

The one in Washington began with an invitation to speak to a large group on sustainable forestry in November 1987, which I did. I was then invited back to work with a group of about thirty people, including an Indian tribe, timber interests (corporate and private), Oregon and Washington Departments of Wildlife, environmental activists from several groups, county government representatives, local community people, and the U.S. Forest Service.

The problem was a growing conflict of interests over a Forest Service's ten-year forest plan. The fight boiled over into the local newspaper, with people criticizing and blaming one another through their letters to the editor. A total impasse was finally reached with the release of the Draft Environmental Impact Statement (Draft EIS) for the Umatilla National Forest.

At this point, Ralph Perkins (district ranger in the Walla Walla Ranger District) and Shirley Muse (chairperson of the Umatilla Forest Resource Council, a local conservation group) met and with bulldog determination decided to work together to resolve, out of court, the deepening crisis over the EIS. That is when I was invited back.

I spent the weekend with a group of people, many of whom had been enemies through the newspaper but had never met face to face. The following is quoted from a February 8, 1994 letter by Shirley Muse concerning the facilitation forum that had taken place in 1988:

> The primary objective of the workshop was to focus on interpersonal and philosophical foundations and the processes that provide the products on U.S. Forest Service lands. Chris Maser worked from the premise that before we could hope to settle land management issues out of court, we must shift our focus from a product only

orientation to a process orientation. For two days we worked, first in small groups and then together in a large group, learning to set [a vision, goals, and] objectives and in the process learning to help each other define areas of agreement and areas that might need to be negotiated. The end product of the workshop was to begin framing a [vision] for the forest based on those areas of agreement. Chris wanted to create a workshop that would help us make a necessary shift in thinking and a change in the process in such a way that all parties involved might retain our dignity—the prerequisite for "winning."

The sessions were based on mutual learning, sharing, defining fear, expectations, hidden agendas and values exercises. We dealt with change and paradigms and perhaps most importantly, with the concept of dignity in consensus groups. Strong points centered around listening actively—not listening is a form of violence and forming rebuttal is a defense mechanism. We shared a common concern for decisions in land management and recognized that the outcome of our work would in the end become a human judgment decision.

With that beginning, the "Guiding the Course" group set ground rules, jelled the make-up of the group and began working together in an effort to develop a sound management plan for the Umatilla Forest.

The group that I facilitated in eastern Oregon asked me to help them because they heard about what I had done in Washington. This group was different, however. It was composed of ranchers, Forest Service personnel, loggers, conservationists, and local community people. While they wanted to work together, they did not know how to. The conflict centered around a Forest Service watershed plan that affected the community.

I spent two days with a group of people trying to reach an accord. We discussed how a forest and watershed function and how livestock affect forests and grasslands, soils, vegetation, riparian zones, stream banks, and so on. We examined the issue of deer and elk use of private property, especially winter hay stacks reserved for domestic livestock, and other wildlife/livestock issues. We talked about lifestyles, economics, and community values. We examined the notion of social/environmental sustainability, the reciprocal relationship between a community and its landscape, and why a vision for the future is important and how to craft such a statement. I then left.

Finally, in 1994 I was asked what the outcome of these two meetings had been. I said that I didn't know. I had not thought about them in years, except that Shirley Muse (the woman who helped to set up the meeting in Washington) had called me now and then for counsel over some particularly sticky point or other. So I contacted the people and asked what the outcome had been. The following is quoted from the same February 8, 1994 letter as cited above:

> Four years and countless meetings later a final plan was released....the group is still intact in 1994, with some changes in individual members, and is still meeting on a regular basis to continue monitoring "our" national forest. Our success has been measured not so much in land management decisions, although there have been great changes there as well, but in the continued respect and dignity we give to each other. We have learned to listen to each other, to respect each other's opinions, to be unafraid to offer a candid opinion and we are all still committed to the process. Perhaps most important, we are friends.

As for the group in eastern Oregon, some months after I left they found someone within the Forest Service to help them with consensus building and the framing of a vision statement. Finally, with vision statement in hand, they revisited the watershed plan. Although they are also still meeting regularly, the group changes as members come and go. Nevertheless, the group is deeply immersed in both land-use planning and monitoring its implementation on the watershed and the landscape surrounding their community.

In June 1992, I spent time in Cergov, northeastern Slovakia, evaluating the condition of the native forest, which is primarily European beech with an admixture of white fir. The group with which I worked had patterned themselves after the militant environmental activists Earth First!, and they were having trouble getting the Slovakian Federal Forest Service to listen to them. Although we had no formal meeting as such, I spent eighteen days with them, in their offices, homes, and in the forest.

The native forest was being rapidly clearcut and replaced with plantations of such nonnative species as Norway spruce, larch, and pine, which are not biologically sustainable in Cergov. The biological errors of forestry made in Germany, the United States, and Canada were all being repeated in the forests of Cergov and for the same reasons—shortsighted, immediate economic gain for areas outside the local communities.

Not only were local native forests being liquidated through clearcutting but also local topsoil was being exported toward the distant sea through uncontrolled erosion. Within one hour after each thunderstorm, all the streams and rivers fed by clearcut slopes went from clear water to water that looked like milk chocolate, as the soil of the forest was washed away.

Enlightened by what I had seen, we talked about many issues, including peace versus violence, one of the main topics. I also put on a day's workshop in the forest for the Federal Forest Service, which, due to Communist rule, was about forty years behind in scientific data. I gave slide presentations to high school classes, university forestry classes, the Federal Forest Service, and the general public. Finally, I wrote a report about our deliberations, which I presented at an international conference on the environment. The report was an outgrowth of what I had seen, our discussions, and a series of recommendations for healing the forest.

Before I left, the chief of the Federal Forest Service said to me: "I don't understand everything you said, and I can't accept everything you said. But if I have learned one thing from you, Chris, it is that the forest is sacred, not the plan."

If nothing else were to come from my trip, this was a great compliment, because it showed that I had earned the chief's trust and that he, after forty years behind the Iron Curtain, could and did change some of this thinking.

Some weeks after I returned home, I received a letter from the group stating that because the people agreed to work peacefully with the Forest Service, the report (translated into Slovak) circulated its way through the Slovakian Parliament. As a result, the group was officially invited to work with the Federal Forest Service in revising at least some parts of the forest plan.

These groups represent the ultimate success, by my measure. They are carrying on with that which is important to them, because I had left enough tools behind to make myself dispensable, which to me is the ultimate goal of transformative facilitation. The process and its outcome are theirs, and that is how it needs to be. If, however, I had expected or wanted perfect land-use plans to emerge from these meetings, I would have failed, because there is no such thing as a perfect plan, only a continuing process.

The labels of success or failure are usually assigned to the perceived outcome or product of an event rather than to the actual process of learning embodied in the event itself. Therefore, when I abdicate my right to interpret the event, such as a facilitation process, success or failure becomes a judgment determined by others, which may be termed the "cultural trance" because the value of an individual's spontaneous creativity usually gets smothered by the prevailing social standards.

The cultural trance is the uncritical acceptance of all the *shoulds*, *oughts*, and *musts* thrust upon us from childhood onward by a myriad of external sources. If I look to *others* for my self-esteem, success involves a visible accomplishment of which "others" must approve. Lack of such visible accomplishment, therefore, is deemed a failure. Success means I do it myself, and failure means I need help. Because success is usually measured in terms of how much money or power I have, failure is simply a measure of perceived lack. Success is a measure of being in control of circumstances, and failure is a measure of not being in control of circumstances.

The real success or failure in life, however, is whether or not I am doing what I really want to do in my heart of hearts. Mythologist Joseph Campbell calls it "following your bliss." If I am doing what I really want to do, regardless of material returns, then I have a success of the heart, no matter what anyone else thinks. Others can measure only the appearance of success based on *their* definition. Yet an apparent failure in the short term can prove a success in the long term. Failure can then be viewed as delayed or postponed success.

If, therefore, I allow others to define me, I allow them to determine my success or failure. If I accept failure on this basis, then the point at which I acquiesce is the point at which I am defeated.

One of my favorite stories is about Babe Ruth, the baseball player. The Babe had struck out two or three times in one game. When the game was over, a sports reporter asked him what he was thinking about as he struck out.

"Hitting a home run," he said.

"Well," asked the reporter, "how does it feel to fail?"

"I didn't fail," replied the Babe. "Every time I get a strike, I'm one swing closer to the next home run, and you know who has to worry about that!"

Babe Ruth had learned two very important lessons. The first was that to be a winner, he had to be willing to risk being a loser, and the degree to which he was willing to risk losing determined the degree to which he was ultimately capable of winning. The Babe was the home run king only because he was first willing to be the strikeout king. Babe therefore had to be willing to be mediocre at something for a while so that, through practice, he could excel.

The second lesson was to be consistent in his efforts, which Winston Churchill put well when he said: "Success is going from failure to failure with enthusiasm." The crowd in the bleachers did not bother Ruth. He smiled at them in the same, quiet way when they booed him as he did when they cheered him. Babe Ruth knew who and what he was—a champ.

8

PRACTICING TRANSFORMATIVE FACILITATION

Good conflict resolution is a meticulous practice in democracy. It is thus critical to understand something about democracy as a practical concept. Democracy is a system of shared power with checks and balances, a system in which individuals can affect the outcome of political decisions. People practice democracy by managing social processes themselves. Democracy is another word for self-directed social evolution.

Democracy in the United States is built on the concept of inner truth, which in practice is a tenuous balance between spirituality and materialism. One such truth is the notion of human equality, in which all people are pledged to defend the rights of each person, and each person is pledged to defend the rights of all people. In practice, however, the whole endeavors to protect the rights of the individuals, while the individuals are pledged to obey the *will* of the majority, which may or may not be just to each person.

The "will" of the majority brings up the notion of freedom in democracy. Nothing that I know of in the Universe is totally free; rather, everything expresses freedom within some sort of limits. Just as there is no such thing as a truly "free market" or an "independent variable," so are individual and social autonomy protected by moral limits placed on the freedom with which individuals and society can act. To this effect, author Anna Lemkow[30] lists four propositions of freedom: "(1) An individual must win freedom of will by self-effort, (2) freedom is inseparable from necessity or inner order, (3) freedom always involves a sense of unity with others beyond differences, (4) freedom is inseparable from truth—or, put the other way around, truth serves to make us free."

Lemkow goes on to say:

> We tend to think of freedom as dependent on circumstantial or external factors, but these propositions point us inward, suggesting rather that freedom is a state of consciousness and...depends on ourselves. Indeed it is something to be won, something to be attained commensurately with becoming more truthful, or more attuned to and aligned with the abiding inner, metaphysical, or moral order or law.
>
> Socio-political and economic freedom or liberty, in turn, would depend (at least in the longer term) on the predominant level of consciousness of the citizenry.

Lemkow is positing that a human being is not completely free to begin with, but possesses the potential capability of self-transformation in the direction of fuller freedom. Beyond this, democracy requires respect for others and excitement in the exchange of ideas. People must learn to listen to one another's ideas, not as points of debate but as different and valid experiences in a collective reality. While they must learn to agree to disagree at times, they must also learn to accept that, like blind people feeling the different parts of an elephant, each person is initially limited by his or her own perspective. When these things happen, people are engaged in the most fundamental aspects of democracy and come to conclusions and make decisions through participative talking, listening, understanding, compromising, and agreeing.

In a democracy, *connection* and *sharing* are central to its viability because a democracy only works when it is being practiced. People are not required to separate feelings from thoughts concerning a topic. Their roles—as teachers, students, leaders, facilitators, and followers—fluctuate within and across the issues. The importance of a democratic system lies in its connection to people's lives, their own experiences, and the real problems and issues they daily face. Practicing democracy can be thought of as education in and for life. And because people have within them the seeds of greatness, as teacher Myles Horton says, "it is not a matter of trying to fill people up but rather of fulfilling them."

The challenge, therefore, is to engage people in the democratic process, which is difficult when they confuse the government with the administration of the government or when the administration becomes so dysfunctional that people despair in their seeming inability to fix it. But then, I know of no perfect government.

A just government must be founded on truth, not knowledge—something we in the United States have all too swiftly forgotten. To achieve such government, it must be based on service (where people are other-serving) rather than power (where people are self-serving). Therefore, environmental protection is only possible if the government is accountable to its people beyond special interest groups and political lobbyists.

We live in an increasingly complex society of intense competition and materialism. In such a society, people commit evil acts in order to gain power, both through positions of authority and financial success. People commit evil acts while falsely expecting to benefit by them, thinking that such benefits will somehow bring happiness. But in the end, as Socrates warned, the guilt of the soul outweighs the supposed material gains. Thus, because people lack perfect knowledge and perfect motives, democracy must be continually practiced and continually improved through that practice.

Nevertheless, the *people* are the government, but they can govern only as long as they elect to use the constitutional system for empowerment. It is important to understand that empowerment is personal self-motivation. No one can empower anyone else; one can only empower oneself. One can, however, give others the psychological space, permission, and skills necessary to empower themselves and then support their empowerment. Beyond that, one can help in the process of empowerment and can increase the chances of success by recognizing another's accomplishments each step of the way. That is true democracy.

Therefore, in the case of the United States, where the government is of the people, by the people, and for the people, when the people empower themselves, they are the government, and it is the administration of that government that resides in Washington, D.C. and not the government itself. The administration becomes the government only when the people turn their power over to the administration and in effect say: I'm a victim and can't change the system, or take care of me.

Democracy is a viable system because it rests on a self-reflective principle; that is, by inviting a constant reinterpretation of itself, it is always in a state of becoming, which continually interweaves it within the intimacy of life. For democracy to remain viable, it must be used, because it is an interconnected, interactive system of balancing and integrating contrasting perceptions of data, fact, and truth. A working democracy is thus predicated on finding the point of balance through compromise in such a way that the rifts between opposites can be minimized and healed.

COMPROMISE AND THE POINT OF BALANCE

Facilitation is the way to compromise and the point of balance that resolves conflicts. The *mandorla*, a symbol of unity, is a prototype of conflict resolution that has long been secreted in the gathering dust of medieval Christianity.

A mandorla is two overlapping circles with an almond-shaped area in the middle where the contents of each circle integrate. When thus put together, their areas of overlap and integration—their common root—can be found and perceived opposites can be balanced. And all opposites have a common root because they are, after all, merely different perceptions of the same reality. For example, a glass of water is half full or half empty, depending on one's point of view, but the level of water is the same in either case.

Once the overlap is identified, acknowledged, and accepted, people can begin working collectively, extending the area of overlap and integration. Although the overlap is tiny at first, like the sliver of a new moon, it is a beginning, the first healing of the split between opposites. With diligent work and the passage of time, the sliver becomes as a quarter moon, then a half moon, and a three-quarter moon, until that point is reached where the two circles become as one—a full moon, unity, total healing.

The mandorla as a symbol, a process, and a metaphor fits every social/environmental problem that I can imagine. The mandorla thus seems a logical metaphor of social/environmental sustainability, which is the necessary next stage of social evolution—the ultimate expression of a working democracy—if society, as we know it, is to survive. If, however, we are to map the country of the mandorla to our best advantage, we must treat one another with compassion and justice while we explore the hidden potential of the almond-shaped land of overlap and integration.

A CURRICULUM OF COMPASSION AND JUSTICE

The transformative facilitation process must be as gentle and dignified as possible, which means that it must be a continual lesson in compassion and justice taught through the facilitator's example. All parties must emerge with their dignity intact if anything is to be resolved. It is therefore important to remember that *now* is always the time for compassion and justice, because, as Mahatma Gandhi pointed out, "An eye for an eye only makes the whole world blind." In this sense, facilitation as a democratic process is perhaps at its best when the people involved must continue dealing with one another after the dispute is resolved.[31]

Compassion is the deep feeling of sharing another's suffering, of giving aid and support to another person in her or his time of need (which is the act of forgiving another's perceived trespass), of extending mercy. The essence of compassion is best acknowledged in a French proverb: "To know all is to forgive all." This is but saying that as I do the level best I can in all I do, so does everyone else, so where, therefore, is the judgment? Thus, when we forgive all, when we fix no judgment and place no blame, we have compassion.

When someone is unkind to me, I try to accept that it is not a personal act, but rather one that reflects the other person's inner distress, and I know that neither of us will gain anything if I shame or shun that person. I do not always succeed in my endeavors, however, and I cannot count the times I have fallen short of my ideal of unconditional compassion, which to me is the understanding through which the act of forgiveness may flow.

Forgiveness, in turn, is to see the fear and the pain out of which another person acts and to extend love as an alternative. To have compassion, therefore, demands far greater courage than does retaliation in any form at any time, because compassion demands that one is responsible for one's behavior and abnegates the role of victim.

Although I cannot experience how the other person is feeling, I can ask. If that person can relax long enough to answer, I may be able to imagine myself for a moment in his or her situation and see if I would act any differently under the particular circumstances. I have inevitably found that I would do the same were I the other person. It is therefore up to me to forgive rather than up to the other person to change, which means that I must do unto others as I would have them do unto me in any given circumstance.

I have often heard it said that "all's fair in love and war" and that "nothing's fair in life." If this is the way people really feel, perhaps we must shift our attention from fairness to justice, or that which is just. If I am just, I am honorable, consistent with the highest morality, and equitable in my dealings and actions. If I do unto others as I would have others do unto me, then I can be a just person.

One can also choose to be just in a practical sense. By being just and equitable with others, I encourage them to treat me justly, which is another lesson I can teach by example. For it is wise to cultivate such kindly behavior for myself by extending it first to others. And if for some reason the person with whom I was just is unjust with me, he or she gives me an opportunity to practice compassion. Being compassionate requires nothing from anyone else—only my courage and the wisdom to love enough to forgive. Such compassion is one of the gifts passed forward through transformative facilitation.

FACILITATION AS A GIFT IS FREE, BUT AS A TRADE HAS A COST

What do a gift and a trade have to do with facilitation? They have much to do with it because transformative facilitation must be an unconditional gift. To define an unconditional gift, consider what I, as a facilitator, might expect out of the facilitation process. Do I want something specific to happen, a certain outcome, for example, or is any outcome okay?

A gift is free of expectations, but a trade has a specific outcome attached to it. Both a gift and a trade are circumstances to which the recipient must respond, and the choice of response is one of either trust or distrust.

A gift is a feeling made visible through an object, but the object is not the real gift. The feeling is the real gift, because it is the cause for giving the object.

A gift, which most people think of as an object, is free of conditions. If I give you a gift, I have, by definition, also given you title and ownership free of encumbrances. You may do with it as you wish, because I have no vested interest in what you do with what you own, which means no strings are attached. Further, your unconditional acceptance of my gift is your unconditional gift to me, because I cannot give you my gift if you refuse to accept it. This thought is in keeping with an Aboriginal American proverb: "You must humble yourself to receive before you can truly give."

If, for example, I give you a chocolate cake but you are on a diet so you graciously accept the cake and give it to someone else, then you have accepted my gift and given me one through your acceptance. In addition, you have given a gift of your own by passing on the cake. If the second person accepts the cake but does not like chocolate and gives the cake to a third person, then the second person has accepted your gift and given one of his or her own. In each case, the apparent or perceived gift was the cake, but the true gift was the unconditional love embodied in the thought of giving by one person and in the thought of receiving by the other. At no time was the real gift the cake itself.

A trade, on the other hand, is an exchange of one thing for another, beginning with the thought or expectation of a specific outcome. By definition, therefore, a trade cannot be a gift, because a gift, truly given and received, is something bestowed without thought of compensation. A trade, however, is a way of realizing a known expectation, a way to control the outcome.

Let's go back to the chocolate cake. If I give you a chocolate cake on the condition that you eat it, I have given you a condition—a prison cell—instead of a gift. I have traded a chocolate cake to you for your compliance with my expectations of your behavior—to eat the cake in spite of your diet. I have used the cake to control you. I have covertly said: "If you really love me, you will

Chapter 8 ■ Practicing Transformative Facilitation 137

eat the cake for me in spite of your diet." The inference is that if you choose to honor your diet and not eat the cake, then you do not really love me. I have laid guilt on you to control your behavior and to give me the outcome I want.

Unless the rules of the trade are agreed to beforehand by all parties, the "trade" is really coercion. Such was the case with the meeting on the livestock grazing fee program, of which I spoke earlier. The facilitators wanted something from us, the participants. They wanted our compliance with their wishes, which, if forthcoming, would please the Interior Secretary and might bring in more business. Although we were not privy to what they wanted, it became clear during the facilitation process that they had a particular hidden agenda.

I trade because an unexpected outcome will force me out of my comfort zone and make me deal with the unknown, and that is not what I want. It is the unknown—that which I think is unknowable, that which demands the risk of uncontrollable change—that frightens me.

One of the many places fear of the unknown can be seen in people is in airports. Passengers have their tickets, and their schedules are confirmed, but not beyond change. A flight is suddenly canceled or baggage is lost, and carefully controlled plans are nowhere to be found. This is distressing because the known expectation suddenly evaporates, and the worst-case scenario of the unknown becomes reality. The dreaded unknown—my not knowing what to expect—has happened. I see no immediate clear choice. I have suddenly lost control!

This is when frightened people get angry and yell at ticket agents. In so doing, they are trying to trade their anger for compliance with their wishes, or more comfortable boundaries within which they can operate "normally." The more frightened they are, the nastier their behavior becomes.

But unknown expectations are also gifts of adventure, which always hold lessons about our lives if we will but look for them. One of my college professors, for example, had such an unexpected experience. He had purchased an expensive microscope in Switzerland, only to have it stolen in Naples, Italy, on his way home. He went to the police station to report the theft. While he stood there waiting, the police chief talked to an American sailor whose wristwatch had been stolen.

"Which pier is your ship docked at?" asked the chief.

"Pier 10," said the sailor.

"I think I know who has your watch. You two come with me," said the chief motioning to both the sailor and the professor.

When they reached the pier, the chief went up to a young boy and said, "Give this man his wristwatch." The boy reluctantly complied.

This, however, did nothing for the professor's microscope. In fact, the chief told him that his problem was much more difficult to solve, probably impossible, and since the microscope was not insured against theft, the professor was probably out of luck.

The professor returned home, angry that he had been ripped off. It had, retroactively, spoiled his whole trip; it was all he could think about. He stewed about the microscope and the money for six months. With time, he finally accepted what was; he let go of what he could not control—the circumstance—and took responsibility for what he could control—his attitude, his response to the circumstance.

Several months later, the professor got a telephone call from customs at the Seattle-Tacoma Airport in Washington advising him that a package had arrived for him. Lo and behold, his microscope had arrived in perfect condition! All of his stewing and internal discord had been a total waste of time and energy.

Thus, I must be detached from the outcome of my facilitation and must become dispensable to all parties as soon as possible by helping them, should they so choose, to establish the processes necessary to resolve their own conflicts and create a vision for their own future. The gift I have to give is helping parties get ready for the next step—bringing the conflict to resolution through a shared vision on which to act.

9

RESOLUTION: DESTRUCTIVE CONFLICT BROUGHT TO A SHARED VISION

An ancient custom of the Aboriginal Americans was to call a council fire when decisions affecting the whole tribe or nation needed to be made. To sit in council as a representative of the people was an honor that had to be earned through many years of truthfulness, bravery, compassion, sharing, listening, justice, being a discreet counselor, and so on. These qualities were necessary because a council fire by its very nature was a time to examine every point of view and explore every possibility of a situation that would in some way affect the whole of the people's destiny.

When someone called a council, that person had to have the courage to accept the council's decision with grace, because when the good of the whole is placed before the good of the few, all are assured a measure of abundance. The timeless teaching of the council fire is that until all of the people are doing well, none of the people are doing well.

The council fire worked well for the Aboriginal Americans because they knew who they were culturally, and they had a sense of place within their environment. Today, however, the global community is in transition, which robs many people of their original sense of place and substitutes some vague idea of location.

This transition is largely the result of massive shifts in human populations over the last three centuries. These shifts have altered the composition of peoples and their cultural structures throughout the world. All of this activity results in growing interconnectedness, interactivity, interdependence, and cultural uncertainty as some political lines change physically and others blur culturally. Cultural uncertainty is particularly true for those people caught between two cultures, such as the warring religious factions around the world, where millions of refugees not only have their sense of culture disrupted but also their sense of place transformed into an alien location where their lives hang in limbo. These changes pose necessary questions for some people (such as "Who are we as a culture?"), which must be answered before a statement of vision and goals can be fruitfully considered.

WHO ARE WE AS A CULTURE?

Who are we now, today? This is a difficult but necessary question for people to deal with if they want to create a vision for the future. They must decide, based on how they define their cultural identity, what kind of vision to create. The self-held concept of who a people are is critical to their cultural future because their cultural self-image will determine what their community will become socially, which in turn will determine what their children will become socially.

Thus, how well a people's core values are encompassed in a vision depends first on how well the people understand themselves as a culture and second on how well that understanding is reflected on paper. Let's consider three examples: the Japanese, Aboriginal Canadians, and Aboriginal Americans.

In Japan, a religious system of belief, today known as Shinto, has been observed since the founding of the country. Shinto gained systematic form spontaneously from within the social life of communities. As a result, it has no specific founder or clearly defined body of scripture. Since ancient times, the Japanese have transmitted the legends and myths of the deities or "kami" as a genealogy of their way of life.

Shinto, in its broadest sense, refers to the entirety of indigenous culture, as opposed to Buddhism and other religious systems imported from outside of Japan. Shinto is established against a background of hydraulic rice agriculture, which is uniquely suited to Japan's warm and humid climate.

When used in the narrow sense, Shinto refers to the rites offered to deities, primarily those deities of heaven and earth listed in classical Japanese works of the ancient period. The physical facility used for the performance of this worship is called "jinju" or shrine.

That Nature and natural phenomena are revered as deities is a result of the Japanese view of Nature as a kind of parent, which nurtures life and provides limitless blessings. Shinto shrines all over Japan are surrounded by luxuriant groves of trees. Backed by the Shinto view that untouched Nature is itself sacred, the groves surrounding the shrines are themselves an important composite element of each shrine.

About 1300 years ago, Emperor Tenmu ordained the practice of removing the old shrine, such as the Grand Shrine of Ise in Ise City, every twenty years and rebuilding a new, exact replica next to it. Why Emperor Tenmu stipulated that the rebuilding of the shrine should take place every twenty years is not clearly known, but it is most likely that twenty years was considered to be the optimum period for allowing the exact replication of the Grand Shrine, considering that it has a thatched roof, unpainted or otherwise preserved structures, and is erected on posts sunk into the ground with only the benefit of foundation stones.

Twenty years is perhaps also the most logical interval in terms of passing from one generation to the next the technological expertise needed for the exacting task of duplicating the shrine. The Shinto shrine can be thought of as sacred architecture created from within the prayer and technical skills of the Japanese people themselves. Passing technical skills and the prayer embodied in the sacred architecture from generation to generation is the context within which lies the real significance of the regular rebuilding. The cultural knowledge has thus far been passed on for 1300 years without change.

Herein lies the challenge for Japan. Although the sacred Shinto architecture can be passed from generation to generation through the perpetuation of the shrines, the belief system is being eroded by the introduction of Western philosophy. This psychic split seems to occur largely because Shinto is based in the belief of Nature's primacy through cycles and processes, whereas Western philosophy is based in the primacy of linear technology and consumer products. The Japanese are therefore caught between two worlds—their ancient ritualized spiritual world and the new Western materialistic free-market one.

The Aboriginal Canadians have a somewhat similar dilemma. They have departed from their old culture because they have—against their will—been forced to adopt European–Canadian ways, which means they have given up or lost ancestral ones. Yet they have not—by choice—totally adopted white culture and want to retain some degree of their ancestral culture. Thus, the question they must ask and answer is: Which of our ancestral ways still have sufficient cultural value for us to keep them? Which of the white ways do we want to adopt? How do we put the chosen elements of both cultures together in such a way that we can today define who we are culturally?

Although Aboriginal Americans have the same task as the Aboriginal Canadians, they have even fewer options because the European–Americans did a much more thorough job of destroying their culture and forcing them to adopt foreign ways. Nevertheless, the question of who we are today is still valid for any vision the people of an Indian reservation in the United States might want to create for their own lands. Here, I suggest, that we all face the question of who we are today as a culture, especially at the community level. This is an important question, because how it is answered will determine the legacy inherited by our children.

For example, in 1993, I was ask to review an ecological brief for a First Nation of Aboriginal Canadians whose reservation was located between the sea and land immediately upslope from the reservation that a timber company wanted to cut. The problem lay in the fact that the timber company could only reach the timber it wanted to cut by obtaining an easement through the reservation, which gave the First Nation some control over the timber company. The First Nation, on the other hand, wanted some control over how the timber company would log the upper-slope forest, because the outcome would for many years affect the reservation, which is just below the area to be cut.

Before meeting with the timber company, the First Nation's chief asked me for some counsel. My reply was as follows:

> Before I discuss the ecological brief I've been asked to review, there are three points that must be taken into account if what I say is to have any value to the First Nation. What I'm about to say may be difficult to hear, but I say it with the utmost respect.
>
> **Point 1**: Who are you, the First Nation, in a cultural sense? You are not your old culture because you have—against your will—been forced to adopted some white ways, which means you have given up or lost ancestral ways. You are not—by choice—white, so you may wish to retain some of your ancestral ways. The questions you must ask and answer are: What of our ancestral ways still have sufficient value that we want to keep them? What of the white ways do we want to or are we willing to adopt? How do we put the chosen elements of both cultures together in such a way that we can today define who we are as a culture?
>
> **Point 2**: What do you want your children to have as a legacy from your decisions and your negotiations with the timber company? Whatever you decide is what you are committing your children, their children, and their children's children to pay for the effects of your decisions unto the seventh generation and beyond.

> This, of course, is solely your choice and that is as it should be. I make no judgments. But whatever you choose will partly answer Point 3.
>
> **Point 3**: What do you want your reservation to look like and act like during and after logging by the timber company? How you define yourselves culturally, what choices you make for your children, and the conscious decisions you make about the condition of your land will determine what you end up with. In all of these things, the choice is yours. The consequences belong to both you and your children.

After they answered this questions for themselves, they had to determine what they wanted to leave for their children.

WHAT LEGACY DO WE WANT TO LEAVE OUR CHILDREN?

Once a group of people, whether a community, such as an Indian tribe or perhaps your own home town, has defined itself culturally, it can then decide what legacy it wants to leave its children. This must be done consciously because whatever decisions the group makes under its new cultural identity, the consequences of those decisions are what the group is committing its children, their children, and their children's children to pay.

Having defined who they are culturally and having determined what legacy they want to leave their children, the people of a community are now ready to craft a vision of what they want because only now do they really know.

The rest of my reply to the First Nation applies here:

> Now to my comments: This is a difficult task at best. As with every definition, it is a human invention and has no meaning to Nature. Therefore, you must tell the timber company, clearly and concisely, what the terms in this ecological brief mean to you and how you interpret them with respect to the company's actions that will affect your reservation.
>
> 1. Every ecosystem functions fully within the limits imposed on it by Nature and/or humans. Therefore, it is the type, scale, and duration of the alterations to the system—the imposed limits—that you need to be concerned with. If your reservation looks the way you want it to and functions the way you want it to, then the question becomes: How must we and the timber company behave to

keep it looking and functioning the way it is? If, on the other hand, your reservation does *not* look the way you want it to and does *not* function the way you want it to, then the question becomes: How must we and the timber company behave to make it look and function the way we want it to? But regardless of your decisions or the company's actions, your reservation will always function to its greatest capacity under the circumstance Nature, you, and the company impose on it. The point is that your decisions and the company's actions, excluding what Nature may do, will determine how your reservation both looks and functions. This reflects the importance of the preceding Point 3 and what you decide.

2. If you want the landscape of your reservation to look and function in a certain way, then how must the timber company's landscape look and function to help make your reservation be what you want it to be? Keep in mind that the landscape of your reservation *and* the company's are *both* made up of the collective performance of individual stands of trees or "habitat patches." Therefore, how the stands look and function will determine how the collective landscape looks and functions.

3. Remember that any undesirable ecological effects are also undesirable economic effects over time. Your interest in your reservation will be there for many, many years, generations perhaps, but the company's interest in the forest may well disappear just as soon as the trees are cut. So, the company's short-term economic decision may be good for them but may at the same time be a bad long-term ecological decision and a bad long-term economic decision for you.

4. To maintain ecological functions means that you must maintain the characteristics of the ecosystem in such a way that its processes are sustainable. The characteristics you must be concerned about are: (1) composition, (2) structure, (3) function, and (4) Nature's disturbance regimes.

The composition or kinds of plants and their age classes within a plant community creates a certain structure that is characteristic of the plant community. It is the structure of the plant community that in turn creates and maintains certain functions. In addition, it is the composition, structure, and function of a plant community that determines which animals can live there and how many. If you change the composition, you change the structure, you change the function, you affect the animals. People and Nature are continually changing a community's structure by altering its composition, which in turn affects how it functions.

For example, the timber company wants to change the forest's structure by cutting the trees, which in turn will change the plant community's composition, which in turn will change how the community functions, which in turn will change the kinds and numbers of animals that can live there. These are the key elements with which you must be concerned, because an effect on one area can—and usually does—affect the entire landscape.

Composition, structure, and function go together to create and maintain ecological processes both in time and across space, and it is the health of the processes that in the end creates the forest. Your forest is a living organism, not just a collection of trees—as the timber industry usually thinks of it.

5. Scale is an often forgotten component of healthy forests and landscapes. The treatment of every stand of timber is critically important to the health of the whole landscape, which is a collection of the interrelated stands.

Thus, when you deal only with a stand, what is ignored is the relationship of that particular stand to other stands, to the rest of the drainage, and to the landscape. It's like a jigsaw puzzle where each piece is a stand. The relationship of certain pieces (stands) makes a picture (drainage). The relationship of the pictures (drainages) makes a whole puzzle (landscape). Thus, relationships of all the stands within a particular area make a drainage and the relationships of all the drainages within a particular area make the landscape.

If one piece is left out of the puzzle, it is not complete. If one critical piece is missing, it may be very difficult to figure out what the picture is. So each piece (stand) is critically important in its relationship to the completion of the whole puzzle (landscape). Therefore, the way each stand is defined and treated by the timber company is critically important to how the landscape, encompassing both the company's land and your reservation, looks and functions over time.

6. Degrading an ecosystem is a human concept based on human values and has nothing to do with Nature. Nature places no value on anything. Everything just is, and in its being it is perfect. Therefore, if something in Nature changes—it simply changes, no value is

either added of subtracted. But whether or not your reservation becomes degraded depends on what you want it to be like, what value or values you have placed on its being in a certain condition, to produce certain things for you. If your desired condition *is* negatively affected by the company's actions, then your reservation *becomes* degraded. If your desired condition is *not* negatively affected by the company's actions, then your reservation is *not* degraded. Remember, your own actions can also degrade your reservation.

7. It is important that you know—as clearly as possible—what the definitions in this brief really mean to you and your choices for your children and your reservation. Only when you fully understand what these definitions mean to you can you negotiate successfully with the timber company.

To negotiate with the timber company, however, the First Nation must have a vision, goals, and objectives for their reservation.

VISION, GOALS, AND OBJECTIVES

Although the word vision is variously construed, it is used here as a shared view of the future. Defining a vision and committing it to paper goes against our training, however, because it must be stated as a positive in the positive, something we are not use to doing. Stating a positive in the positive means stating what we mean directly. For example, a town has an urban growth boundary that it wants to keep within certain limits, which can be stated one of two ways: (1) we don't want our urban growth boundary to look like that of our neighbor—a negative stated as a positive, or (2) we want our urban growth boundary to remain within a half a mile from where it is now situated—a positive stated as a positive.

Further, to save our planet and human society as we know it, we must be willing to risk changing our thinking in order to have a wider perception of the world and its possibilities, to validate one another's points of view or frames of reference. The world can be perceived with greater clarity when it is observed simultaneously from many points of view. Such conception requires open-mindedness in a collaborative process of intellectual and emotional exploration of that which is and that which might be, the results of a shared vision.

The movie *Spartacus* depicted the story of a Roman slave forced to become a gladiator, who led an army of slaves in an uprising in 71 B.C. They twice defeated the Roman legions, but were finally conquered by General Marcus Licinius Crassus after a long siege and battle in which they were surrounded by and had to fight three Roman legions simultaneously.

The battle over, Crassus faces the thousand survivors seated on the ground as an officer shouts: "I bring a message from your master, Marcus Licinius Crassus, Commander of Italy. By command of his most merciful excellency, your lives are to be spared. Slaves you were, and slaves you remain. But the terrible penalty of crucifixion has been set aside on the single condition that you identify the body or the living person of the slave called Spartacus."

After a long pause, Spartacus stands up to identify himself. Before he can speak, however, Antoninus leaps to his feet and yells, "I am Spartacus!" Immediately, another man stands and yells, "No, I'm Spartacus!" Then another leaps to his feet and yells, "I'm Spartacus!" Within minutes, the whole slave army is on its feet, each man yelling "I'm Spartacus!"

Each man, by standing, was potentially committing himself to death by crucifixion. Yet their loyalty to Spartacus, their leader, was superseded only by their loyalty to the vision of themselves as free men, the vision that Spartacus had inspired. The vision was so compelling that, having once tasted freedom, they willingly chose death over submitting to slavery. By withholding their obedience from Crassus, they remain free because slavery requires that the oppressed submit their obedience to the oppressor.

In more recent times, a vision of freedom and equality inspired thirteen colonies to formally declare their independence from England on July 4, 1776. The vision of human freedom and equality was so strong that a whole nation, the United States of America, was founded on it. In 1836, the fall of the Alamo, the Franciscan mission in San Antonio, Texas, and the slaughter of the men defending it inspired Texans in their vision of freedom from Mexican rule. In both cases, the strength of the vision carried a people to victory against overwhelming odds.

Although a vision may begin as an intellectual idea, at some point it becomes enshrined in one's heart as a palpable force that defies explanation. It then becomes impossible to turn back, to accept that which was before, because to do so would be to die inside. Few, if any, forces in human affairs are as powerful as a shared vision of the heart.[32]

In its simplest, intellectual form, a shared vision asks: What do we want to create? Beyond that, it becomes the focus and energy to actively create that which is desired. Few people, however, know what a vision, goal, or objective is, how to create them, how to state them, or how to use them as guidelines for development.

A statement of *vision* is a general declaration that describes what a particular person, group of people, agency, or nation is striving for. A vision is like a "vanishing point," the spot on the horizon where the straight, flat road on which you are driving disappears from view over a gentle rise in the distance. As long as you keep that vanishing point in focus as the place you want to go, you are free to take a few side trips down other roads and always know where you are in relation to where you want to go, your vision. It is therefore necessary to have at hand a dictionary and a thesaurus when crafting a vision statement, because it must be as precise as possible; through it, you must say what you mean and mean what you say.

Gifford Pinchot, the first chief of the U.S. Forest Service, had a vision of protected forests that would produce commodities for people in perpetuity. In them he saw the "greatest good for the greatest number in the long run." Through his leadership, he inspired this vision as a core value around which everyone in the new agency could, and did, rally for almost a century.

In a more recent example, I spoke in 1989 to a First Nation of Aboriginal Canadians who owned a sawmill in central British Columbia. I had been asked to discuss how a coniferous forest functions, both above- and belowground, so that the First Nation could better understand the notion of productive sustainability, something they were greatly concerned about. After I spoke, a contingent from the British Columbia provincial government told the Aboriginal Canadians what they could and could not do in the eyes of the government. The government officials were insensitive at best. The Aboriginal Canadians tried in vain to tell the officials how they *felt* about their land and how they were personally being treated. Both explanations fell on deaf ears.

After the meeting was over and the government people left, I explained to the Aboriginal Canadians what a vision is, why it is important, and how to create one. In this case, they already knew in their hearts what they wanted; they had a shared vision, but they could not articulate it in a way that the government people, whose dealings with the First Nation were strictly intellectual, could understand.

They committed their feelings to paper as a vision statement for their sawmill in relation to the sustainable capacity of their land and their traditional ways. They were thus able to state their vision in a way that the government officials could understand, and it became their central point in future negotiations.

In another instance, also in 1989, I helped a president and vice-president frame a vision, goals, and objectives for their new company. Although the president became frustrated during the two-day process, he told me a couple of years later that it had been the most important exercise that he had ever been through for his company, and he had used it constantly as the company grew.

Chapter 9 ■ Resolution: Destructive Conflict Brought to a Shared Vision

In contrast to a vision, a *goal* is a general statement of intent that remains until it is achieved, the need for it disappears, or the direction changes. Although a goal is a statement of direction, which may be vague and is not necessarily expected to be accomplished, it does serve to further clarify the vision statement. A goal might be stated as: "My goal is to see Timbuktu."

There is, however, a saying in Nova Scotia for a person without a goal: "If you don't know where you're going, any path will take you there." Thus, without a goal, we take "potluck" in terms of where we will end up, which was Alice's dilemma when she met the Cheshire-Cat in Lewis Carroll's story of *Alice's Adventures in Wonderland*.[33] Alice asked the Cheshire-Cat:

> "Would you tell me, please, which way I ought to go from here?"
> "That depends a good deal on where you want to get to," said the Cat.
> "I don't much care where—" said Alice.
> "Then it doesn't matter which way you go," said the Cat.
> "—so long as I get somewhere," Alice added as an explanation.
> "Oh, you're sure to do that," said the Cat, "if you only walk long enough."

An *objective*, on the other hand, is a specific statement of intended accomplishment. It is attainable, has a reference to time, is observable and measurable, and has an associated cost. The following are additional attributes of an objective: (1) it starts with an action verb, (2) it specifies a single outcome or result to be accomplished, (3) it specifies a date by which the accomplishment is to be completed, (4) it is framed in positive terms, (5) it is as specific and quantitative as possible and thus lends itself to evaluation, (6) it specifies only the "what, where," and "when" and avoids mentioning the "why" and the "how," and (7) it is product oriented.

Let's consider the previously goal: "My goal is to see Timbuktu." I will now make it into an objective: "I will see Timbuktu on my twenty-first birthday." My stated objective is action oriented: I will see. It has a single outcome: seeing Timbuktu. It specifies a date, the day of my twenty-first birthday, and is framed in positive terms: I will. It lends itself to evaluation of whether or not I achieved my stated intent, and it clearly states "what," "where," and "when." Finally, it is product or outcome oriented: to see a specific place.

As I strive to achieve this objective, I must accept and remember that my objective is fixed, as though in concrete, but the plan to achieve my objective must remain flexible and changeable. A common human tendency, however, is to change the objective—devalue it—if it cannot be reached in the chosen way or by the chosen time. It is much easier, it seems, to devalue an objective than it is to change an elaborate plan that has shown it will not achieve the objective as originally conceived.

It is important to understand what is meant by vision, goal, and objective because collectively they tell us where we are going, the value of getting there, and the probability of success. Too often, however, we "sleeve shop." Sleeve shopping is going into a store to buy a jacket and deciding which jacket we like by the price tag on the sleeve.

The alternative to sleeve shopping is to first determine what I want by the perceived value and purpose of the outcome. Second, I must make the commitment to pay the price, whatever it is. Third, I must determine the price of achieving the outcome. Fourth, I must figure out how to fulfill my commitment—how to pay the price—and make a commitment to keep my commitment. Fifth, I must act on it.

Alexander the Great, the ancient Greek conqueror, provides an excellent example of knowing what one wants and how to achieve it. When he and his troops landed by ship on a foreign shore that he wanted to take, they found themselves badly outnumbered. As the story goes, he sent some men to burn the ships and then ordered his troops to watch the ships burn, after which he told them: "Now we win or die!"

Once I have completed my statement of vision, goals, and objectives, I will be able to answer the following questions concisely: (1) What do I want? (2) Why do I want it? (3) Where do I want it? (4) When do I want it? (5) From whom do I want it? (6) How much (or many) do I want? (7) For how long do I want it (or them)? If a component is missing, I may achieve my desire by default, but not by design.

Only when I can concisely answer all of these questions am I ready for planning. Only then do I know where I want to go, the value of going there, and can calculate the probability of arrival. Next I must determine the cost, make the commitment to bear it, and then commit myself to keeping my commitment.

Although it is we who define our vision, goals, and objectives, it is the land that limits our options, and we must keep these limitations firmly in mind. At the same time, we must recognize that they can be viewed either as obstacles in our preferred path or as solid ground on which to build new paths. Remember, Nature deals in trends over various scales of time. Habitat (food, cover, space, and water) is a common denominator among species; we can use this knowledge to our benefit. Long-term social/environmental sustainability requires that short-term economic goals and objectives be considered within the primacy of environmental postulates and sound long-term ecological goals and objectives.

How might such a process work? As an example, in 1989, I was asked to help the staff of a national forest in New Mexico come to grips with a vision, goals, and objectives for moving their forestry practices toward biological sustainability and hence economic sustainability. In so doing, I had to be very careful of my boundaries, which was sticky because I was, of necessity, wearing three hats.

I helped plan, participated in, and facilitated the outcome of a week-long conference on the management of old-growth timber within a biologically sustainable forest. This conference was requested because of a long-standing and growing conflict, which was becoming increasingly destructive both environmentally and culturally, among conservationists, three groups of Pueblo Indians, Chicanos, Anglos, the timber industry, and the U.S. Forest Service. The conflict was over old-growth forests, logging practices, traditional forest uses by both the Aboriginal Americans and the Chicanos, and changes necessary for sustainable forestry.

The first three days were spent viewing slides accompanying scientific presentations on how a forest and its streams function above- and belowground (soils, water, trees, microbiology, mycology, animals, and people). (Simultaneously with the ecological data, my task was to walk the audience through systems thinking, understanding the consequences of decisions, and how to ecologically and culturally link social/environmental sustainability.) The scientific presentations were followed by presentations from each participating ethnic group, which dealt with their core values and points of view. Throughout this period, there was free and open discussion among the collective group (over fifty people).

During this time, people were asked to look at numbered color photographs on a wall and rank them from the most old-growth-like forest to the least. The participants were also asked to write a short description of what old-growth was to them, including poetry if they wished.

The fourth day was spent in the field with an open discussion in several age classes of forest in which the participants expressed verbally which one(s) felt the most "old-growthy" to them and why. The point was for people to be able to express themselves in whatever way they were most comfortable, and in the process convert the abstractions of the conference room into concrete social/environmental experiences.

The last day was again spent in the field, using a flip chart to come to grips with the notion of a collective vision and goals. Not only did a collective vision and goals gel but also the group agreed to rewrite the forest plan together. This was subsequently accomplished within a few months, as opposed to the year within which the forest supervisor had originally hoped to be able to revise the plan.

During this whole process, there were two detractors, both from the timber industry. Both of these gentlemen thought systems thinking (social/environmental sustainability) was "just philosophy" and beyond the purview of both science and such "emotional things" as visions. The rest of the group, however, outvoted them in the democratic process.

There was another gentleman, however, who purchased timber for one of the companies. After tentative beginnings as the timber industry's representative on the planning committee, he became so caught up in the vision of biologically sustainable forestry that he departed from the industry's hard-line stance. The power of the vision was so great for him that when the company he worked for fired him because he changed his mind and heart, he said that while it was tough and frightening, he felt better about himself. His willingness to give up his job to accommodate his expanding consciousness is the kind of courage that continually strengthens my faith in humanity and in the power of transformative facilitation.

As we build our shared visions of a sustainable future in which each person's core values and expertise are acknowledged, we must exercise the good sense and humility to ask our children, beginning at least with second and third graders, what they think and how they feel about their future.

I say this because I remember that as a child whenever I expressed my opinion about what I thought the world needed to be like or how I wanted it to be, I was inevitably invalidated as being "just a child who knew nothing" and was therefore summarily dismissed. But consider for a moment that the children must inherit the world and its environment as we adults leave it for them. Our choices, our generosity or greed, our morality or licentiousness will determine the circumstances that must become their reality.

Why, then, do adults assume that we know what is best for the children, their children, and their children's children when we are blatantly destroying their world with our blind greed and competitiveness? Why are children never asked what they expect of us as the caretakers and the trustees of the world they must inherit? Why are they never asked what they want us to leave them in terms of environmental quality? Why are they never asked what kinds of choices they would like to be able to make when they grow up? (For that matter, why do we not ask our elders where we have come from, how we are repeating history's mistakes, and what we have lost, such as fundamental human values, along the way?)

Where do we, the adults of the world, get the audacity to assume that we know what is good for our children when all over the world they are being abused at home by parents who are out of control of themselves, are being slaughtered in the streets in the egotistical squabbles of adults over everything imaginable, and are being starved to death by adults using the allocation of food for political gain? We do not even know what is good for us. How can we possibly speak for them?

This lack of responsible care was keenly felt at the June 1992 worldwide Conference on the Environment, held in Rio de Janeiro. A twelve-year-old girl delivered to the entire delegation a most poignant speech about a child's perspective of the adult's environmental trusteeship. I saw a video of the speech in which a child was pleading for a more gentle hand on the environment so that there would be some things of value left for the children of the future. I saw an adult audience moved to tears—but not to action!

In the society of the future, it is going to be increasingly important to listen to what the children say because they represent that which is to come. Children have beginners' minds. To them, all things are possible until adults with narrow minds, who have forgotten how to dream, put fences around their imaginations.

We adults, on the other hand, too often think we know what the answers should be and can no longer see what they might be. To us, whose imaginations were stifled by parents and schools, things have rigid limits of impossibility. We would do well, therefore, to consider carefully not only what the children say is possible in the future but also what they want. The future, after all, is theirs.

Each generation must be the conscious keeper of the generation to come—not its judge. It is therefore incumbent upon us, the adults, to prepare the way for those who must follow. This will entail, among other things, wise and prudent planning, beginning with the idea of sustainable development.

PART II

BEYOND DESTRUCTIVE CONFLICT: SOCIAL/ ENVIRONMENTAL SUSTAINABILITY

Pessimism comes from the repression of creativity.
Otto Rank

Thus far, we have discussed some of the reasons for and the principles of facilitating the resolution of destructive environmental conflicts. As mentioned, I conclude each facilitation by helping the parties create a shared vision for a future in which they can all benefit. I consider the dispute largely, but not entirely, resolved when the vision is completed.

But what is there left to facilitate if the vision is completed? The answer depends on just how functional the parties have become during the facilitation process. In some instances, there is nothing left to facilitate. In others, the parties require help to implement their vision, and that means facilitation. There is still another answer to the question, however, one concerning entire communities.

Not all facilitation revolves around destructive conflict. Sometimes it is required simply to help people, or even entire communities, develop and implement a vision for the future. Circumstantial changes in a community's resource base may require a dramatic shift in its frame of reference, its identity, such as a community built around lumbering when harvestable timber runs out or a coastal town built around commercial fishing when the fish stocks are depleted.

A community's challenge is to change from being narrowly specialized, and therefore dependent on a given resource for its cultural identity and economic survival, to becoming diversified in a sustainable fashion, ecologically, economically, and culturally. For a democratic community to be sustainable, it must be active with intelligence, which means that it must take time to reflect on the meaning, purpose, and direction of its activity. Here, again, facilitation plays a vital role in helping people cope with loss, change, and hope for a more sustainable future.

Instead of focusing on the fear of loss or fear of change by ruminating in the past, facilitation can help a community shift its focus to using change as a fulcrum of hope and choice for a more sustainable direction in the present for the future. Think of a community as a scale in which the balance of people's fears and aspirations tips it either toward the negatives of the past or the potential positives of the future. Then facilitation can become the instrument through which the balance is tipped toward a positive, more sustainable future.

The rest of this book accepts and goes beyond the previously discussed principles of facilitating the resolution of destructive environmental conflicts. Assuming that the initial conflict has been resolved, the rest of this book examines the notion of sustainable community development as a facilitated process. Through the transformative facilitation process, the initial note of short-term social/environmental discord can be turned into one of long-term social/environmental harmony.

10

SUSTAINABLE DEVELOPMENT

by Chris Maser and Christine Kirk

What is sustainable development? In 1992, when *Global Imperative* was published, sustainable development, as expressed in Norwegian Prime Minister Brundtland's report for the World Commission on Environment and Development, was taken to be an oxymoron. It was thought of as being automatically confined to our traditional linear thought process in which it necessarily juxtaposed two mutually exclusive concepts: sustainability and development. In this sense, sustainability was the language of balance and limits over time, whereas development was the language of expansion, of expecting ever-more in some limitless fashion.

Today, however, we perceive sustainable development as a nonlinear process of systems thinking through which the social significance of nonmaterial wealth and qualitative values can be accounted for in social decision making. Sustainable in this context has at least two essential elements: (1) intergenerational equity and the responsibility of the current generation to its own members and to its descendants, and (2) the specification of what is to be sustained. Development, in this context, is a process of directed change, of social evolution if you will. Although we, as a society, do not have many answers, we can find guiding principles for action in the questions we ask. Questions based on a unified world view will bring new answers and spawn new questions.

Development as evolution is a social, psychological transformation that is nevertheless accountable for the effects present decisions cause in the future. When put in the context of sustainability, it becomes a process of change guided by the principles of social and environmental justice—for all living things, not just for humans.

Sustainable development enables us to transcend our crisis in perception because it requires that decisions be based on assumptions different from those of the reductionistic mechanical world view to which we have heretofore subscribed. In basing decisions on a unified world view, society can guide itself toward behaviors and lifestyles that are environmentally sustainable and thereby ensure, to the greatest extent possible, its own cultural sustainability.

SUSTAINABLE DEVELOPMENT WITHIN THE CONTEXT OF OUR WORLD VIEW

A world view has incredible power in directing the way people think. It often seems, for example, that the assumptions embodied in our world view have become so much "second nature" that we are unaware they exist. We perceive them to be absolute truths when in reality they are illusions accepted as truths. We must therefore examine carefully our present, obsolete, mechanistic world view and begin a conscious transition to a world view with a far greater sense of social/environmental sustainability (a unified world view) if our society is to survive the twenty-first century.

Mechanistic World View

Our behavior, the extension of our feelings, thoughts, and values, is out of harmony with the world because we insist on applying a mechanistic world view as it was founded over 300 years ago. Although the mechanistic world view seemed correct in its time and place, the more we study the problems of our time, the more apparent it becomes that the root of our current social/environmental imbalance is a spiritual crisis brought about by our clinging to this mechanistic view and its associated value system. Our clinging to the mechanistic world view has spawned profoundly lopsided and unhealthy ideologies, technologies, institutions, and lifestyles.

Whatever we discuss, be it disease, child abuse, crime, economics, energy shortages, extinction of species, forestry, pollution, or nuclear power, the dynamics are the same: an underlying crisis of perception. The values and attendant assumptions of the mechanistic world view on which we still base our decisions are irrelevant to both the present and the future. Yet our continued acceptance of this world view as the absolute truth and the only valid way to knowledge has led to our current global crises and is propelling us ever closer to social oblivion through environmental destruction.[34]

It should come as no surprise, therefore, that our attempts to "overcome these problems" are part of the exact mindset that created them in the first place. Put differently, yesterday's solutions to yesterday's problems have become today's problems, and today's solutions to today's problems, such as fragmentation, competition, and reactiveness, will become tomorrow's problems. Today's problems are not solvable with our obsolete, mechanistic world view because it is based on dysfunctional thought patterns concerning our current issues and must be transcended.

Today, for instance, we are so focused on our national and personal security that we do not see the price we pay for living in and with dysfunctional bureaucratic organizations where wonder, joy, and the thrill of learning find no dwelling place. Not only are we losing the open, emotionally safe places to dance with the ever-changing patterns of life but also we are continuing to ask the same old, tired questions and thereby limit our imagination and new possibilities.

How did our contemporary world view come about? It was fashioned by such rationalist thinkers as Bacon, Galileo, Descartes, Locke, and Adam Smith.

Francis Bacon (1561–1626), an English philosopher and essayist, felt that through his invention of the "scientific method" humans could disengage themselves from Nature and become objective observers of the natural world. Scientific method, as it is practiced, is a process of thinking that fosters the notion of human superiority over Nature, which in Bacon's view had to be "hounded into service," "put into constraint," and made a "slave." To him, the aim of the scientist was to "torture nature's secrets from her."[34]

Galileo Galilie (1564–1642), an Italian scientist and philosopher, believed that only measurable and quantifiable things—his distinction between "primary" and "secondary" qualities—were "real or relevant" and could be studied.[35]

René Descartes (1596–1650), a French philosopher and mathematician, thought of Nature as a "giant clockwork mechanism," run by mechanical principles that could be understood by disassembling it into small, more manageable pieces and then arranging the pieces in a "logical" order. His primary thesis was the mind/body and human/Nature separation.

John Locke (1632–1704), an English philosopher, saw only utilitarian value in

Nature—its preordained requirement to serve human desires. He believed in the ideals of individualism, rights of private property, and free markets with which the government should not interfere.

Adam Smith (1723–1790), a Scottish political economist and philosopher, provided the rationale for a society where people must compete with one another in pursuit of their own self-interests. He believed that the "Invisible Hand" would guide an individual's self-interest for the betterment of society if only the pursuit of material wealth was protected.[34] While Adam Smith's "Invisible Hand" has spiritual connotations, they are out of keeping with his pursuit of self-interests in the form of material wealth. Further, his notion of a Higher Moral guiding humanity was already overshadowed by the accepted reductionistic mechanical posits of Bacon, Galileo, Descartes, and Locke.

Such rationalistic thinkers as these legitimated and institutionalized the lust of material wealth over which feudal society had so long fought. Thus was born the reductionistic mechanical world view.

Consider the collective paradigm of Francis Bacon, Galileo Galilie, René Descartes, John Locke, and Adam Smith: Nature's sole value is in service to the material desires of humanity. But Nature must be tortured before her secrets will be revealed for human use. Once wrested from Nature, only those things that are measurable and quantifiable are "real" or "relevant" and can be studied. Because "real" things are both measurable and quantifiable, they must operate through linear mechanical principles that can be understood by disassembling the things themselves into smaller and smaller more manageable pieces, which can then be rearranged in an order deemed "logical" to the human mind.

Finally, major segments of human society confer upon themselves the unlimited rights of individual private property for which people must compete with one another in pursuit of their own self-interests. Note that self-interest is to be free from government (local, regional, national, or global) interference because the "Invisible Hand" of moral guidance will temper self-interest in the pursuit of material wealth—for the betterment of society.

The mind/body split and the human/Nature separation are thus the legacy of the mechanistic world view, a view that is ever increasing our sense of isolation from one another and from Nature. This dualism has led us to treat Nature as a commodity from which we are independent and separate. By separating ourselves from Nature, we have justified our trying to control the uncontrollable.

Our analytical perspective involves a four-part process: (1) disarticulate the system into its component parts, (2) study each part in isolation, (3) glean a knowledge of the whole by studying its parts, and (4) rearrange the parts in such a way that they satisfy our human sense of logic. The implicit assumption is that systems are aggregates of interchangeable parts that function in a linear fashion. Thus, by optimizing each part, we optimize the whole. We continually fragment our problems into smaller, more "manageable" pieces while our challenges are increasingly systemic.

Today, fragmentation, which looks at the parts and ignores the whole, continues to disintegrate our social structure by obliterating the sense of a society as a living system. Fragmentation—specialization, special interest groups, and political lobbyists—is the very foundation of today's professionalism, and yet it is making our society increasing ungovernable. The triumph of such reductionist thinking has given rise to a whole set of conditions under which we try to operate in isolation from the system itself.

This kind of fragmentation led quantum physicist David Bohm to say: "Starting with the agricultural revolution, and continuing through the industrial revolution, increasing fragmentation in the social order has produced a progressive fragmentation in our thought." Such fragmentation, for example, is at the very heart of the Catholic Church. According to Elaine Pagels, professor of religion at Princeton University, it was the main strategy used to separate the sect that eventually became *the* church from other early Christian sects espousing different interpretations of Jesus's teachings.[36]

Our social predicament is a legacy of our mechanistic world view, which finds value only in those material things that can be measured and quantified and discounts all spiritual things that defy material valuation. We therefore live in frantic pursuit of fulfillment, but a fulfillment based on substitute gratifications, the material things our culture creates to feed its spiritual emptiness.

The trouble with substitute material gratifications is that we never get enough of what we do not need. In addition, we often do not even know what we are looking for and what we are trying to fill. In our frenzied consumerism to fill our empty spiritual wells, we are blind to the very foundation of our humanness—the qualitative spiritual values of such things as love, trust, respect, and meaningful relationship.

Finally, we must recognize and accept that our communities are microcosms of the larger society. Thus, at the heart of any serious effort to change how communities function lies the need to address the basic dysfunction of our larger culture and vice versa.

The Transition

Having been long steeped in the reductionistic mechanical world view, it is too easy to dismiss as impractical idealism any attempt to refocus from bread-and-butter issues to ideas and processes. Yet our world view is counter to the law of entropy, which says that the current theory of social development, our social trance, is seriously flawed relative to the "real world," a notion repeatedly demonstrated by history and repeatedly ignored by society. People therefore fail to see how their accustomed way of life is based on unviable thoughts rooted deeply within our present-day social trance.

So it is that a different world view, one that brings the material and the spiritual into harmony and heals the mind/body, human/Nature schism, is needed to heal society. Today's clutching at cheap material substitutes for spiritual truth can satisfy only temporarily before setting up the need for more and more cheap material substitutes, the pursuit of which squanders the world's resources. Is there a way out of this morass? Yes.

The answer lies in recognizing the value of relationships and accepting that the only way anything can exist is encompassed in its interdependent and interactive relationship to everything else. As such, every relationship is dynamic, constantly adjusting itself to fit precisely into all other relationships, which consequently are adjusting themselves to fit precisely into every other relationship, and so on *ad infinitum*. The change is from a linear, commodity-oriented thought process to a systems approach where the indicators of health are rooted in the quality of the relationships between and among the parts.

Can so fluid a notion as ever-adjusting relationships be made to work within our current, rigid, mechanistically oriented social construct? The answer is no, because, through self-reinforcing behavioral feedback loops, our present social paradigm condemns change as a condition to be avoided at almost any cost. Nevertheless, the perceived security we have long sought through ever-increasing consumption, militaristic technology, and domination over Nature has actually threatened our long-term social survival. This threat is quickly approaching, if not already here, which prompted Czech President Vaclav Havel to observe: "Without a global revolution in human consciousness a more humane society will not be possible."

If, on the other hand, we have the courage and the willingness to adopt and implement the concept of sustainable development as social evolution in which change is accepted as a process to be embraced, then the notion of ever-adjusting relationships becomes the creative energy that guides a vibrant, adaptable, ever-renewing society through the present toward the future. And because sustainable development honors the integrity of both society and its environment, the outcome is a unified world view in which a system's function defines the system. That is to say that the function defines the composition, which in turn defines the structure, and it is by the visible structure that we tend to characterize a system.

Unified World View

The unified world view is predicated on the notion of holism, in which reality consists of organic and unified wholes that are greater than the simple sum of their parts. The following are basic assumptions on which the unified world view is founded: (1) everything, including humans and nonhumans, is interconnected, interdependent, and interactive; (2) the whole is greater than the sum of its parts; (3) processes have primacy over components; (4) the integrity of the environment and its ecological processes has primacy over human desires when such desires would destroy the system's integrity for future generations; (5) Nature determines the limitations of human endeavors; (6) the relevancy of knowledge depends on its context; (7) the disenfranchised as well as future generations have rights that must be accounted for in present decisions and actions; and (8) nonmonetary relationships have value.[37]

In the unified world view, the behavior of a system depends on how individual parts *interact* as functional components of the whole—as opposed to what each isolated part is doing—because the whole is understood through the relation/interaction of its parts. To understand a system, therefore, we need to understand how it fits into the larger system of which it is a part. This gives us a view of systems supporting systems supporting systems, *ad infinitum*. We thus move from the primacy of the parts to the primacy of the whole, from insistence on absolute knowledge as truth to the relatively coherent interpretations of constantly changing knowledge, from isolated self to self in community, and from attempting to solve old problems to creating new concepts.

In a unified world view, individual people—as well as their relationships among one another, Nature, and their communities—both have value and are valued, as are all living beings. It is this combined sense of personal value and contributive value that makes sustainable development a workable proposition for the present and into the future.

SUSTAINABLE DEVELOPMENT: A CONSCIOUS PROCESS OF SELF-DETERMINATION AND SOCIAL EVOLUTION

The problems in our communities cannot be isolated. Nor can they be understood without first understanding their context. This means that one must understand the various parts of a community and their interactions before one can understand why something is the way it is.

In developing this understanding, process has primacy over the parts because process directs the outcome, the function of each part. A part does not control the process, although it may influence it.

In placing development within a new context of thinking, the answers to such questions as "what is poverty" will be very different than they are today. If a lifestyle promotes sustainability through self-provisioning and recognizes the relationships between one's own sustenance and the livelihood of the planet, that life is not necessarily perceived as one of poverty. This leaves the way open to change the indicators of poverty.

Progress, therefore, would be any action that moves society towards social/environmental sustainability. For society to progress, decisions must be made that recognize and respect the requirements and rights of future generations, as well as the requirements and intrinsic value of all species and the Earth's carrying capacity with respect to its human population. (Carrying capacity is the number of individuals that can live in and use a particular landscape without impairing its ability to function in an ecologically specific way.) This position is very different from our blind faith in material progress.

We must recognize and accept that ignorance and unknown outcomes do not give us a right to continue blindly along our present course in the name of material progress. Rather, it is our responsibility to move cautiously in order to minimize our effects on our home planet.

Sustainable development is thus about the notions of "enoughness" and "reversibility." Here the operative questions are: "When is enough enough?" and "If we err in our decision, is the outcome reversible?" Such questions are crucial because sustainable development is necessary to promote a change in the content of social/environmental decisions. What is needed to resolve our social/environmental problems goes beyond environmentally safe commodity production and technology.

Instead of the current tinkering with symptoms of our social/environmental malaise, problems must be solved at their source—world view assumptions and values—because these drive our decisions, policies, and plans. Sustainable development therefore questions the very purpose of society and our participation with our home planet and demands social/environmental justice, which challenges the very heart of our perceived relationship with Nature and one another.

We as planetary citizens must learn to think at least seven generations ahead when making decisions because the great and only gift we have to give those who follow is potential choices and some things of value from which to choose.

Today's decisions become tomorrow's consequences, a notion that highlights the word "responsibility." Responsibility is a double-edged sword in that our responsibility, our moral obligation, is to choose carefully today so that the generations to come can respond viably to the circumstances we have created for their time of choice. Intelligent decisions on our part are possible only when we both recognize and accept the intrinsic value of Nature as a living organism rather than accepting Nature only as a collective resource from whose body we extract a variety of commodities as the life blood of our dysfunctional, linear economic system.

Development must be flexible and open to community definition because the values promoted must meet various needs and situations while safeguarding sustainability. The process of valuation embodied in sustainable development addresses social/environmental justice in recognizing the necessity of equal access to resources as well as equal distribution of goods and services while simultaneously protecting the long-term ecological sustainability of the system that produces them.

Sustainable development also addresses the need to promote education and feelings of self-worth in people, allowing them to act as catalysts in the process of change, whether in their own lives or in the life of society. For change to be a creative process, each person must respect every other person as well as the intrinsic value of his or her environment.

Finally, the valuation/decision process through which sustainable development works must flow within and promote the democratic frame of reference because democracy only works when it is actually practiced. In this sense, most of the change must be directed by the people from the bottom up—the grass roots.

AT WHAT SCALE IS SUSTAINABLE DEVELOPMENT POSSIBLE?

Thinking about the scale at which sustainable development is possible calls to mind a catchphrase: think globally; act locally. But when considering the global community from an individual's standpoint, helping to heal the world seems like a hopeless task, even an unintelligible abstraction. Yet as people come to understand their effect on the global community and the effect of their world view, they want to do something to change the worn-out paradigm. If global and national strategies are abstractions too far removed from the average person's realm of experience, at what level can they act and be effective? What will make people act at any level?

Sustainable development must be implemented where people are able to learn, feel, and be empowered to act—at the local level. Sustainable development must be integrated into policies and decisions in local communities where people have the power to effect change and make decisions based on a unified world view, one that begins healing the environment in the present for the future.

Here, as he so often does, author Wendell Berry cuts to the core: "That will-o'-the-wisp of the large-scale solution to the large-scale problem, so dear to governments and universities and corporations, serves mostly to distract people from the small, private problems that they may in fact have the power to solve. The problems, if we describe them accurately, are all private and small. Or they are so initially."[38] It is thus imperative that we address the fundamental causes of our problems at their roots—our thinking and behavior at the local community level—or we will always be dealing with symptoms and band-aid solutions that compound the problem by denying the cure.

LOCAL COMMUNITY DEVELOPMENT

by Chris Maser and Christine Kirk

A local human community is a group of people with similar interests living under and exerting some influence over the same government in a shared locality. They have a common attachment to their place of residence, where they have some degree of local autonomy. People in a community share social interactions with one another and organizations beyond government and through such participation are able to satisfy the full range of their daily requirements within the local area. The community also interacts with the larger society, both in creating change and in reacting to it. Finally, the community as a whole interacts with the local environment, molding the landscape within which it rests and is in turn molded by it.

It is important to recognize that community components will change when the social focus shifts from the reductionistic mechanical world view to a unified one, examples of which still exist in the few remaining unspoiled aboriginal cultures. When the world view becomes unified, people will realize that they are but one species among the many, and a new sense of community will encompass all living things, including soils, within the common area.

As yet, however, we are so overdependent on and mesmerized by competition that it is our only model for learning and change. Historically, our vision has been directed by competition. There is nothing intrinsically wrong with competition; it can even be fun and promote invention and daring. Our problem is that we have lost the balance among competition, cooperation, and coordination at precisely the time we most need to work with one another. We thus find ourselves oftentimes competing with the very people with whom we need to collaborate.

In a unified world view, a local community serves five purposes:[39] (1) social participation—where and how people are able to interact with one another to create the relationships necessary for a feeling of value and self-worth; (2) mutual aid—services and support offered in times of individual or familial need; (3) economic production, distribution, and consumption—jobs, import and export of products, as well as the availability of such commodities as food and clothing in the local area; (4) socialization—educating people about cultural values and acceptable norms; and (5) social control—the means for maintaining those cultural values and acceptable norms.

With the current disintegration of family and community in American life, it is unlikely that most people in this country really have an intimate sense of belonging. We have largely lost our sense of connection to and with community. Much of this lack of community may result from our lopsided mechanistic world view in which material possessions take the place of spirituality, as manifested in quality relationships and mutual caring. If, however, human society and its environment are ever to become sustainable, it is necessary to rediscover or recreate our sense of local community in order to balance the material with the spiritual, which is the essential balance required in a unified world view.

IS LOCAL COMMUNITY THE APPROPRIATE SCALE FOR SUSTAINABLE DEVELOPMENT?

Through the concept and practice of local community, people can empower themselves and support one another through decisions that promote a sustainable world as well as increase their quality of life. Within a local community, people can act as the force driving change in their political system even as they change their lifestyles. Through their actions, people partake in guiding destiny, despite the fact that a local community is part of a larger more impersonal governmental system.

Local community governments, as opposed to county, state, or national governments, have both a greater degree of understanding and the interaction necessary to amend local problems, such as land use, waste reduction, political representation, and education. They are therefore better able to implement and adjust to aspects of sustainability in the social/environmental arena.

People both define their local communities and are defined by them in that communities play a primary role in maintaining cultural values within and among generations. The collective of individual values determines familial values; the collective of familial values determines community values and determines what appropriate behavior, poverty, and success are. As we are growing up and are taught at home, educated in schools, and participate in community, socialization occurs, norms are set, and societal control takes place.

People make most of their decisions, do most of their consuming and waste production, and develop many personal relationships within their local community. It is not surprising, therefore, that lifestyle becomes a political issue.

Citizens at the local level can also begin drawing connections between personal consumption and its effects on local, regional, and global economic well-being and environmental health. Although political pressure must be exerted continuously on national governments, both at home and abroad, lifestyles in each and every local community have direct and immediate effects on the biosphere.[40]

Local communities, through their collective effects on world society, act as catalysts for change in local, regional, state, and national communities and finally in the world itself. Through the behavior of their individuals, they contribute greatly to environmental health and the global climate. And because we as individuals collectively comprise local communities, which in the collective comprise regional, state, and national communities, we can heal our global environment simply by changing our individual behaviors.

Local communities, as the force that drives change for better or worse, are thus the appropriate scale for dealing with sustainable development. Before discussing sustainable development, however, we must understand local community development.

UNDERSTANDING LOCAL COMMUNITY DEVELOPMENT

Local community development is a process of organization, facilitation, and action that allows people to help create a community in which they *want* to live. It is a process in which the ideals of sustainable development can be implemented by both allowing and encouraging people to act as catalysts for sustainable change.

Local Community Development

Local community development may well be the instrument through which people can create the means to invigorate society. Given the current state of our economy, politics, disintegrating families, social relations, sense of security, and the confused condition of our guiding values, it may be that community development, which is the democratic process at the local level of our domestic lives, is the best opportunity for applying the democratic process.[41]

Community development is the mechanism through which people empower themselves by increasing their ability to control their own lives in order to create a more fulfilling existence through mutual efforts to resolve shared problems. Community development works on the belief that through collective action people can successfully resolve their issues as well as organize and implement change. It thus promotes a sense of accomplishment and belonging through shared learning and service.

Another way local community development enhances people's potential is by helping them dissolve barriers. Barriers can be dissolved by bringing all parties affected into the decision-making process. While prejudice and a sense of inequality suppress relationships among people due to their perceived differences, community development helps them learn to cope collectively with the many problems affecting their lives by uniting them in common cause when they might not otherwise choose to associate with one another.

Because local community development is a democratic process that works only when it is accessible to and implemented by the majority of the population, it is necessary to involve as many members of a community as possible in the process of improving democracy through participation. The more diverse the participants in the democratic process of community development, the more accurately the community will be represented, the greater will be the sense of equality in rights and duties, and the truer the outcome. Local people are thus empowered by acting collectively through organizations to influence decisions, policies, programs, and projects that affect them as a community.

The important word here is "empowerment," which addresses people's perceived capacity to influence decisions that affect their lives through active participation in and hence improvement of the democratic process. Central to the notion of empowerment is people's willingness to accept responsibility for their own behavior, first by overcoming interpersonal barriers and learning to work with one another for a greater good and second by directing formal authority within the democratic process. To accomplish the foregoing, it is usually necessary to engage the facilitation process.

Local Community Development and the Local Economy

Community development and economic development differ in that economic development is only one aspect of community development just as economy is only one aspect of community. Economic development works to increase activity and stability in the production, distribution, and consumption of products and services within a community, but that is not enough. According to economists Robert Constanza and Herman E. Daly: "To effect a true synthesis of economics and ecology [and hence community] is the second most important task of our generation, next to avoiding nuclear war. Without such an integration we will gradually despoil the capacity of the earth to support life. Gradual despoilation is certainly preferable to destroying it all at once in a nuclear war, but is still an unhappy prospect."[42]

Thus, while it is important to recognize that economic development contributes to community stability, its primary focus is to increase economic activity within the local area through business retention, expansion, and attraction, as well as job training. It must of course be recognized that economic development within the context of sustainable community development must be in harmony both with the productive capacity and integrity of the environment over time and with human dignity and a sense of well-being. Community development, on the other hand, focuses on increasing socialization, mutual aid, economic activity, social participation, and control, which in turn increases the social, educational, and cultural stability of a community.

Community development—planning the local process (vision, goals, and objectives)—is a necessary step to undertake before an economic development plan can be successfully implemented. This becomes clear when a community tries to identify its vision and goals for a business plan, which must be related to and interact with all aspects of community development. Many skills are necessary to organize people, run meetings, and facilitate the creation of a vision, goals, and objectives with which to draft a business plan, which then must be implemented and monitored.

Citizen input and local control of the economic process are as vitally important to the long-term integrity, solidarity, and stability of a community as are the locally owned, diversified businesses themselves. Because community development seeks to create a unique circumstance in which human and economic sustainability are mutually reinforcing, the economic content of community development must be carefully thought out and skillfully integrated within the social content.

It is therefore improbable that large, absentee-owned businesses are a realistic answer to local employment needs because such owners are seldom committed to the welfare of the community. They are unlikely to purchase local products, hire local people, or contribute to and remain loyal to the community in difficult times. The question then becomes: how sustainable is community development?

The Sustainability of Local Community Development

Community development as a tool does not in and of itself promote sustainability. No one is safe from the many environmental and social problems that threaten our planet and our health, but we are not all endangered equally. In light of this thought, consider today's notion that local cultures must change and adapt to national and international influences—influences that promote and produce nonsustainable activities and results.

For example, a timber company exporting whole logs from local forests to Japan or a sawmill owner installing state-of-the-art equipment to reduce the number of employees while increasing production of milled lumber for shipment to Japan and other Pacific Rim countries may help short-term economic stability but simultaneously fosters a local community's dependency on outside markets and their influences. Through such activities, communities become increasingly dependent on external markets and political forces over which they have decreasing amounts of control. Under such circumstances, the importance of the local people and their shared place declines in the face of outside influences. Unfortunately, this is happening in virtually all societies because of the mechanistic cookie-cutter ideas about progress and development.

Consider the native forest in Cergov, northern Slovakia, which was being clearcut to benefit areas outside the local communities. Prior to importing the technology of clearcutting, the forest of Cergov was logged with horses. Horse logging, even under the benign neglect of the early Communist regime, had been biologically sustainable for centuries and so too had been the cultures and economies of the small mountain villages. Now in the villages, located in the upper valleys near the edge of the forest, the jobs once sustained by horse logging are gone, as is the topsoil.

Today, because of the uncritical acceptance of outside technology as the panacea of short-term national economic problems, the local people who once made their living from the local forest must commute to the cities to find work, and the villages have lost—perhaps forever—part of their cultural heritage. These are but two of the costs of imported technology used blindly for short-term economic gain.

From these examples it should be clear that community development is only as sustainable as the values, perceptions, and questions that drive it. Here one might ask what community and sustainability have in common. Their commonality is that both must abide by and enhance the local culture over time.

SUSTAINABLE COMMUNITY DEVELOPMENT

As we have discussed, local community development is a process of educating, organizing, and acting, which empowers local people to influence their destiny through self-determined democratic governance. What happens if we now add the notion of sustainability to the equation?

Bear in mind that there is little real chance of moving forward without communities of people and dynamic leaders who are genuinely committed to sustainable types of change. The search for quick fixes usually results in superficial changes with respect to some problematic symptom but leaves untouched the deeper cause of the symptom. The nature of the commitment, which encompasses the need for change in the larger world, uses our local communities as vehicles for bringing about such change, which necessitates the willingness to learn.

Real learning—the remembrance of things forgotten and the development of things new—occurs in a continuous cycle over time. Learning encompasses theoretical conceptualization, practical conceptualization, action, and reflection, including equally the realm of the intellect and that of the intuition. Real learning is important because overemphasis on action, one part of which is competition, simply reinforces our fixation on short-term quantifiable results. Our overemphasis on action precludes the required discipline of reflection, which is a persistent practice of deeper learning that often produces measurable consequences for long periods of time.

As previously stated, many of today's problems resulted from yesterday's solutions, and many of today's solutions are destined to become tomorrow's problems. This simply means that our quick-fix social trance blinds us because we insist on little ideas that promote fast results regardless of what happens to the system itself. What society really needs are big, systemic ideas that both promote and safeguard social/environmental sustainability.

Where, asked the late publisher Robert Rodale, are the big ideas, those that change the world? They probably lie unrecognized in everyday life because our culture lacks sufficient free spaces for general thought.

A big idea, according to Bob Rodale, has the following characteristics: (1) it must be generally useful in good ways, (2) it must appeal to generalists and give them an advantage over specialists, (3) it must exist in both an abstract and a practical sense, (4) it must be of some interest at all levels of human concern,

(5) it must be geographically and culturally viable over extensive areas, (6) it must encompass a multitude of academic disciplines, and (7) it must have a life over an extended period of time.[43]

Let's see if sustainable community development could be such a big idea. Local community development is a tool that is subject to the beliefs of those who use it. The context—the shared vision—that guides the process of local community development determines the outcome. Sustainable community development therefore places local community development within the context of sustainability.

Development as a process means building capacity, and community development means building the capacity of people to work collectively in addressing their common interests in the local society.[44] Sustainable community development means building the capacity of people to work collectively in addressing their common interests in the local society within the context of sustainability—that which is sustainable biologically, culturally, and economically.

Sustainable community development is therefore a community-directed process of development that is based on: (1) transcendent human values of love, trust, respect, wonder, humility, and compassion; (2) sharing generated through communication, cooperation, and coordination; (3) a capacity to understand and work with the flow of life as a fluid system, recognizing the significance of relationships; (4) patience in seeking an understanding of a fundamental issue rather than applying band-aid-like quick-fixes to a symptom of a problem; (5) consciously integrating the learning space into the working space into a continual cycle of theory, experimentation, action, and reflection; and (6) a shared societal vision that is grounded in long-term sustainability, both culturally and environmentally.

Sustainable community development seems to fit all of Rodale's requirements. It also helps people to understand that life is not condensable, that any model is an operational simplification, a working hypothesis that is always ready for and in need of improvement. With the understanding that there are neither short-cuts nor concrete facts, communication functions as a connective tool for invention, cooperation, and coordination.

When people speak from their hearts and unite through active listening, they produce tremendous power to invent new realities and bring them into being through collective actions. Thus, while today's environmental users with special interests will not all be around in the next century, all of the environmental uses and all of the sustainable local communities can be if we achieve sustainable development at the local community level as a "big idea."

Sustainable Community Development Means Change as a Local Creative Process

The time for sustainable development in local communities is fast approaching because citizens all over the United States, indeed the world, are realizing that *they* must take the lead in addressing their own social/environmental problems rather than waiting for their leaders to limply take the initiative. As a society, however, we have largely chosen to waste time pointing fingers at universities, agencies, and Congress, rather than risk taking charge of our own destinies.

Nevertheless, many people, regardless of their particular walks in life, are awakening to the need for change. People are realizing that their democratic society is changing and will continue to change without them unless they begin actively participating in the process of governance. They are awakening to their own powers of self-support and self-management. Given their own tools, local communities are more effective in defining and meeting their own needs, at lower costs, than are any government or private service providers, and so begins a populist movement.

A populist movement reaches its peak whenever the fundamental institutions of a nation (large corporations and organized religions, as well as the federal government) consolidate vast powers but collapse inwardly from corruption and collusion among policy and business elites. Real issues are then ignored or weakly addressed through a series of political charades, because while science and media thrive on controversy, politics is paralyzed by it.

For example, current public environmental debates are so politicized that we become preoccupied with relatively minor details, which causes us to run around looking for knowledge while we are drowning in information. This happens whenever we fail to proceed from a basic frame of reference that allows us to focus on the fundamental issues and real reforms without getting lost in a confusion of isolated details.

Although most people admit that far-sighted, far-reaching reforms are urgently needed, the shallowness of political dialogue causes public cynicism and feelings of being manipulated. Thus, in an atmosphere of growing crises, local communities discover that they must resolve their own problems—the very basis of sustainable community development.

In the community development process, values are shared and learned. The question is not whether we transmit values, because we do; the question is what values we transmit and how.[44] The values that need to be learned and transmitted in order to move toward sustainability are those of a unified world view: values of love, dignity, relationship, equality, compassion, justice, respect, democracy, responsibility, and process.

These values, which underlie sustainable development, can be transmitted and implemented through education, self-actualization, self-help, and collective action—the process of local community development. There are, however, no teachers with correct answers; there are only guides, such as facilitators, with different areas of expertise and experience that may help along the way.

Through community development, a process is created that provides a suite of applied strategies for bringing about change in such a way that tools are available for public adoption and use. By placing the community development process within the context of sustainability—shifting from a reductionistic mechanical world view to a unified systems way of thinking—one builds a description and analysis of change as a process based on sustainable values and aspirations.

Placing the process of change within the realm of sustainability directs local communities towards a better understanding of the effects of individual and collective participation within the community itself and on its immediate environment within its surrounding landscape. It also encourages people to change from nonsustainable activities to sustainable ones.

A prerequisite for working towards sustainable outcomes from decision making and developmental action is to increase people's awareness of: (1) their connection to one another within their local community, (2) their communal connection to their immediate environment and its surrounding landscape, and (3) their community's place within the larger regional, state, national, and global communities. As people come to understand and feel their role as a contributor to the many issues that we as a society face, the need for action and change will become increasingly powerful.

People's sense of empowerment and belief in their potential to resolve problems is crucial to sustainable community development. People are a powerful catalyst for change both as activists within their local communities and as examples in changing their behaviors to promote more sustainable lifestyles. Such change relies on creativity, which is fragile and easily stifled. It is therefore the facilitator's task to encourage and protect each person's creativity during the facilitation process.

When people are inspired by their own interests and enjoyment, there is a better chance they will explore unlikely paths, take risks, and produce something that in the end is useful. Motivation is internal to people themselves. So, while people must motivate themselves, they can be helped to analyze, understand, and use their own experiences to new and greater ends. This brings up a Chinese proverb: "I hear and I forget; I see and I remember; I do and I understand." In this sense, people are not trained; they are liberated and train themselves, providing examples for others.

When goals are imposed on them, however, or when they are goaded by fear of firing, creativity withers. Sustainable community development therefore depends on intrinsic motivation, which is conducive to creativity.

Although our larger social system is designed to insist on conformity, to go along with mass thinking, local sustainable community development by its very nature is designed as an advocate and protector of the freedom and space necessary for creativity to flourish. The single most important component of creativity is freedom—the power to decide what to do and how to do it, a sense of control over one's own ideas and work. "Genius," according to inventor Thomas Alva Edison, "is 1 percent inspiration and 99 percent perspiration." His observation seems to be true. To physicist Albert Einstein, what genius needs most is the freedom of pursuit.

Because many local issues can and must be addressed simultaneously through the process of sustainable community development, it is a potentially powerful strategy for change. By addressing the needs and concerns of both individuals and community groups, it increases the solidarity and adaptability of a local community, which means that the issues on which a community focuses become increasingly centered within the context of long-term sustainability.

Long-term social/environmental sustainability is a consciously directed process within the democratic system; it is the development phase of a sustainable community. The development process begins with the creation of a shared vision and goals. Grasping a shared vision creates momentum, which demands a well-conceived strategy to achieve that vision. Such a strategy must include clearly communicated directions and workable means that enable everyone to participate initially in creating the development plans and later in being publicly accountable for achieving them.

The development process, however it evolves, is important because only through it can people participate in a shared vision of the future. If we cannot share a vision for the future towards which to build, then we are, as professor Aldo Leopold wrote in 1933, confronted by a contradiction: "To build a better motor we tap the uttermost powers of the human brain; to build a better countryside we throw dice."

Local people who empower themselves to work together in tapping the utmost powers of their minds and developing their own sustainable community will reap the following benefits:

1. A defined course of action, which helps ensure that the selected course has a good chance of success.

2. A process that serves as the foundation on which all community activities are based and, as such, must result in answers to what, where, when,

why, and how actions are to be taken and who will conduct the actions for whom. If these questions are answered in a manner satisfactory to all, the chance of a destructive conflict is greatly reduced, but if perchance conflict arises, it can usually be resolved, often within the context of sustainable community development.

3. A well-conceived plan that allows those responsible to determine what they are responsible for and provides people with the opportunity to gain a clear insight with respect to their specific tasks in relationship to the function of a community as a whole.
4. A process that helps a particular group of people communicate to others that the group is thoughtful in what it is doing and stands a good chance of accomplishing its stated purpose.
5. A process that will aid in monitoring and evaluating a community and its achievements.
6. A periodic evaluation of a group's progress towards meeting its vision, goals, and objectives identified in the plan, which is critical for evaluating whether it is providing the promised services to its customers and supporters. This step is essential for the health and growth of any community or organization within a community.
7. A vehicle through which the collective long-range (100+-year) vision of the people involved with a community can be realized. Planning, which is looking at options and solutions, helps people focus their energy on their vision, goals, and objectives and thereby helps a community achieve maximum utilization of its human talents and financial resources.
8. A process that helps people to influence what the present is and the future might be for the benefit of both today's citizens and tomorrow's generations.

In addition to all the goals, parameters, and legal requirements embedded in the planning process, it is fundamental that facilitators and leaders endorse the concept of persons, which begins with recognition and understanding of people's diversity in their gifts, talents, and skills.

The Role of Local Government

A prerequisite for sustainable development in a local community is that it must be inclusive, relating all relevant disciplines and special professions from all walks of life. Setting a good example is one of the most important functions of any local government involved in implementing the principles and practices of sustainable community development. Leading by example—breaking down bureaucratic barriers through interdisciplinary crossing of departmental lines, recycling and buying recycled goods, providing day care, car pooling, flexible working hours—increases not only the capacity of a government to govern but also its effectiveness *and* efficiency.

It is thus important for governments to both identify departmental and community links concerning mutually interrelated issues and to bring all people affected to the table in an effort to collectively resolve shared problems, which means dealing with human diversity. Understanding and accepting diversity allows us to acknowledge that each of us has a need to be needed, to contribute in some way. It also enables us to begin admitting that we do not and cannot know or do everything and that we must rely on the strengths of others with complete trust.

For example, in writing this book, Chris is the first to acknowledge that the quality of the outcome, the difference between good and excellent, is not in his writing, but rather in the reviewers' comments and in the final editing. Nine people reviewed the manuscript before it ever went to the publisher, each adding his or her own gift to the quality of the outcome.

Four reviewers challenged the concepts, each selecting different ones; another helped balance the use of abstract and concrete examples. One reviewer was particularly adept at finding typos and misspellings and another at focusing on the clarity and economy of sentence structure. Two reviewers were concerned with the overall tenor of the message and three suggested organizational changes in the presentation.

Diversity of thought, culture, and expertise thus allows all persons to contribute to the development process in a special way, making their unique gift a part of the effort necessary to create a sustainable local community. Accepting diversity helps us to understand the need each person has for equality, identity, and opportunity in the process. Recognizing diversity gives us all a chance to provide meaning, fulfillment, purpose, and a gift of our talents to our community and future generations.

Assuming people accept the notion of diversity, what is it that they most want from the development process? People want the most effective, productive, and rewarding way of working together to achieve a common end. They want the process and the relationships forged therein to meet their personal needs for belonging, meaningful contribution, having the opportunity to make a commitment to a special place—their community, having the opportunity for personal growth, and having the ability to exert reasonable control over their destinies.

Increasing Local Adaptability

Societies around the globe are in the throws of change, some because of diminishing resources and others because of social upheaval, but all are losing control over their destinies. Regardless of the cause, sustainable local community development provides vision, planning, and direction in times of crisis as well as in times of peace.

The focus of the local government under the auspices of sustainable community development must be on balancing the ability of a community to meet its own needs and to maintain relative economic stability as outside markets fluctuate, all the while protecting the ability of future generations to meet their needs in the same area. Sustainable community development works to maintain a dynamic equilibrium through consciously directed, systemic, self-reinforcing feedback loops. It offers a process that can mobilize citizens to direct information towards long-term community sustainability, which in some measure equates to the economic stability of a local community.

Sustainable community development increases the adaptability of a community by creating and maintaining a diversified social and economic base with local shared ownership and access to basic human services. Community adaptability, and therefore stability, is based on its ability to meet the majority of its own needs within itself instead of being dependent on outside resources. This means, however, that the adaptability of a community also encompasses the ecological integrity of its surrounding landscape (to be discussed later in this chapter).

Improving Citizen Participation

A vitally important component of sustainable community development is local citizen participation in planning, implementing, and monitoring programs, policies, and projects. The goal is to improve the quality of popular participation instead of merely its quantity.

Sustainable community development is based on the assumption that the best ideas usually come from the people, not the policy makers. Therefore, active participation in a local community is necessary to direct the process, which means, for example, taking part in citizen administrative boards, in town hall meetings, and through local grass roots activities.

As a process, sustainable community development exposes citizens to the ramifications of their thoughts and actions on others, their local environment, and the surrounding landscape, as well as motivating and organizing people to direct change. Its aim is for citizens to control the developmental process by feeding ideas and information to the governing body through self-empowered organizations.

People want the most effective development process possible, one that is honestly used through participation in a truly democratic way. Participative development must begin with a firm belief in the potential of people. It arises both out of a leader's heart and his or her personal commitment to people and out of the heart of the democratic principle: the right to an open, accessible process; the right and duty to influence decision making; and the right and duty to understand the results.

To accomplish participative development, leaders must create and maintain emotionally safe environments within which people can develop quality relationships with one another. Creating such an environment requires at least five things: (1) respect for one another; (2) understanding and accepting that what people believe precedes policy and practice; (3) agreement on the rights of participation in and access to the planning process; (4) understanding that most people work as volunteers and need personal covenants, not legal contracts; and (5) understanding that relationships count more than structure because people—not structures—build trust.

The development team's needs are best met by meeting the needs of its individuals. If this is done, development can be productive, rewarding, meaningful, maturing, enriching, fulfilling, healing, and joyful. Participative development is one of the greatest privileges in our democracy and one of our greatest responsibilities.

Nevertheless, the creative development process is difficult to handle because in such a process almost everyone at different times and in various ways plays four roles: one as creator, another as implementor, a third as temporary leader with a specific expertise demanded by a given circumstance, and finally as follower, supporter, and helper.

Although implementation is often as creative as the questions to which it is responding, it is at this very point that leaders and managers may find it most difficult to be open to the influence of others. Nevertheless, by conceiving a shared vision and pursing it together, a local community's problems of cultural adaptability and sustainable development can be resolved, and the community members may simultaneously and fundamentally alter their concept of adaptability, sustainability, and development. But this requires "joint ownership" of the development process.

The heart of sustainable development is joint ownership of the process for each person involved. Because owners cannot walk away from concerns, everyone's accountability begins to change. Ownership demands increasing maturity on everyone's part, which is probably best expressed in a continually rising level of literacy: participative literacy, ownership literacy, sustainable development literacy, and so on. And ownership demands a commitment to be as informed as possible about the whole.

Joint ownership is an intimate, personal experience in that each person commits himself or herself not only to the process but also to the outcome. One's beliefs are connected to the intimacy of one's experience and come before and have primacy over policies, standards, or practices. This intimate, personal commitment to the development process affects one's accountability and draws out one's personal authenticity.

No development process can amount to anything without the people who make it what it is. It is initially what the people are and finally what the people become. People do not grow by knowing all the answers; they grow by living with the questions and their possibilities. The art of working together thus lies in how people deal with change, how they deal with conflict, and how they reach their potential.

The intimacy of ownership arises from translating personal and community values into a plan for a sustainable future that seeks its excellence in a search for truth, wisdom, justice, and knowledge—all tempered with intuition and compassion. The people of a community must therefore make a covenant, a promise with one another: to honor and protect the sacred nature of their relationships so that each may reflect unity, grace, poise, creativity, and justice. If they base decisions on the intrinsic value of human diversity, and if they base decisions on the notion that every person brings a unique offering to the development process, then inclusivity will be the only path open to them.

Including people—really including people—in the development process means helping them to understand the process, their place within it, and their accountability for the outcome. It means giving others the chance to do their best according to the diversity of their gifts, which is fundamental to the equality that environmental justice requires and democracy inspires. Finally, a community must be committed to using wisely and responsibly its environment and its finite resources, which means a conscious, sustainable, reciprocal relationship between the local community and its surrounding landscape.

To create the desired change, however, it is essential that all affected groups in the community are involved in the process. It is further necessary that the people responsible for a local program, policy, or project be involved in its creation and monitoring to increase the probability of a successful outcome, because sustainable community development is initially site specific.

Sustainable Community Development in Relation to Its Landscape

Sustainability means that development programs must, to the extent possible, integrate the local people's requirements, desires, motivations, and identity in relation to the surrounding landscape. It also means that local people, those responsible for development initiatives and their effect on the immediate environment and the surrounding landscape, must participate equally and fully in all debates and discussions from the local level to the national.[45] Here, a basic principle is that programs must be founded on local requirements and cultural values in balance with those of the broader outside world.

Some time ago, Chris attended a meeting on the development of rural communities in which economic diversification was the sole focus of discussion. It soon became apparent that the group had no idea of the importance of landscape to the identity of a community. For example, a logging community is set within a context of forest; a ranching community is set within the context of lands for grazing, often grasslands or shrub-steppe; and a community of commercial fishers is usually set along a coastline, be it a great lake or an ocean.

The setting of a community helps define the community because people select a community for what it has to offer them within the context of its landscape. The setting therefore helps create many characteristics that are unique to the community. By the same token, the values and development practices of a community alter the characteristics of its surrounding environment.

In addition to the surrounding environment, the constructed environments within a community are also part of its setting and therefore its identity. This includes the buildings, zoning, design of transportation systems, and the allowance of natural occurrences within the structured setting.

In turn, a community's world view defines its collective values, which in turn determines how it treats its surrounding landscape. As the landscape is altered through wise use or through abuse, so are the community's options altered in like measure. A community and its landscape are thus engaged in a mutual, self-reinforcing feedback loop as the means by which their processes reinforce themselves and each other.

Each community has physical, cultural, and political qualities that make it unique and more or less flexible. The degree of flexibility of these attributes in a community is important because sustainable systems must be ever flexible, adaptable, and creative.[46] The process of sustainable community development must therefore remain flexible, because what works in one community may not work in another or may work for different reasons. Beyond this, the power of sustainable community development comes from the local people as they move forward through a process of growing self-realization, self-definition, and self-determination. Such personal growth opens the community to its own evolution within the context of the people's sense of place, as opposed to coercive pressures applied from the outside.

Sustainable community development encompasses any process that helps people meet their requirements, from self-worth to food on the table, while simultaneously creating a more ecologically and culturally sustainable and just society for the current generation and those that follow. Due to its flexibility and openness, it is perhaps more capable than other forms of development in creating such outcomes because it integrates the requirements of a local community with those of the immediate environment and surrounding landscape, while instilling a relative balance between the local community and the larger world of which it is a part.

With this in mind, it is imperative that local communities not only consider but also involve their surrounding landscapes in all aspects of sustainable development because the spatial patterns of topography and vegetation result from complex interactions among physical, biological, and social forces. For example, in the vicinity of Taos, New Mexico, the Pueblos (Aboriginal Americans) had long used the surrounding old-growth piñion pine forest for both food (its seeds) and firewood. Then the Spanish invaded the area and also began using old-growth pine for firewood. It became traditional.

Later the Anglos invaded and the population grew. Since old-growth piñion pine was the best firewood, everyone wanted an equal share. In recent years, however, there has been a great influx of retired Anglos from Texas and southern California, most wanting their "fair share" of the firewood.

The result of this continual and growing onslaught on the slow-growing, centuries-old piñion pine forest is the potential for its imminent demise, because there is relatively little of it left. Along with the biological decline of the old-growth forest surrounding Taos is the rapidly growing problem of air pollution from the continual increase in wood smoke.

The people of Taos, by ignoring the reciprocal nature of the participation of their community with its surrounding landscape, are seeing the cultural ambiance of the town's setting fading into history with its rapid growth in population, increased cutting of the old-growth piñion forest for firewood, increasing air pollution with the burning of that firewood, and the loss of its ancient forest by clinging to the tradition of cutting it down for firewood.

Thus, while sustainable community development is site specific in one sense, in another sense communities within close proximity to their neighbors affect those neighbors because the landscape and its ecological patterns form a common denominator among adjacent communities. While each community must determine how its proposed actions will affect its immediate surroundings, it must also consider its indirect effects on its neighbors.

In order to address the likely consequences that the proposed actions of a community may create in the larger context of shared landscape patterns, it is imperative to understand that the value of doing so must be built on the aggregate of communal shared visions from the bottom up, from cooperation and coordination among the communities themselves. It cannot be imposed by state authority from the top down. A simple example is the myriad ways in which a community near the headwaters of a river can affect all communities downstream by its actions within the upper watershed.

Thus, while a state's government may generally impose a top-down statewide vision on the communities within its borders, it will be of relatively little consequence if the communities choose not to comply with the dictated values. It is the net affect of the collective visions of all the communities as implemented on the ground that actually governs the future landscape patterns within the state. Therefore, the state's vision is *de facto* the collective of the communities' visions because each community in its development must and will change something. It is thus necessary that change be consciously understood, accepted, and directed as an ongoing process of hidden opportunities yet to be discovered if sustainable community development is to be achieved. (For a further discussion of this subject see *Global Imperative*.[5])

Information Feedback Loops

People's values, belief in process, and the empowerment to act and collectively resolve problems is the first component of sustainable community development. Education that allows people to learn of their connection to societal/environmental problems, both local and global, is the second part of the mechanism. The democratic system of government is the third and all-encompassing piece. It is all encompassing because its processes of public representation funnel people's knowledge, feelings, requirements, desires, and concerns into an informational feedback loop that directs change. In this manner, sustainable community development can have a significant effect in directing societal change towards social/environmental sustainability.

Sustainable community development can instill a sense of purpose and a sense of belonging that are defined and maintained by a local community within its social/environmental context. It does this by integrating all aspects of society in working toward a dynamic balance of sustainable outcomes.

Such balance can only be maintained if information is fed back into the system in a way that fosters new questions and new practices appropriate for changing circumstances while simultaneously discarding only inappropriate old questions and old ways. Sustainable community development is based on information feedback, not insanity, which is the act of trying the same old thing over and over while each time expecting a different, more desirable outcome.

Sustainable community development creates a mechanism for information to feed through the political system and direct change towards a dynamic equilibrium between the community and its environment. In the case of adjacent communities, a collective mechanism of information feedback is also essential if sharing the same landscape and its common products, such as water, is going to be just and sustainable.

Wise and sustainable development requires our total presence in the present. It also requires that decisions are based on true human/environmental indicators, such as feelings, a balance between logic and intuition, a balance between social and environmental necessities, self-worth, responsibility in the present for the future, social/ecological adaptability, and so on. This may sound easy, but it is extremely demanding in terms of concentration and energy. Yet difficult as that may seem, the most difficult part of developing social/environmental sustainability is that we will all have to let go of some of our old, cherished beliefs and desires, such as the long-held simplistic notion that economic development is the sum total of community development.

12

MODIFYING OUR BELIEF SYSTEMS REGARDING CHANGE

In 1969, Elisabeth Kübler-Ross published a book titled *On Death and Dying*,[47] which simultaneously is a book "On Life and Living." Elisabeth described five stages that a terminally ill person goes through when told of her or his impending death: denial and isolation, anger, bargaining, depression, and acceptance. Before relating these stages to our thought processes and how we change, let's examine each stage:

1. Denial, refusing to admit reality or trying to invalidate logic, is the first stage a terminally ill person goes through. Denial leads to a feeling of isolation, of being helpless and alone in the Universe. At some level, however, the person knows the truth but is not yet emotionally ready or able to accept it.

2. Anger, which is a violent outward projection of fear, can be called emotional panic. The person is emotionally out of control because she or he can no longer control circumstances.

3. Bargaining is when a person attempts to bargain with God to change the circumstances, to find a way out of having to deal with what is.

4. Depression is a somewhat different type of issue because it comes in two stages. In the first stage, a person is in the immediate process of

losing control of circumstances, such as a job and his or her identity with that job. The second stage is one in which a person is no longer concerned with past losses, such as a job, but is taking impending losses into account, such as leaving loved ones behind.

5. Acceptance, the final stage, is creative and positive. With acceptance returns trust, a faith in the goodness and the justice of the outcome. Acceptance allows us to acknowledge our problem, which allows us to define it, which in turn allows us to transcend it. But first we must *accept what is*, which is to *know the truth that sets us free*.[48]

Now let's see how understanding these stages of dying helps the living to understand the dying and the living. Although we are alive, we die daily to our ideas and belief systems, and in so doing, we go through the five stages of dying, which really are five stages of grieving. These stages are necessary as a process that prepares the way for change, a dying of the old thoughts and their attendant values and relationships within our lives to make way for the birth of the new:

1. Denial of or resistance to change is the first stage of a dying belief system in which we isolate ourselves because we see change as a condition to be avoided at almost any cost. We become defensive, fearful, and increasingly rigid in our thinking; we harden our attitudes and close our minds. If one becomes defensive about anything, starts to form a rebuttal before someone is finished speaking, filters what is said to hear only what one wants to hear, one is in denial.

2. Anger is the violent projection of uncontrollable fear. One is so afraid of change, of the dying of an old belief system, that one becomes temporarily insane: "I won't accept this!" One's anger, however, is not aimed at the person on whom it is projected; it is aimed at one's own inability to control the circumstances that seem so threatening.

3. Bargaining is looking for a way to alter the circumstances based on more "acceptable" conditions, which is the purpose of such things as labor unions.

4. Depression is when one becomes resigned to his or her inability to control or change the "system," whatever that is, to suit his or her desires. One feels helpless and deliberately gives up trying to alter circumstances. One becomes a "victim" of "outside forces," and one's defense is to become cynical—distrustful of human nature and motives. A cynic is a critic who stresses faults and raises objections but assumes

Chapter 12 ■ Modifying Our Belief Systems Regarding Change

no responsibility. A cynic sees the situation as hopeless and is therefore a prophet of doom who espouses self-fulfilling prophecies of failure regardless of the effort invested in success.

5. Acceptance of what is allows one to transcend the purely emotional state of mind and reach an integrated point of logic. In so doing, one can define the problem and in turn transcend it. Acceptance of the problem, however, must come before a resolution is possible.

Why do we fear unwanted, uncontrollable change so much? We resist such change because we are committed to protecting our existing belief system. Even if it is no longer valid, it represents the safety of past knowledge in which there are no unwelcome surprises. We try to take our safe past and project it into an unknown future by skipping the present, which represents change and holds both uncertainty and accountability.

When confronted with change, we try to control the thoughts of others by accepting what to us are "approved" thoughts and rejecting "unapproved" thoughts. We see such control as a defense against unwanted change. But as author George Bernard Shaw said: "My own education operated by a succession of eye-openers each involving the repudiation of some previously held belief."

Change is the death of an accepted, "tried and true" belief system through which we have coped with life and which has become synonymous with our identity and therefore our security. When we get "too comfortable" with our belief systems, we might think of the turtle, for which only two choices in life exist: pull its head into its shell where in safety it starves to death or stick its neck out and risk finding something to eat and live.

Dysfunctional communities and their organizations with vested interests tend to hide within their self-serving ways by systematically distorting information. Such distortions do not depend on deliberate falsifications by individuals. Instead, people who are competent, hard-working, and honest can sustain systematic distortions by merely carrying out their organizational roles in an uncritical—and therefore personally safe—manner. Unchecked by outside influences or the undeniable realities of catastrophic failures, organizational systems can sustain self-serving distortions, even though the potential for catastrophic consequences is significant.

A technological culture, such as ours, faces two choices: it can wait until catastrophic failures expose systemic deficiencies, distortions, and self-deceptions (the turtle with its head sucked into its shell) or it can provide social checks and balances to correct for systemic distortions prior to catastrophic failures (the turtle with its head outside its shell, risking a view of the world).

The second more desirable alternative, however, requires the active involvement of independent people who must ask "uncomfortable" questions and pursue "unfavorable" inquiries. Without such initiatives, checks and balances are undermined and catastrophic possibilities are likely to increase as the scope and power of organizational technology expand.[5]

As we move forward in sustainable community development, remember that success or failure is a crisis of the will and the imagination, not the possibilities. Remember also that to protect the best of what we have in the present for the present and the future, we must all continually change our thinking and our behavior to some extent. Society's saving grace is that we have a choice. Therefore, whatever needs to be done can be—if enough people want it to be done and decide to do it.

ENDNOTES

1. Robert A. Baruch Bush and Joseph P. Folger. 1994. *The Promise of Mediation: Responding to Conflict through Empowerment and Recognition,* Jossey-Bass, San Francisco, 296 pp.

2. USDA Forest Service. 1988. Maser: a man with a mission. *Southwest Region News,* pp. 6, 16.

3. Colin Greer. 1994. The well-being of the world is at stake. *Parade Magazine,* January 23:4–5.

4. Donald Ludwig, Ray Hilborn, and Carl Walters. 1993. Uncertainty, resource exploitation, and conservation: lesson from history. *Science,* 260:17, 36.

5. Chris Maser. 1992. *Global Imperative: Harmonizing Culture and Nature,* Stillpoint Publishing, Walpole, N.H.

6. See the books by Alice Miller. 1981. *The Drama of the Gifted Child,* Basic Books, New York; 1984. *For Your Own Good,* Farrar, Straus, Giroux, New York; 1984. *Thou Shalt Not Be Aware,* New American Library, New York; 1986. *Pictures of a Childhood,* Farrar, Straus, Giroux, New York; 1990. *The Untouched Key,* Anchor Books, New York; 1990. *Banished Knowledge,* Doubleday, New York; 1991. *Breaking Down the Wall of Silence,* Dutton Books, New York. I recommend them highly.

7. John G. Stoessinger. 1974. *Why Nations Go to War,* St. Martin's Press, New York.

8. D.W. Schindler, K.G. Beaty, E.J. Fee, D.R. Cruikshank, et al. 1990. Effects of climatic warming on lakes of the central boreal forest. *Science,* 250:967–970.

9. John H. Baldwin. 1984. *Environmental Planning and Management,* Westview Press, Boulder, Colo., 280 pp.

10. Chris Maser. 1994. *Sustainable Forestry,* St. Lucie Press, Delray Beach, Fla.
11. Edward Bach. 1931. *Heal Thyself,* C.W. Daniel Company, Limited, Essex, England.
12. *A Course in Miracles, Workbook for Students.* 1975. Foundation for Inner Peace, Tiburon, Calif., p. 247.
13. E. Saunders. 1989. Another way to get a diploma. *Corvallis Gazette-Times* (Corvallis, Ore.), March 12.
14. *The Holy Bible,* Authorized King James Version, World Bible Publishers, Iowa Falls, Iowa, Leviticus 16:21–22.
15. T.J. Fleming and A. Fleming. 1970. *Develop Your Child's Creativity,* Association Press, New York.
16. *A Course in Miracles, Manual for Teachers.* 1975. Foundation for Inner Peace, Tiburon, Calif., p. 26.
17. *The Holy Bible,* Authorized King James Version, World Bible Publishers, Iowa Falls, Iowa, Proverbs 15:1.
18. James Allen. 1981. *As a Man Thinketh,* Grosset & Dunlap, New York.
19. Don Costar. 1995. No need to change grazing practices. Letters to the editor. *Reno-Gazette Journal* (Reno, Nev.), January 13.
20. J.P. Carse. 1985. *The Silence of God,* Macmillan, New York.
21. T. Merton. 1965. *The Way of Chuang Tzu,* New Directions, New York.
22. Richard Attenborough. 1982. *The Words of Gandhi,* Newmarket Press, New York, 111 pp.
23. The Associated Press. 1988. British Columbia wood companies face challenges. *The Sunday Oregonian,* August 7.
24. Bill Devall (Ed.). 1993. *Clearcut: The Tragedy of Industrial Forestry,* Sierra Club Books/Earth Island Press, San Francisco.
25. Gerald Corey. 1986. *The Theory and Practice of Counseling and Psychotherapy* (3rd ed.), Brooks/Cole, Monterey, Calif.
26. C.S. Hall, G. Lindzey, J.C. Loehlin, and M. Manosevitz. 1985. *Introduction to Theories of Personality,* John Wiley & Sons, New York.
27. U.S. Department of Transportation, Federal Aviation Administration. 1977. Aviation Instructor's Handbook, U.S. Government Printing Office, Washington, D.C.
28. John F. Kennedy. 1961. *Profiles in Courage,* Harper & Row, New York, 266 pp.
29. Jeffrey Mishlove. 1994. Intuition, the source of true knowing. *Noetic Sciences Review,* 29:31–36.

30. Anna F. Lemkow. 1994. Our common journey toward freedom. *The Quest,* 7(1):55–63.
31. Robert D. Garrett. 1994. Mediation in Native America. *Dispute Resolution Journal,* March:38–45.
32. Peter M. Senge. 1990. *The Fifth Discipline: The Art and Practice of the Learning Organization,* Doubleday, New York, 424 pp.
33. Lewis Carroll. 1933. *Alice's Adventures in Wonderland,* Doubleday, Doran, & Co., New York, 162 pp.
34. Fritjof Capra. 1988. *The Turning Point: Science, Society, and the Rising Culture,* Bantam Books, New York, 464 pp.
35. R.D. Laing. 1982. *The Voice of Experience,* Ballantine Books, New York.
36. Elaine Pagels. 1989. *The Gnostic Gospels,* Vintage Books, New York.
37. Carolyn Merchant. 1992. *Radical Ecology: The Search for a Livable World,* Routledge, New York.
38. Wendell Berry. 1990. Word and flesh. *Whole Earth Review,* Spring:68–71.
39. Ronald L. Warren. 1972. *The Community in America* (2nd ed.), Rand McNally College Publishing, Chicago.
40. Jeremy Rifkin. 1991. *Biosphere Politics: A Cultural Odyssey from the Middle Ages to the New Age,* Harper, San Francisco.
41. M. Ravitz. 1982. Community development: challenge of the eighties. *Journal of the Community Development Society,* 13:1–10.
42. Robert Constanza and Herman E. Daly. 1987. Toward an ecological economics. *Ecological Modelling,* 38:1–7.
43. Robert Rodale. 1988. Big New Ideas—Where Are They Today? Unpublished speech given at the Third National Science, Technology, Society (STS) Conference, Arlington, Va., February 5–7.
44. James A. Christenson and Jerry W. Robinson, Jr. (Eds.). 1989. *Community Development in Perspective,* Iowa State University Press, Ames.
45. Stephen Ameyaw. 1992. Sustainable development and the community: lessons from the KASKA Project Botswana. *The Environmentalist,* 12:267–275.
46. Sustainable Energy: A Local Government Planning Guide for a Sustainable Future. 1992. The Energy Task Force of the Urban Consortium Energy, Environment, and Economic Development Unit, Portland, San Francisco, and San Jose.
47. Elisabeth Kübler-Ross. 1969. *On Death and Dying,* Macmillan, New York.
48. *The Holy Bible,* Authorized King James Version, World Bible Publishers, Iowa Falls, Iowa, John 8:23.

REFERENCES

A Course in Miracles, Manual for Teachers. 1975. Foundation for Inner Peace, Tiburon, Calif.

A Course in Miracles, Text. 1975. Foundation for Inner Peace, Tiburon, Calif.

A Course in Miracles, Workbook for Students. 1975. Foundation for Inner Peace, Tiburon, Calif.

Allen, J. 1981. *As a Man Thinketh,* Grosset & Dunlap, New York.

Ameyaw, Stephen. 1992. Sustainable development and the community: lessons from the KASKA Project Botswana. *The Environmentalist,* 12:267–275.

Andrews, Cecile. 1992. Study circles: schools for life. *In Context,* 33:22–25.

Bach, Edward. 1931. *Heal Thyself,* C.W. Daniel Co., Saffron Walden, Essex, England.

Boorstin, D.J. 1985. *The Discoverers, The History of Man's Search to Know His World and Himself,* Vintage Books, New York.

Brandt, E. 1988. To cherish life. *Parade Magazine,* October 16, pp. 4–6.

Bush, R.A.B. and J.P. Folger. 1994. *The Promise of Mediation: Responding to Conflict through Empowerment and Recognition,* Jossey-Bass, San Francisco, 296 pp.

Capra, Fritjof. 1988. *The Turning Point: Science, Society, and the Rising Culture,* Bantam Books, New York.

Carter, E.A. and M. McGoldrick. 1980. The family life cycle and family therapy: an overview. In: *The Family Cycle: A Framework for Family Therapy,* Carter, E.A. and M. McGoldrick (Eds.), Gardner Press, New York.

Chambers, Robert E. and Mark K. McBeth. 1992. Community encouragement: returning to the basis for community development. *Journal of the Community Development Society,* 23:20–37.

Christenson, James A. and Jerry W. Robinson, Jr. (Eds.). 1989. *Community Development in Perspective,* Iowa State University Press, Ames.

Cousins, William J. 1957. Community development—some notes on the way and the how. *Community Development Review,* 7:24–30.

Covington, W.W. and M.M. Moore. 1991. Changes in Forest Conditions and Multiresource Yields from Ponderosa Pine Forests since European Settlement. Unpublished report, submitted to J. Keane, Water Resources Operations, Salt River Project, Phoenix, 50 pp.

Crutzen, P.J. and M.O. Andreae. 1990. Biomass burning in the tropics: impact on atmospheric chemistry and biogeochemical cycles. *Science,* 250:1669–1678.

DePree, Max. 1989. *Leadership Is an Art,* Dell, New York.

de Steiguer, J.E., J.M. Pye, and C.S. Love. 1990. Air pollution damage to U.S. forests. *Journal of Forestry,* 88:17–22.

Drengson, Alan. R. 1985. The virtue of Socratic ignorance. In: *Occasions for Philosophy,* J.C. Edwards and D.M. MacDonald (Eds.), Prentice-Hall, Englewood Cliffs, N.J., pp. 34–42.

Dunham, Arthur. 1963. Some principles of community development. *International Review of Community Development,* 11:141–151.

Durrant, M. 1987. Therapy with young people who have been the victims of sexual assault. *Family Therapy Case Studies,* 2:57–63.

Edgar, C. and B. Adams. 1992. *Ecology and Decline of Red Spruce in the Eastern United States,* Springer-Verlag, New York.

Erikson, Erik. 1963. *Childhood and Society* (2nd ed.), Norton, New York.

Esher, R.J., D.H. Marx, S.J. Ursic, R.L. Baker, L.R. Brown, and D.C. Coleman. 1992. Simulated acid rain effects on fine roots, ectomycorrhizae, microorganisms, and invertebrates in pine forests of the southern United States. *Water, Air, and Soil Pollution,* 61:269–278.

Ferguson, Marilyn. 1980. *The Aquarian Conspiracy, Personal and Social Transformation in the 1980s,* J.P. Tarcher, Los Angeles.

Feuerstein, Georg. 1994. Cultivating the power of intuition. *The Quest,* 7(3):32–38, 40–41.

Frankl, V.E. 1963. *Man's Search for Meaning,* Pocket Books, New York.

Franklin, J.F. and R.T.T. Forman. 1987. Creating landscape patterns by forest cutting: ecological consequences and principles. *Landscape Ecol.,* 1:5–18.

Friedman, John. 1992. *Empowerment: The Politics of Alternative Development,* Blackwell, Cambridge, Mass.

Garrett, R.D. 1994. Mediation in Native America. *Dispute Resolution Journal,* March: 38–45.

Gentry, A.H. and J. Lopez-Paradi. 1980. Deforestation and increased flooding of the upper Amazon. *Science,* 210:1354–1356.

Goldenberg, I. and H. Goldenberg. 1985. *Family Therapy, An Overview* (2nd ed.), Brooks/Cole, Monterey, Calif.

Gordon, John C. 1993. *The New Face of Forestry: Exploring a Discontinuity and the Need for a Vision,* Grey Towers Press, Milford, Pa., 15 pp.

Hansen, J., I. Fung, A. Lacis, D. Rind, S. Lebedeff, R. Ruedy, G. Russell, and P. Stone. 1988. Global climate changes as forecast by Goddard Institute for Space Studies three dimensional model. *Journal of Geophysical Research,* 93:9341–9364.

Hardin, G. 1984. An ecolate view of the human predicament. *The Environ. Fund, Monogr. Ser.,* 14 pp.

Harding, Anna K. and Marsha L. Greer. 1993. The health impact of hazardous waste sites on minority communities: implications for public health and environmental health professionals. *Journal of Environmental Health,* 55:6–10.

Harding, Anna K. and George R. Holdren, Jr. 1993. Environmental equity and the environmental professional. *Environmental Science and Technology,* 27:1990–1993.

Harmon, Mark E., William K. Ferrel, and Jerry F. Franklin. 1990. Effects on carbon storage of conversion for old-growth forests to young forests. *Science,* 247: 699–702.

Harris, L.D. 1984. *The Fragmented Forest,* University of Chicago Press, Chicago, 211 pp.

Harris, L.D. and C. Maser. 1984. Animal community characteristics. In: *The Fragmented Forest,* L.D. Harris, University of Chicago Press, Chicago, 211 pp.

Heider, John. 1986. *The Tao of Leadership: Leadership Strategies for a New Age,* Bantam Books, New York.

Heilbronn, Gary N. (Ed.). 1993. *Environmental Law in Hong Kong: Problems and Prospects,* Faculty of Law, University of Hong Kong, Hong Kong, 117 pp.

Hyatt, Carole and Linda Gottlieb. 1987. *When Smart People Fail,* Simon and Schuster, New York, 240 pp.

Jacob, N. 1989. Towards a theory of sustainability. *Trumpeter,* 6:93–97.

Johnson, Kirk. (in press). Emerging lessons for reconciling community and environment. *The Changing Northwest.*

Johnson, Robert A. 1987. *Ecstasy, Understanding the Psychology of Joy,* Harper & Row, San Francisco.

Johnson, Robert A. 1991. *Owning Your Own Shadow,* Harper, San Francisco.

Keepin, W. 1994. David Bohm: a life of dialogue between science and spirit. *Noetic Sciences Review,* 30:10–16.

Kershaw, J.A., C.D. Oliver, and T.M. Hinckley. 1993. Effect of harvest of old-growth Douglas-fir stands and subsequent management on carbon dioxide levels in the atmosphere. *Journal of Sustainable Forestry,* 1:61–77.

Knox, Robert J. 1993. Environmental equity. *Journal of Environmental Health,* 55: 32–34.

Kofman, Fred and Peter M. Senge. 1993. Communities of Commitment: The Heart of Learning Organizations. Unpublished paper on file at the Sloan School of Management, MIT, Boston, 24 pp.

Kolb, D.M. and associates. 1994. *When Talk Works: Profiles of Mediators,* Jossey-Bass, San Francisco, 513 pp.

Laing, R.D. 1982. *The Voice of Experience,* Ballantine Books, New York.

Lashof, D.A. and D.R. Ahuja. 1990. Relative contribution of greenhouse gas emissions to global warming. *Nature,* 344:529–531.

Lélé, Sharachandra M. 1991. Sustainable development: a critical review. *World Development,* 19:607–621.

Leopold, Aldo. 1933. The conservation ethic. *Journal of Forestry,* 31:634–643.

Leopold, Luna B. 1990. Ethos, equity, and the water resource. *Environment,* 2:16–42.

Maathai, W. 1995. Bottlenecks of development. *Resurgence,* 169(March/April):4-10.

Maser, Chris. 1992. *Global Imperative: Harmonizing Culture and Nature,* Stillpoint Publishing, Walpole, N.H.

Maslow, A.H. 1968. *Toward a Psychology of Being* (2nd. ed.), D. Van Nostrand, Princeton, N.J.

Maslow, A.H. 1970. *Religions, Values, and Peak-Experiences,* Viking Press, New York.

Meadows, Donella H. 1992. Change is not doom. *ReVision,* 14:56–60.

Merchant, Carolyn. 1992. *Radical Ecology: The Search for a Livable World,* Routledge, New York.

Merton, Thomas. 1991. The Sacred City. In: *Preview of the Asian Journey,* Crossroads, New York.

Myers, N. and R. Tucker. 1987. Deforestation in Central America: Spanish legacy and North American consumers. *Environmental Review,* 11:55–71.

Olson R.K. and A.S. Lefohn (Eds.). 1989. *Transactions Effects of Air Pollution on Western Forests,* Air and Waste Management Association, Pittsburgh.

Pagels, Elaine. 1989. *The Gnostic Gospels,* Vintage Books, New York.

Papalia, D.E. and S.W. Olds. 1979. *A Child's World,* McGraw-Hill, New York.

Perry, D.A. 1988. Landscape pattern and forest pests. *Northwest Environmental Journal,* 4:213–228.

Perry, David A. and Jeffrey G. Borchers. 1990. Climate change and ecosystem responses. *Northwest Environmental Journal,* 6:293–313.

Perry, David A., Michael P. Amaranthus, Jeffery G. Borchers, Susan L. Borchers, and R.E. Brainerd. 1989. Bootstrapping in ecosystems. *BioScience,* 39:230–237.

Perry, David A., Jeffery G. Borchers, Susan L. Borchers, and Michael P. Amaranthus. 1990. Species migrations and ecosystem stability during climate change: the belowground connection. *Conservation Biology,* 4:266–274.

Price, Joan. 1994. Socrates: midwife to the soul. *The Quest,* 7(3):58–61.

Rapport, David J. 1989. What constitutes ecosystem health? *Perspectives in Biology and Medicine,* 33:120–132.

Rapport, David J., H.A. Regier, and T.C. Hutchinson. 1985. Ecosystem behavior under stress. *American Naturalist,* 125:617–640.

Rifkin, Jeremy. 1991. *Biosphere Politics: A Cultural Odyssey from the Middle Ages to the New Age,* Harper, San Francisco.

Robert, Karl-Hendrik. 1991. Educating a nation: the natural step. *In Context,* 28:10–15.

Robinson, Jerry W., Jr. and James A. Christenson. 1980. *Community Development in America,* The Iowa State University Press, Ames.

Rubin, Herbert J. and Irene Rubin. 1986. *Community Organizing and Development,* Macmillan, New York.

Sams, Jamie. 1990. *Sacred Path Cards: The Discovery of Self through Native Teachings,* Harper, San Francisco.

Savonen, C. 1990. Ashes in the Amazon. *Journal of Forestry,* 88:20–25.

Schlesinger, M.E. and F.F. Mitchell. 1985. Model predictions of the equilibrium climatic response to increased carbon dioxide. In: Projecting the Climatic Effects of Increasing Carbon Dioxide, DOE/ER-0237, U.S. Department of Energy, Washington, D.C., pp. 83–147.

Senge, Peter. 1990. *The Fifth Discipline: The Art and Practice of the Learning Organization,* Doubleday, New York.

Shearman, R. 1990. The meaning and ethics of sustainability. *Environmental Management,* 14:108.

Shiva, Vandana. 1992. *Staying Alive: Women, Ecology, and Development,* Zed Books, N.J.

Shortle, W.C. and E.A. Bondietti. 1992. Timing, magnitude, and impact of acidic deposition on sensitive forest sites. *Water, Air, and Soil Pollution,* 61:253–267.

Smith, Emily T. 1992. Growth vs environment: in Rio next month a push for sustainable development. *Business Week,* 3256:66–75.

Solo, R. 1974. Problems of modern technology. *Journal of Economic Issues,* 8:859–876.

Steiner, Rudolf. 1985. The threefold social order. Translation from *The Renewal of the Social Organism,* 1919. Anthroposophic Press, Hudson, N.Y.

Stensland, G. 1960. Some prerequisites for community development. *International Review of Community Development,* 6:81–90.

Swetnam, Thomas W. 1990. Fire history and climate in the southwestern United States. In: Effects of Fire in Management of Southwestern Natural Resources, J.S. Krammers (Tech. Coord.), USDA Forest Service General Technical Report RM-191, Rocky Mountain Research Station, Fort Collins, Colo., pp. 6–17.

Tims, Doug. 1991. Vision for the '90s: responsible, shared use. *American Forests,* May/June:17–20.

Toman, Michael A. 1993. Economics, Ecology, and "Sustainability." Unpublished manuscript on file at Resources for the Future, Washington, D.C., 14 pp.

Turner, M.G. 1989. Landscape ecology: the effect of pattern on process. *Annu. Rev. Ecol. Syst.,* 20:171–197.

U.S. Department of Transportation, Federal Aviation Administration. 1977. Aviation Instructor's Handbook, U.S. Government Printing Office, Washington, D.C.

World Commission on Environment and Development. 1987. *Our Common Future,* Oxford University Press, New York.

Young, Rob and Grant Power. 1992. Self-sustaining communities: the current upsurge of grassroots activity could well transform our society. *In Context,* 33:10–12.